Cover illustration:

The seal impression of "ʾAḥaz (son of) Yehotam, King of Judah"

Messages from the Past

Hebrew Bullae from the Time of Isaiah Through the Destruction of the First Temple

Robert Deutsch

Messages from the Past

Hebrew Bullae from the Time of Isaiah Through the Destruction of the First Temple

Robert Deutsch

ARCHAEOLOGICAL CENTER PUBLICATIONS
TEL AVIV, ISRAEL
1999

ARCHAEOLOGICAL CENTER PUBLICATIONS
7 Mazal Dagim street
Old city of Jaffa 68036 Israel

ISBN 965-90240-3-7

Photos by Zeev Radovan and the author.
Drawings by Rodica Pinchas and the author.

Printed in Israel at Graphit press Ltd., Jerusalem, 1999

CONTENTS

Foreword 7
Introduction 9

Chapter One

The seal 13
Seal manufacture 13
The bulla 14
Use of the seal 15
The script and the inscription 16
Iconography 16
The ethnic definition 16

The biblical evidence

The seal in the Old Testament 16
The gemstones 17
The manufacturing and the engraving 17
Wearing practices according to the OT 17
Other uses 18
The document sealing custom 18
The use of seals and bullae in the Mishnah 19
The Onomasticon 19
The iconography of the Hebrew seals 20
Phoenico-Egyptian motifs 20
Floral motifs 21
Faunal motifs 21
Anthropomorphic motifs 21
The register dividers as ornament 21
Flora motifs 21
Geometric motifs 22
The border as ornament 22
The question of authenticity 22

Chapter Two

Hebrew bullae from controlled excavations

Tell el-Judeideh 27
Beth-Zur 27
Lachish 27
Beer-Sheba 28
Tell el-Ḥesi 28
Jerusalem 28

Unprovenanced published Hebrew bullae

The British Museum collection 30
255 Hebrew bullae (from Tell Beit Mirsim area?) 30
Two Hebrew fiscal bullae 42
The Josef Samel collection 42
Thirty five Hebrew bullae from private collections 43
Five Hebrew bullae in the Israel Museum 45
A Hebrew bulla from the Victor Barakat collection 46
A Hebrew bulla from the W. Stern collection 46
Three Hebrew bullae in the Bible Lands Museum 46
A Hebrew bulla from the Jerusalem antiquities market 46

Unpublished Hebrew bullae of unknown provenance

Two Hebrew bullae from the private collection of Dr. Elie Borowski 46
Twenty Hebrew bullae in the Hecht Museum, Haifa 47

Iron Age bullae from the neighboring states

Two Ammonite bullae 48
A Moabite bulla 48
Two Edomite bullae 48
Eleven Assyrian Aramaic bullae 48
A bulla from Zenjirli (Samʾal) 48
The Marzeaḥ papyrus bulla 48
A Phoenician bulla from Tell el-Ḥeres 49

Persian period bullae

A hoard of 65 Aramaic bullae from Judah 49
An Aramaic bulla of unknown provenance 49
Summary and conclusions to chapters One and Two 50

Indexes for chapters One and Two

Personal names 53
Titles and professions 57
Toponyms, words and numerals 58

Chapter three

109 Hebrew Bullae from the Time of Isaiah Through the Destruction of the First Temple

A bulla of Ahaz, son of Yehotam, King of Judah 61
Three bullae bearing the title "Servant of Hezekiah" 63
Two bullae bearing the title "Who is over the House" 68
Four bullae bearing the title "Servant of the King" 71
Three bullae bearing the title "Governor of the City" 76
Five bullae which belonged to women 79
A bulla which belonged to "The daughter of the King" 79
Personal bullae 84
Fiscal bullae 166
Summary and conclusions to chapter three 174
The List of bullae in Chapter Three 176

Indexes for chapter Three

Personal names 179
Royal names 180
Toponyms 180
Titles 180
Words 181
Numerals 181
Bibliography 182

Plates

I–VIII, The letters
IX–XIII, The iconography
XIV–XV, Thermoluminescence analysis
XVI, Color pictures of the Royal bullae of Ahaz and Hezekiah
XVII, Drawings of the Royal bullae of Ahaz and Hezekiah

Foreword

The subject of this study is the Hebrew epigraphic evidence from Hebrew seal-impressions (bullae) from the 8th through the beginning of the 6th century B.C.E., from Judah. The Hebrew inscribed seal-impressions are of great importance as they are reliable extra-biblical evidence from the time of the First Temple. They reflect the day-to-day reality in the most exciting period of Jewish history: the biblical period. The main goal of this study is to bring together all the published Hebrew seal-impressions and to add to it unpublished material which is currently held in private collections. Such a corpus is of major importance for the improvement of our paleographic, iconographic, onomastic, chronological and statistical knowledge of the history of Israel in the First Temple period. Seal-impressions carry written information such as personal names, nouns, titles, professions, city names, dates etc. The most important aspect of this information is its comparison to the biblical and the extra-biblical texts. This will allow us to identify seal owners with people mentioned in the Old Testament. Such identifications will enable a better understanding of both the epigraphic material, and the biblical text. The large corpus of personal names found on epigraphic seals and seal-impressions is equally important as the biblical list of names. Moreover, new unrecorded names which are revealed on these small finds, enrich and reconstruct the mosaic of First Temple period onomasticon.

Several bullae, called by Avigad "fiscal bullae", bear biblical city names. These are important extra-biblical sources to support the historical core of the OT. The comparison of this data with the OT text provides us a better understanding of the finds. The credibility of the text found on seals and seal-impressions is beyond doubt, due to the fact that these are free of bias — not written by tendentious authors. These are first-hand inscriptions used by their owners in every day routine activities of sealing documents or other objects.

The study extends the corpus of the published Hebrew bullae from 376 to 510 items, an impressive, updated number, valuable due to its heterogeneity and credibility.

This book is based on the author's MA thesis written in 1996, in Hebrew, under the guidance of Prof. Anson F. Rainey and presented to the Dept. of Archaeology and Ancient Near Eastern Studies at the Tel Aviv University. This English version is an updated translation by the author from the Hebrew version first published in 1997.

It gives me great pleasure to thank to all who assist me and made this research possible: Mrs. Ofra Rimon, chief curator of the Hecht Museum at Haifa; Dr. Arie Kindler, director of the Kadman Numismatic Dept. at the Eretz Israel Museum in Tel Aviv; Dr. Elie Borowski of the Bible Lands museum in Jerusalem; and Mr. Yoav Sasson of Jerusalem. I am grateful to Mr.

Shlomo Moussaieff, collector and Bible scholar, for allowing me to examine and publish the bullae from his collection.

It is a pleasant task to thank Prof. Anson F. Rainey, Prof. Michael Heltzer and Dr. Gabriel Barkay who read the Hebrew manuscript. Their valuable comments and suggestions were instrumental in shaping of this book. Finally, and most importantly, my thanks to Prof. David Ussishkin and Prof. Israel Finkelstein for their encouragement and support during my studies at the Tel Aviv University.

Introduction

The subject of this study is the Hebrew epigraphic evidence from the biblical period, in the form of Hebrew seal-impressions (bullae) from the 8th through the beginning of the 6th century B.C.E., from Judea.

The corpus presented here is divided into three chapters: The first chapter deals at length with the historical phenomenon of sealing and the definitions of the "seal" and "bulla". A review of the materials and manufacturing process, the script and inscriptions, the iconography and decorations, and the use of the seals and bullae in ancient time is presented. The relevant biblical evidence recording the use of seals and sealing, is brought to light. A discussion about the authenticity of material published from unknown provenance ends this chapter.

The second chapter presents all the material published to date. This includes 61 bullae discovered during controlled excavations at Tell el-Judeideh, Beth Zur, Lachish, Beer-Sheba, Tell el-Ḥesi and Jerusalem, and 315 bullae published with unknown provenance. In addition, 25 bullae from public and private collections are listed. These are to be published in the near future by several scholars. A total of 401 bullae published to date, or in preparation to be published, are listed.

The third chapter presents 109 hitherto unpublished bullae from the collection of Mr. Shlomo Moussaieff in London. This group includes a unique example of a Hebrew royal seal-impression, the bulla of "Ahaz the King of Judah", seal-impressions of high officials such as: "Servants of Hezekiah", "Who is over the house (of the King)", "Servants of Kings", "Governors of cities" and two persons bearing no titles, but known as officials from the Bible. Five seal-impressions of women are also presented, one of which belonged to "The daughter of the King". This chapter ends with five "fiscal" bullae, on which are mentioned three city names: Lachish, ʾAravot and Naṣiph.

Chapter One

The seal

The earliest seals are known from Mesopotamia and Anatolia as early as the 7th and 6th millennium B.C.E. But the seal only becomes common with the invention of cuneiform writing in Mesopotamia, and simultaneously, hieroglyphic writing in Egypt around 3300 B.C.E (Collon 1990:11–20). Seal-impressions are found on clay tablets, jars and sealings (bullae). The shapes of the seals vary: in Mesopotamia they are cylindrical and lengthwise-perforated and are called "cylinder seals". They were in use throughout the ancient world and are found in Syria, Egypt, Anatolia and also in Canaan. The Hyksos (in Canaan) used seals called *scarabs* which are found in all Middle Bronze Age tells (Giveon 1988; Rowe 1936). In the Iron Age II period in Judah (900–586 B.C.E.), the time of the First Temple, the stamp seals are characterized by their small size (average of 1.5 cm.), elliptical form, dome shape, flat base and lengthwise perforation in order to be set in a ring or pendant bezel. Such a seal is called *scaraboid* according to its similarity to the shape of the Egyptian scarab beetles. Seals of other forms are also known, such as conoid, cubic, rectangular etc., but they are rare during the Iron Age II (Hestrin and Dayagi-Mendels 1979:7).

In manufacturing seals, all kinds of local and imported stones, both common and semi-precious, were used. Other seals were cast in bronze and, rarely, silver. Glass, faience and even clay were also used. Organic materials were also used, such as ivory (elephant and hippopotamus), bone and wood. Surprisingly, gold Hebrew seals are missing from those we would expect to find belonging to high officials.

Hebrew epigraphic seals have appeared in the land of Israel since the beginning of the Hebrew script in the 9th century B.C.E. (Naveh 1994:21). The base of the seal is usually divided into two, three or four registers, widthwise or lengthwise, which contains the script. The inscription indicates the owner's name and patronym (the name of his father and occasionally the name of his grandfather). On seals of high officials, their titles are mentioned. Several others bear the profession of the owner. Some seals are decorated with motifs from the flora or fauna of Israel, as well as with mythological creatures, mainly from the Phoenico-Egyptian world (Sass 1993:194–256).

Seal manufacture

The process of seal manufacturing begins with choosing a stone. The selection is made according to several characteristics such as: size, weight, hardness, color, shading, purity, rarity and value. The most common stones in the land of Israel are the hard limestones of different colors, from white, yellow, reddish, through brown and black. The sources for the semi-precious stones are from trade with both neighboring countries and more distant ones. The most common imported stones used for seal manufacture are the red carnelian and the lined brown with white agate. More rare are purple amethyst, transparent quartz, red or green jasper, white chalcedony, black hematite, green malachite and blue lapis lazuli. In the Bible we find several accounts which relate to semi-precious stone trade: "And also the ship of Hiram, that brought gold from Ofir, brought in from Ofir a great amount of almug wood and precious stones" (I Kgs. 10:11). The selection of a seal is based mainly on the type of stone and its color. This reflects the faith which people had in the mystic properties of a stone.

The second stage in seal manufacturing is in bringing the raw material into the desired shape. This shape is usually elliptic in form, dome shaped and with a flat base. Yet, other shapes such as conoid, rectangular, bead-shaped and duck-shaped seals were also made.

The third stage in seal manufacturing is the perforation, usually lengthwise. This was made by hand with a bow and drill. The technique was in drilling halfway from each side. The meeting place in the middle of the hole is characterized by a ridge. This perforation is made in order to set the seal into a bezel.

The fourth stage in seal manufacturing is the engraving of the flat base with a decorative motif. Sometimes the back is also decorated. The carving was made with three main tools: chisel, disk and drill. The decoration ranges from minimalist, serving only to divide the space into registers by simple lines, through elaborate ornamentation. The motifs used in decorating Hebrew seals were borrowed from the flora and fauna as well as from the Phoenico-Egyptian, Babylonian and Assyrian mythological world. We can observe different styles and recognize particular craftsmen or workshops. Decorated seals are common in Israel and Judah in the 8th century B.C.E., but rare in Judah in the 7th and in the beginning of the 6th century B.C.E.

The fifth stage in seal manufacturing is the engraving of the inscription. The inscription was engraved into the surface of the seal in incuse and mirror image. This to ensure that the impression will be in readable relief. Several seals called votive seals did not serve signet purposes, therefore the incuse script is not in mirror image but straight.

The seals were mounted in rings or pendants or simply hung on a cord.

The bulla

The *bulla* is a lump of clay impressed by a seal, originally attached to a document or another object to be sealed by it. In antiquity, a document was rolled and tied by a cord. On the knot, or the cord itself, was attached the wet lump of clay and sealed with a seal. After the clay was sealed it was allowed to dry. The concept was that a sealed object can be opened only by violating the bulla or cutting the cord. A document could be sealed with one or several bullae, and sealed by one or several seals (Avigad 1986:123, figs. 1–4). The behavior of the wet lump of clay under the pressure of the seal is mentioned in the Bible with a borrowed meaning: "It is changed like clay under the seal" (Job 38:14).

The bulla is a product of the seal and preserves additional data to that preserved by the seal itself. Usually on the reverse of the bulla, the grooves left by the cord which tied the sealed object are visible, as well as the imprint of the material to which the bulla was affixed, for example, imprints of papyrus, textile or wood. A close examination will reveal the fingerprints of the person who impressed the seal while it was wet (Avigad 1986:19). The bullae are dried but not fired; fire will burn to ashes all the organic materials connected with the bullae, but will also harden and preserve them. Ironically, they survived thanks to fire and destruction. Petrographic analysis of the clay allows us to determine the area from which the material has been extracted. The color of the bulla depends on the clay from which it is made and the heat, if it suffered fire. The colors vary, from very bright, through red, brown, grey and black.

The script on the bulla appears in relief as a result of the incuse script on the seal. The seal bears the script in mirror image, therefore the impressed inscription on the bulla is readable. A seal could be used to impress many bullae, and such duplicates are common. For example, fourteen bullae of "Neriyahu (son of) ʾAdoniyahu" were found (Avigad 1986, no. 126). Bullae which were used other than to seal objects are also known. The reverse of such bullae is conical or convex and carries no impressions of textures or cord. Avigad was the first to call them "fiscal bullae" (Avigad 1990). These were used as documents or receipts and also as means of payment. The purchase of "seals", which are probably bullae, is mentioned in the Mishna: מי שהוא מבקש נסכים הולך לו אצל יוחנן שהוא ממונה על החותמות, נותן לו מעות ומקבל ממנו חותם. בא לו אצל אחיה שהוא ממונה על הנסכים, ונותן לו חותם ומקבל ממנו נסכים. ולערב באין זה אצל זה, ואחיה מוציא את החותמות ומקבל כנגדן מעות. — "Who wishes to get libations, goes to Yohanan who is over the seals, hands him over coins and receives a seal. He goes to ʾAhiya who is over the libations, hands him over a seal and receives libations. At evening they meet, and ʾAhiya presents the seals and exchanges them for coins" (Moed, Shekalim 5:4). This means that the libations for the temple were purchased by or exchanged for "seals" or bullae and not directly for coins. At the end of the day, the appointed official "over the libations" had to display the "seals" he received during the day, and sell them for money to the official who was "over the seals".

Use of the seal

Seals were mainly used to seal documents, but also sacks, wooden boxes, and pottery vessels containing valuables such as grains, oil or wine. Jar handles were sealed before firing. Windows and doors were also sealed. In addition, the seal served as an ornament or amulet, as a security deposit and as an offering.

The seal was valuable also according to its material. Seals belonged to private people, to public officials and royal ministers. Seals are also known for recording their possessive familial relationship. Herodotus attested that in Babylon every person carried a seal (Herodotus I:195). The large number of inscribed Hebrew seals, together with other Hebrew epigraphic material such as ostraca and engraved inscriptions in stone, points toward the existence of a large literate population in Judah and Israel in the First Temple period. On the seals, which mainly belonged to men, the personal name of its owner and his patronym are mentioned. Only a few dozen recovered seals belonged to women. These are divisible into three groups according to their familial connection: daughters, wives and maids. Women's seals recording only their personal names without the patronym, are also known. The right of sealing is evidence for the equality and high positions of these women.

The script and the inscription

The inscription is in the ancient Hebrew script *ktb dʿṣ*, which developed together with the Phoenician from the Proto-Sinaic or Proto-Canaanite alphabetic script. The language is the ancient Hebrew used in the First Temple period (Avigad 1986:113–115). The legend is an ownership inscription which is usually formulated: Personal name + Patronym. As mentioned above, the inscription has been engraved into the surface of the seal in incuse and mirror image. This is to ensure that the impression, which is made in soft clay, will be in readable relief. Seals called votive seals bear straight incuse inscriptions.

The iconography

The majority of the Hebrew seals of the end of the 7th century and beginning of the 6th century B.C.E. are aniconic (Avigad 1986:118–119). Those which are iconic bear Egypto-Phoenician and Syro-Mesopotamian iconography, flora and fauna motifs, every day objects, mythological creatures and religious topics (Sass 1993:194–256). The decoration appears on the surface of the seal, yet seals with decorated back are also recorded (Pls. IX–XIII).

The ethnic definition

The ethnic definition of a seal owner is based on several criteria: the origin of the seal, the material, the typology, its iconography, the script and language, the name and its theophoric element.

The biblical evidence

The seal in the Old Testament

The term "seal", חותם, appears in the OT 14 times in masculine and once in feminine, חותמת (Even-Shoshan 1990:353). The term "signature", חתימה, appears nine times, the term "sealed", חתום, appears six times and the term "end", חתום, appears once (ibid.: 407).

The gemstones

In the book of Exodus (39:10–13), the 12 different semi-precious gemstones set in the high priest's breastplate are mentioned: "And they set in four rows of stones: the first row was a ruby, a chrysolithe, and a beryl: this was the first row. And the second row, a turquoise, a sapphire, and a diamond. And the third row, a ligure, and an agate, and a jasper. And the fourth row, an emerald, a shoham, and a jade: they were inclosed in fixtures of gold in their settings".

The manufacture and the signet engravings

Several biblical verses mention the act of manufacturing seals. There is no description of the tools used, but the manufacturing technique included drilling (Ezek. 28:13). In the Bible the term פתוחי חותם "signet engravings", is used as a well known idiom. The book of Exodus is our richest source concerning the manufacture of seals:
"מעשה חרש אבן פתוחי חתם תפתח את שתי האבנים על־שמת בני ישראל מסבת משבצות זהב תעשה אותם" — "With the work of an engraver in stone, like the engravings of a signet, shalt thou engrave the two stones with the names of the children of Yisra'el: thou shalt make them to be set in fixtures of gold" (Exod. 28:11).

"על־שמת בני ישראל שתים עשרה על־שמתם פתוחי חותם איש על־שמו תהייו לשני עשר שבט" — "And the stones shall be with the names of the children of Yisra'el, twelve, according to their names, like the engravings of a signet; every one with its name shall they be, according to the twelve tribes" (Exod. 28:21).

"ויעשו את־אבני השהם מסבת משבצת זהב מפתחת פתוחי חותם על שמות בני ישראל" — "And they arranged the shoham stones enclosed in fixtures of gold, graven, as signets are graven, with the names of the children of Yisra'el" (Exod. 39:6).

The idiom "signet engravings", was used for incuse inscriptions upon artifacts other than seals, such as gold jewelry:
"ועשית ציץ זהב טהור ופתחת עליו פתוחי חתם קדש ליהוה" — "And thou shalt make a plate of pure gold, and engrave upon it, like the engravings of a signet, Holiness to the Lord" (Exod. 28:36).

The wearing practices according to the OT

According to the OT, seals were worn on the chest, on the arm, on the right hand, or on the finger:
"ויסר פרעה את־טבעתו מעל ידו ויתן אתה על־יד יוסף" — "And Par'o took off his ring from his hand, and put it on Yosef's hand" (Gen. 41:42).

"שימני כחותם על לבך כחותם על זרועך" — "Set me as a seal upon thy heart, as a seal upon thy arm" (Songs 8:6).

"ושמתיך כחותם כי בך בחרתי" — "and will make thee like a signet ring: for I have chosen thee" (Hag. 2:23).

"חותם על־יד ימין" — "signet upon my right hand" (Jer. 22:24).

Other uses of seals according to the OT

In addition to documents, the custom of sealing with personal seals was performed on other items. In several biblical verses this custom is mentioned. For example, the rock which blocked the lion's den in which Daniel had been cast was sealed with two seals, one belonging to the King and the second to one of his ministers:

"והיתית אבן חדה ושמת על־פי גבא וחתמה מלכא בעזקתה ובעזקת רברבנוהי" "And a stone was brought, and laid upon the mouth of the den; and the king sealed it with this own signed, and with the signet of his lords" (Daniel 6:18).

In the OT period the seal-impression and the seal itself served as an identifying object. Moreover, it could be used as a security deposit. This we learn from Tamar's request to have Judah's seal as a pledge and the use she made of it:

"מה הערבון אשר אתן־לך ותאמר חתמך ופתילך ומטך אשר בידך ויתן לה" — "And he said, What pledge shall I give thee? And she said, Thy signet, and thy cord, and thy staff that is in thy hand" (Gen. 38:18).

"הכר־נא למי החתמת ופתילים והמטה האלה" — "Discern, I pray thee, whose are these, the signet, and the cord, and the staff" (Gen. 38:25).

The document sealing custom according to the OT

The personal seal and the custom of sealing documents is significantly important in the OT period and it is clear from many verses:

"ותכתב ספרים בשם אחאב ותחתם בחתמו" — "So she wrote letters in Ah'av's name, and sealed them with his seal" (I Kgs. 21:8).

"ואכתב בספר ואחתם" — "And I subscribed the deed, and sealed it" (Jer. 32:10).

"וכתוב בספר וחתום והעד עדים" — "And subscribe deeds, and seal them, and take witnesses" (Jer. 32:44).

"אתה חותם תכנית מלא חכמה וכליל יפי" — "Thou art a seal and paragon, full of wisdom, and perfect in beauty" (Ezek. 28:12).

"לקוח את־הספרים האלה את ספר המקנה הזה ואת החתום ואת ספר הגלוי הזה ונחתום בכלי חרס למען יעמדו ימים רבים" — "Take these documents, this deed of the purchase, both that which is sealed, and this open deed; and put them in an earthen vessel, that they may last for many days" (Jer. 32:14).

"ותהי לכם חזות הכל כדברי הספר החתום אשר־יתנו אתו אל־יודע הספר לאמר קרא נא־זה ואמר לא אוכל כי חתום הוא" — "And the vision of all this is become to you as the words of a book that is sealed, which men deliver to one that is learned, saying, Read this, I pray thee: and he says, I cannot: for it is sealed" (Isa. 29:11).

"יד־כל־אדם־יחתום" — "He seals up the hand of every man" (Job 37:7).

"צור תעודה חתום" — "Bind up the testimony" (Isa. 8:16).

"כי כתב אשר נכתב בשם המלך ונחתם בטבעת המלך אין להשיב" — "But the writing which is already written in the king's name, and sealed with the king's ring, cannot be revoked" (Esth. 8:8).

"ויכתב בשם המלך אחשורש ויחתם בטבעת המלך" — "And he wrote in the name of the king Ahashverosh, and sealed it with the king's ring" (Esth. 8:10).

These documents were made of rolled parchment or papyrus, bound up and tied with a cord. To the cord, or to the knot, was attached a lump of clay called a "bulla" which was impressed with a seal. A document was sealed with one or several bullae.

The use of seals and bullae according to the Mishna

In the Mishna (Kedoshim, Tamid 3:3), the "chamber of the seals" which was in the temple is mentioned. There the seals were kept whose impressions on bullae served as evidence of the payment for the sacrifice. Also, there is mentioned a functionary "who is in charge over the seals" (Shekalim, 5:3–4).

The onomasticon

The onomastic list formed by names found on seals and sealings, is equivalent in its volume and heterogeneity to that which is known from the Old Testament. Moreover, it is a first-hand, reliable apparatus. The owner's name on seals, like those in the Bible, is composed of his personal name and that of his father. Rarely, the name of his grand father is also mentioned. On one bulla, even the name of the grand father's father is given; where we witness the paponym phenomenon, the seal owner is named after his great-grand father (Deutsch and Heltzer 1997, no. 96). Personal names with no patronym are also recorded. In general, the names are theophoric. The theophoric element may appear as a prefix or as a suffix. Such names are **יהו**עזר and עזרי**הו** "Yehoʿazar" and "ʿAzaryahu". A hypocoristicon is a shortened name which has lost its theophoric element. Such names are ברוך (ברכיהו) "Baruch" (Berekhyahu) or סמך (סמכיהו) "Samakh" (Samakhyahu). The theophoric element יו "Yau", is typical to the northern Israelite kingdom, while the theophoric element יהו "Yahu (Yahweh)" is typical to the southern Judean kingdom. The theophoric element serves as a criterion to define and classify the name as Israelite, Judean or foreign.

The Hebrew names are usually sentences. Such names are:

Verbal sentence: עזריהו — "ʿAzaryahu" (The God Yahweh, has helped) or יהונתן — "Yehonatan" (The God Yahweh, has given).

Interrogative, rhetorical sentence: מיכאל — "Mikhaʾel" (Who is like the God El) or מכיהו — "Mikhayahu" (Who is like the God Yahweh).

Declarative sentence: אביהו — "Abiyahu" (My father is the God Yahweh) or מלכיהו — "Malkiyahu" (My King is the God Yahweh).

Request sentence: שבניהו — "Shebanyahu" (Pray, God Yahweh, return).

Another common phenomenon was the adoption of names from the flora and fauna of Judah such as: תמר — "Tamar" (Palm), אפרח — "ʾEphraḥ" (To blossom), שעל — "Shuʿal" (Fox), עכבר — "Achbor" (Mouse), פרעש — "Parʿosh" (Flea), עורב — "ʿOreb" (Crow), חגב — "Ḥagab" (Grasshopper), etc. In this study, four new, hitherto unknown, personal names are revealed: איעם "ʾEyʿam", אליכן "ʾEliyakhin", מנחמו "Menaḥemo" and מקמיהו "Meqimyahu". Two city names, ʾArubboth and Naṣib, recorded only in the Old Testament, are also presented here for the first time in extra-biblical sources.

The iconography of the Hebrew seals

The manufacture of Hebrew iconographic personal seals, starts with the adoption of the Phoenician script by the Hebrew language. Iconic seals are common until the conquest of Samaria in 720 B.C.E., become significantly diminished in the 7th century B.C.E. and are very scarce by the end of the 7th century B.C.E. (Avigad 1986:118–119). A rich variety of subjects was used to decorate the Hebrew seals. A list of such motifs are presented below:

Phoenico-Egyptian motifs

Two-winged beetle (Avigad 1986, no. 199)
Four-winged beetle (Hestrin and Dayagi-Mendels 1979, nos. 47, 48, 133)
Winged sun (Deutsch and Heltzer 1995, nos. 65, 66)
Two-winged *Uraeus* (Hestrin and Dayagi-Mendels 1979, no. 36)
Four-winged *Uraeus* (Avigad 1986, nos. 200, 201)
Griffin, standing, seated or crouching (Hestrin and Dayagi-Mendels 1979, nos. 41–44)
The bust of Sekhmet, the Egyptian lioness-headed goddess (Deutsch and Heltzer, 1995, no. 63)

Floral motifs

Phoenician-style palmette (Avigad 1986, nos. 6, 47, 58, 75, 129)
Proto-Aeolic (palmette) capital (ibid., no. 206)
Palm tree (ibid., no. 205)
Pillar with Proto-Aeolic (palmette) capital (ibid., nos. 116, 137; and no. 54 below)
Palm branch (ibid., nos. 20, 42; and nos. 38, 92, 102 below)
Pomegranates (ibid., no. 24; Deutsch and Heltzer 1995, no. 66; and no. 66 below)

Faunal motifs

Horse (Deutsch and Heltzer 1994, no. 21)
Lion (Hestrin and Dayagi-Mendels 1979, no. 3)
Grazing doe (Avigad 1986, no. 169; Hestrin and Dayagi-Mendels 1979, nos. 45, 46; Deutsch and Heltzer 1994, nos. 23, 27; and nos. 32, 37, 51 below)
Fox (Deutsch and Heltzer 1994, no. 25)
Horned quadruped (Avigad 1986, nos. 203, 204)
Alligator (Deutsch and Heltzer 1995, no. 65)
Rooster (Hestrin and Dayagi-Mendels 1979, nos. 5, 6)
Bird (Avigad 1986, no. 202; Deutsch and Heltzer 1994, no. 19)
Fish (Avigad 1986, no. 132; Hestrin and Dayagi-Mendels 1979, nos. 34, 51; and no. 65 below)
Locust (Hestrin and Dayagi-Mendels 1979, no. 42)
Scorpion (Deutsch and Heltzer 1995, no. 66)

Anthropomorphic motifs

Ruler (Avigad 1986, no. 10; Barkay 1994)
Priest (Avigad 1986, no. 77)
Youth with griffin (Deutsch and Heltzer 1995, no. 75)
Egyptian-style youth (Hestrin and Dayagi-Mendels 1979, nos. 39, 40)
Chain of (dancing?) human figures (Deutsch and Heltzer 1995, no. 68)

The register divider as ornament

Floral motifs

Lotus-bud (Avigad 1986. nos. 38, 147,152; and below nos. 7, 21, 47, 49, 59, 93)
Parallel lines terminating in a lotus or palmette (Avigad 1986, nos. 30, 37, 138, 165; and below no. 52)
Parallel lines terminating in pomegranates (Avigad 1986, no. 70; Deutsch and Heltzer 1995, no. 55, 66)

Geometric motifs

Ladder-pattern (Avigad 1986, nos. 80, 127, 150, 153, 157; and below nos. 15, 16, 36, 55, 64, 88)
Thunderbolt pattern (Avigad 1986, nos. 123, 136)
Parallel lines terminating in a loop (Hestrin and Dayagi-Mendels 1979, nos. 53, 60)
Parallel lines terminating with dots (Hestrin and Dayagi-Mendels 1979, nos. 63, 64; and below no. 61)
Two parallel lines with a row of dots (pearls) between them (Hestrin and Dayagi-Mendels 1979, no. 76; Deutsch and Heltzer 1995, no. 74)

The border as ornament

Two parallel lines with a row of dots (pearls) between them (Avigad 1986, nos. 52, 69, 83)
A chain of pomegranates (Deutsch and Heltzer 1997, no. 86; and no. 66 below)
Ladder-pattern (Avigad 1986, no. 25; Deutsch and Heltzer 1995, no. 61)

This list includes the majority of the patterns but it is not complete and new motifs are frequently discovered (See plates IX–XIII).

The question of authenticity

Most of the Hebrew bullae have no provenance. These reached the antiquity market, mainly in Jerusalem, and from there they found their way to public and private collections. This fact obliges us to question the authenticity of the bullae. We learn about the existence of seals and sealings from the bullae uncovered in controlled excavations at the City of David, Lachish, Beth-Zur, Beer-Sheba, Tell el-Ḥesi and Tell el-Judeideh (See below the section Bullae uncovered from controlled excavations). Also to be mentioned are seals uncovered in controlled excavations such as Megiddo, Lachish, Arad, etc., which testify to the extensive use of seals and sealings in the First Temple period.

The other rich source of knowledge about seals and sealings is the Bible (See above the section: The seal in the Old Testament).

The authenticity question has been raised in the past by N. Avigad within his publication of 255 bullae from non-controlled excavation. Avigad (1986:13) states: "There was no reason to suspect their authenticity, and I seriously doubt whether it would be possible to forge such burnt and damaged bullae".

The group composed of 109 bullae, presented here for the first time (Chapter Three), were examine under a powerful (x40) microscope. As a result of the microscopic analysis, several phenomena, which argue for their authenticity, were observed:

1. All the bullae suffered from corrosion and from much climateric damage during the 2700 years. These symptoms were observed on the surfaces, on the edges, in the cracks and on the reverse of the bullae.

2. Crystals of different sizes and shapes were present on the surfaces of the bullae. These also

grow in the clay, toward the outside, causing cracks and breakages to the surfaces.[1]

3. Corrosion and crystals are present on fractured surfaces, and in cracks made while the lumps of clay were being impressed in antiquity. These are not visible on recently-damaged surfaces.

4. Environmental contaminations, such as wires, hairs or other organic materials, were not detected in or on the clay. These probably existed in antiquity, at the time they were made, but they decomposed and vanished over time.

5. Professionally magnified black and white, and color pictures of all the bullae were taken.[2] Some were enlarged 40 times. These contribute to a better visual examination of the weathering phenomena on the surfaces of the seal-impressions.

6. The royal bulla of Ahaz (Chapter Three, no. 1), has been examined by some preeminent scholars. Among them are F. M. Cross, A. Lemaire, P. Bordreuil, K. McCarter, W.G. Lambert and G. Barkay. They all express a unanimous opinion about the authenticity of the royal seal-impression.

7. Several bullae which are first presented in Chapter Three (below), have published duplicates, i.e. were sealed with the same seals. These are:

a. Bulla no. 2: *lyhwzr/ḥ bn ḥlq/yhw ʿbd ḥ/zqyhw* — "Belonging to Yehozaraḥ son of Ḥilqiyahu, servant of Ḥizqiyahu", identical with the bulla published by Hestrin and Dayagi-Mendels (1974; 1979, no. 4).

b. Bulla no. 59: *lmlkyhw b/n ywʿlyhw* — "Belonging to Malkiyahu, son of Yoʿaliyahu", identical with a bulla published by Deutsch and Heltzer (1994, no. 20).

c. Two identical bullae, nos. 66a-b: *lnrʾ / mlkyhw* — "Belonging to Neraʾ, son of Malkiyahu", identical with another two bullae: one unpublished, kept in a private collection in Tel Aviv, and the second one published by Deutsch and Heltzer (1997, no. 86).[3]

d. Bulla no. 86: *lškny/h/w / ʾlʿśh* — "Belonging to Shekanyahu (son of) ʾElʿaśa", identical with the bulla published by Deutsch and Heltzer (1994, no. 16).

e. Bulla no. 65: *lnḥmyhw / yhwʾb* — "Belonging to Neḥemyahu, son of Yehoʾab", identical with an unpublished bulla kept in a private collection in Tel Aviv.

8. Two bullae were chosen randomly from among those which are in a poor state of preservation, but look fired.[4] These are no. 76c and no. 85 (below). Bulla no. 76c was sent to Germany (R. Kotalla Laboratory in Haigerloch), and bulla no. 85 to England (Research Laboratory for Archaeology in Oxford). Both laboratories performed thermoluminescence tests and reached the conclusion that they are ancient (See plates XIV–XV).

---

1. See an enlarged color photo x7, of the Royal Bulla of Ahaz (plate XVI). Notice the crystals of dot and ring shapes which grew on the surface and especially a large white one above the letter *alef* which grew from inside the clay toward the outside causing a crack and breakage in the surface.
2. The black and white pictures were taken by Mr. Zeev Radovan of Jerusalem.
3. The bulla no. 66a (below) has been recently published in WSS (no. 583) erroneously as: "Belonging to Neriyahu(?), son of Malkiyahu".
4. Clay bullae were normally not fired but dried naturally as a result of their use in antiquity to seal objects. Still, some of them come from destruction strata which suffered fire. Therefore thermoluminescence analysis can be performed on some of them. Such tests were made for two bullae in our group (See plates XIV–XV).

Chapter Two

Hebrew bullae from controlled excavations

1. Tell el-Judeideh

Two bullae were discovered in the 1899–1900 archaeological excavations, first published by Bliss (1900:221–222):

1. כברה *kbrh* — "(Belonging to) *kbrh*?". Only a drawing has been published by Bliss (WSS 536).

2. ..לשמרנ *lšmrn..* — "Belonging to *šmrn..*", damaged bulla which depicts a two-winged beetle. Only a drawing has been published by Bliss (WSS 639).

2. Beth-Zur

A bulla found in 1931 (Sellers and Albright 1931:8):

1. לגאליהו / בן המלך *lgʾlyhw / bn hmlk* — "Belonging to Geʾalyahu, the son of the king" (WSS 412).

3. Lachish

Nineteen bullae were discovered at Lachish. Two in 1936 (Tufnell et al. in *Lachish* III:348, nos. 172,173):

1. לגדליהו / אשר על הבית *lgdlyhw / ʾšr ʿl hbyt* — "Belonging to Gedalyahu, who is over the house". Chance find on the surface (WSS 405).

2. לחלקיהו / בן מאס *lḥlqyhw / bn mʾs* — "Belonging to Ḥilqiyahu son of *mʾs*". Found in Locus H15, room 1003 (WSS 498).

In the 1966 expedition to Lachish headed by Y. Aharoni, a terracotta juglet containing 17 Hebrew bullae was uncovered from the floor of a store-room (*Lachish* V:19–22, Pl. 20–21). Only seven are legible and two, partly legible. Bullae nos. 8 and 9 are duplicates and bulla no. 5 belonged to a high official:

3. (no. 1a) ליהוכל / בן יהו[ח]י *lyhwkl / bn yhw[ḥ]y* — "Belonging to Yehukal son of Yehoḥai" (WSS 524).

4. (no. 2a) לנחם ב/ן ענניהו *lnḥm b/n ʿnnyhw* — "Belonging to Naḥum son of ʿAnaniyahu" (WSS 571).

5. (no. 3a) לנריהו / [בן] פרעש *lnryhw / [bn] prʿš* — "Belonging to Neriyahu son of Parʿoš" (WSS 577).

6. (no. 4a) ליהואל / מיאמן *lyhwʾl / myʾmn* — "Belonging to Yhoʾel (son of) Miʾamen" (WSS 523).

7. (no. 5a) לשבניהו / [בן or עבד] המלך *lšbnyhw / [bn* or *ʿbd] hmlk* — "Belonging to Shebanyahu, son/servant of the king" (WSS 416).

8. (no. 6a) לירמיהו / בן צפניהו / בן נבי *lyrmyhw / bn ṣpnyhw / bn nby* — "Belonging to Yirmiyahu, son of Ṣepanyahu, son of Nobai" (WSS 530).

9. (no. 7a) לירמיהו / בן צפניהו / בן נבי *lyrmyhw / bn ṣpnyhw / bn nby* — "Belonging to Yirmiyahu, son of Ṣepanyahu, son of Nobai" (WSS 530).

10. (no. 9a) ... ליהורם *lyhwrm ..* — "Belonging to Yehoram .."

11. (no. 11a) ... / ..יהו *yhw.. / ...* — "(Belonging to) Yeho..."

4. Beer-Sheba

In the 1971 expedition to Beer-Sheba, headed by Y. Aharoni of the Tel Aviv University, a Hebrew bulla impressed with a square seal was uncovered in Locus 435, an Iron Age II room of Stratum II (*Beer-Sheba* I:75–76, Pl.32, no. 1). The bulla is damaged, yet is very large, the largest of its kind (impression size 50x55 mm.). The reading of the patronym is not certain:

1. לעבדיהו / נריהו *lʿbdyhw / nryhw* — "'Belonging to ʿObadyahu (son of) Neriyahu?" (WSS 661).

5. Tell el-Ḥesi

In the 1977 excavations at Tell el-Ḥesi (O'Connell 1977), a bulla dated to the late 8th century B.C.E. has been found. The inscription is complete and in a good state of preservation:

1. למתניהו / ישמעאל *lmtnyhw / yšmʿʾl* — "Belonging to Mattanyahu (son of) Yishmaʿʾel" (WSS 568).

6. Jerusalem

In the 1982 area G excavation at the City of David in Jerusalem, headed by Y. Shiloh of the Hebrew University (Shoham 1994), 51 bullae were uncovered. 47 are Hebrew epigraphic, although four fragments belonged to two bullae. The remaining four are iconic unepigraphic:

1. [לאחָ]זיהו or [לע]זיהו / [אל]שמע or [יהו]שמע *[lʾḥ]zyhw* or *[lʿ]zyhw / [ʾl]šmʿ* or *[yhw]šmʿ* — "Belonging to ʾAḥazyahu / ʿUzziyahu (son of) ʾElishamaʿ / Yehoshamaʿ" (S 26; WSS 660).

2. לאחיאב / בן יהואב *lʾḥyʾb bn yhwʾb* — "Belonging to ʾAḥyʾab son of Yehoʾab" (S 37, WSS 427).

3. לאחימה / חנניה *lʾḥymh / ḥnnyh* — "Belonging to ʾAḥymo (son of) Ḥananyah" (S 28, WSS 429).

4. לאליקם / בן אוהל *lʾlyqm / bn ʾwhl* — "Belonging to ʾElyaqim son of ʾOhel", duplicate of no. 5 (S 29, WSS 437a).

5. לאליקם / בן אוהל *lʾlyqm / bn ʾwhl* — "Belonging to ʾElyaqim son of ʾOhel", duplicate of no. 4 (S 30, WSS 437b).

6. [ל]אלנתן / בן בלגי *[l]ʾlntn / bn blgy* — "Belonging to ʾElnatan son of Bilgai". Register divider: double line terminating in loops (S 20, WSS 440).

7. לאלנתן / [ב]ן בלגי *lʾlntn / [b]n blgy* — "Belonging to ʾElnatan son of Bilgai". Register divider: lotus-bud (S 21, WSS 441).

8. לאלשמע / בן יהואב *lʾlšmʿ / bn yhwʾb* — "Belonging to ʾElishamaʿ son of Yehoʾab" (S 18, WSS 447 *yhwʾb or yhwʾur*).

9. לאלשמע ב/ן סמכיהו *lʾlšmʿ b/n smkyhw* — "Belonging to ʾElishamaʿ son of Semakyahu (S 7, WSS 448).

10. לאפרח / אחיהו *lʾprḥ / ʾḥyhw* — "Belonging to ʾEfraḥ (son of) ʾAḥiyahu". Duplicate of no. 11 (S 9, WSS 450a).

11. לאפרח / אחיהו *lʾprḥ / ʾḥyhw* — "Belonging to ʾEfraḥ (son of) ʾAḥiyahu". Duplicate of no. 10 (S 10, WSS 450b).

12. לבלגי ב/ן דליה[ו] *lblgy b/n dlyh[w]* — "Belonging to Bilgai son of Delayahu" (S 1, WSS 458).

13. לבניהו ב/ן הושעיהו *lbnyhw b/n hwšʿyhw* — "Belonging to Benayahu son of Hoshaʿyahu" (S 31, WSS 459).

14. לברכיהו / בן מלכי *lbrkyhw / bn mlky* — "Belonging to Berekyahu son of Malki" (S 33, WSS 463 *mlky* or *mlkyhw*).

15. לברכי[הו] / בן ע... *lbrky[hw] / bn ʿ...* — "Belonging to Berekyahu son of ʿA..." (S 40, WSS 464).

16. לגא[ליהו] / ... *lgʾ[lyhw] / ...* — "Belonging to Gaʾalyahu ..." (S 22, WSS 466).

17. לגדיהו / בן עזר *lgdyhw / bn ʿzr* — "Belonging to Gaddiyahu son of ʿEzer" (S 13, WSS 467).

18. לגמריה / בן מגן *lgmryh / bn mgn* — "Belonging to Gemaryah son of Magen" (S 19, WSS 469 *gmryhw*).

19. לגמריהו / [ב]ן שפן *lgmryhw / [b]n špn* — "Belonging to Gemaryahu son of Shafan" (S 2, WSS 470).

20. לדלי[הו] ב/[ן] הושעיהו *ldly[hw] b/[n] hwšʿyhw* — "Belonging to Delayahu son of Hoshaʿyahu" (S 25, WSS 474).

21. להושעיה[ו] / ...יהו *lhwšʿyh[w] / ...yhw* — "Belonging to Hoshaʿyahu (son of) ...yahu" (S 11, WSS 482).

22. לחנמלך / ישמעאל *lḥnmlk / yšmʿʾl* — "Belonging to Ḥannamelek (son of) Yishmaʿʾel" (S 3, WSS 500).

23. לחנניה[ו] ב/ן אחא *lḥnnyh[w] b/n ʾḥʾ* — "Belonging to Ḥananyahu son of ʾAḥʾa" (S 34, WSS 503).

24. לטבשלם / בן זכר *lṭbšlm / bn zkr* — "Belonging to Ṭobshallem son of Zakkur" (S 4, WSS 508).

25. לטבשלם / בן בנזכר *lṭbšlm / bn bnzkr* — "Belonging to Ṭobshallem son of Benzakar" (S 5; WSS 509).

26. לי.. / בן עזריהו *ly.. / bn ʿzryhw* — "Belonging to Y... son of ʿAzaryahu" (Shiloh 1986, 38+44, S 38, WSS 510).

27. ליאזניה[ו] / [ב]ן מעשיהו *lyʾznyh[w] / [b]n mʿśyhw* — "Belonging to Yaʾazanyahu son of Maʿaśeyahu" (S 41, WSS 511).

28. לידעיהו / בן משלם *lydʿyhw bn mšlm* — "Belonging to Yedaʿyahu son of Meshullam" (S 12, WSS 515).

29. ליה[ו] ... / בן ב... *lyh[w].. / bn b..* — "Belonging to Yeho.. son of B.." (S 43, WSS 518).

30. למכי[הו] / בן חצי *lmky[hw] / bn ḥṣy* — "Belonging to Mikayahu son of Ḥaṣi" (S 8, WSS 541).

31. [ל]נחם בן / שאלה [l]nḥm bn / š'lh — "Belonging to Naḥum son of She'ila" (S 45, WSS 573).

32. לנריהו / דמליהו lnryhw / dmlyhw — "Belonging to Neriyahu (son of) Domleyahu" (S 36, WSS 581).

33. לנתנ[יהו / ב]ן רח[ם]? lntn[yhw / b]n rḥ[m]? — "Belonging to Natanyahu son of Raḥam?" (S 16, WSS 586).

34. לסילא / [ב]ן אלשמע lsyl' / [b]n 'lšm' — "Belonging to Sila' son of 'Elishama'" (S 35, WSS 588 *syl'* or *yl'*).

35. לעזריהו / בן א[חא]? l'zryhw / bn '[ḥ'] — "Belonging to 'Azaryahu son of 'Aḥa'?" (S 42, WSS 595).

36. לעזריהו ב/ן חלקיהו l'zryhw b/n ḥlqyhw — "Belonging to 'Azaryahu son of Ḥilqiyahu" (S 27, WSS 596).

37. לעזרקם / מכיהו l'zrqm / mkyhw — "Belonging to 'Azriqam (son of) Mikayahu" (S 32, WSS 599).

38. לעמ[דיהו] / אשיהו l'm[dyhw] / 'šyhw — "Belonging to 'Immadiyahu (son of) 'Ashyahu" (Shiloh 1986, 6+24; S 24; WSS 605).

39. לרפאיהו / בן אפרח lrp'yhw / bn 'prḥ — "Belonging to Rapa'yahu son of 'Efraḥ" (S 17, WSS 626).

40. לשמעיהו / בן יאזני[הו] lšm'yhw / bn y'zny[hw] — "Belonging to Shema'yahu son of Ya'azanyahu" (S 15, WSS 636 *y'zny*).

41. לשמעי[הו] / מחסי[הו] lšm'y[hw] / mḥsy[hw] — "Belonging to Shema'yahu (son of) Maḥseyahu" (S 14, WSS 637).

42. לשמעיהו / [ב]ן פלטיהו lšm'yhw / [b]n plṭyhw — "Belonging to Shema'yahu son of Pelaṭyahu" (S 23, WSS 638).

43. לשפטיהו / בן דמלי[הו] lšpṭyhw / bn dmly[hw] — "Belonging to Shefaṭyahu son of Domleyahu" (S 44, WSS 643).

44. לשפטיהו / בן צפן lšpṭyhw / bn ṣpn — "Belonging to Shefaṭyahu son of Ṣapan" (S 39, WSS 644).

45. [לטבשלם]? / בן זכר / הרפא [lṭbšlm]? / bn zkr / hrp' — "Belonging to Ṭobshallem son of Zakkur, the Healer" (S 6, WSS 420 *zkr* or *bnzkr*).

Unprovenanced published Hebrew bullae

7. The British Museum collection

A bulla purchased by the museum in 1965 from the Shlomo Moussaieff collection:

1. לחנניהו ב/ן גדליהו lḥnnyhw b/n gdlyhw — "Belonging to Ḥananyahu son of Gedalyahu" (Avigad 1964:193, WSS 504).

8. 255 Hebrew bullae (from Tell Beit Mirsim area?)

The unprovenanced find appeared on the antiquities market in Jerusalem in 1975 and was published by Avigad in 1986. The assumed origin of the group (Tell Beit Mirsim) has no sufficiently reliable support (Avigad 1986:13).[5]

A1. לאדניהו / אשר על הבית *lʾdnyhw / ʾšr ʿl hbyt* — "Belonging to ʾAdoniyahu who is over the house" (WSS 403).

A2a. לאדניהו / אשר על הבית *lʾdnyhw / ʾšr ʿl hbyt* — "Belonging to ʾAdoniyahu who is over the house" (WSS 404a).

A2b. לאדניהו / אשר על הבית *lʾdnyhw / ʾšr ʿl hbyt* — "Belonging to ʾAdoniyahu who is over the house" (Duplicate of the previous bulla, WSS 404b).

A3. לנתן אשר / [ע]ל בית *lntn ʾšr / [ʿ]l byt* — "Belonging to Natan who is over (the) house" (WSS 406).

A4. לאלשמע / [ע]בד המלך *lʾlšmʿ / [ʿ]bd hmlk* — "Belonging to ʾElishamaʿ servant of the king" (WSS 408).

A5. לגדליהו / עבד המלך *lgdlyhw / ʿbd hmlk* — "Belonging to Gedalyahu servant of the king" (WSS 409).

A6. לגאליהו ב/ן המלך *lgʾlyhw b/n hmlk* — "Belonging to Geʾalyahu son of the king". In the upper register a Phoenician-style palmette motif is depicted (WSS 413).

A7. לנרי[הו ב]/ן המלך *lnry[hw b]/n hmlk* — "Belonging to Neriyahu son of the king" (WSS 415).

A8. לירחמאל / בן המלך *lyrḥmʾl / bn hmlk* — "Belonging to Yeraḥmeʾel son of the king" (WSS 414).

A9. לברכיהו / בן נריהו / הספר *lbrkyhw / bn nryhw / hspr* — "Belonging to Berekhyahu son of Neriyahu, the scribe" (WSS 417a).

A10. שר הער *śr hʿr* — "The Governor of the city". Two male figures, in pseudo-Assyrian style, stand opposite one another. The figure on the left holds a bow and arrows. The script appears in a cartouche (WSS 402a). A duplicate of this bulla is on display in the Kadman Numismatic Museum in Tel Aviv (Barkay 1994; WSS 402b).

A11. לאדניהו ב/ן יקמיהו *lʾdnyhw b/n yqmyhw* — "Belonging to ʾAdoniyahu son of Yeqamyahu" (WSS 423).

A12. לפדיהו / יהוקם *lpdyhw / yhwqm* — "Belonging to Pedayahu (son of) Yehoqam" (WSS 608).

A13. [לא]חיהו / [א]ביהו *[lʾ]ḥyhw / [ʾ]byhw* — "Belonging to ʾAḥiyahu (son of) ʾAbiyahu" (WSS 428).

A14. לאחקם בנ[ן] / טביהו *lʾḥqm b[n]ṭbyhw* — "Belonging to ʾAḥiqam son of Ṭobiyahu". In the upper register a Phoenician-style palmette motif is depicted (WSS 433).

A15. לאחקם / נריהו *lʾḥqm / nryhw* — "Belonging to ʾAḥiqam (son of) Neriyahu" (WSS 434).

A16. לאחקם / אחאב *lʾḥqm / ʾḥʾb* — "Belonging to ʾAḥiqam (son of) ʾAḥʾab" (WSS 432).

A17. לאלעז / בן אחאב *lʾlʿz / bn ʾḥʾb* — "Belonging to ʾEl(i)ʿaz son of ʾAḥʾab" (WSS 444).

A18a. לאלעז בן / אחאב *lʾlʿz bn / ʾḥʾb* — "Belonging to ʾEl(i)ʿaz son of ʾAḥʾab" (WSS 445a).

5. If not mentioned otherwise, the bulla is aniconic.

A18b. לאלעז בן / א]חאב *l'l'z b[n / ']ḥ'b* — "Belonging to 'El(i)'az son of 'Aḥ'ab" (Duplicate of the previous bulla, WSS 445b).

A18c. ל]אלעז בן] / אחאב *l[']l'z bn]/ 'ḥ'b* — "Belonging to 'El(i)'az son of 'Aḥ'ab" (Duplicate of the previous bulla, WSS 445c).

A19. לאחאב / בן אפרח *l'ḥ'b / bn 'prḥ* — "Belonging to 'Aḥ'ab son of 'Ephraḥ" (WSS 426).

A20. [לא]פרח בן / יהושע *[l']prḥ bn / yhwš'* — "Belonging to 'Ephraḥ son of Yehoshua'" (WSS 451).

A21. לאפרח ב/ן יהושע בן / מתניהו *l'prḥ b/n yhwš' bn / mtnyhw* — "Belonging to 'Ephraḥ son of Yehoshua' son of Mattanyahu" (WSS 452).

A22. [לא]פרח / [בן] שחר *[l']prḥ / [bn]šḥr* — "Belonging to 'Ephraḥ son of Shaḥar" (WSS 453).

A23. לאפרח / [בן שח]ר בן / [ג]דיהו *l'prḥ / [bn šḥ]r bn / [g]dyhw* — "Belonging to 'Ephraḥ son of Shaḥar son of Gaddiyahu" (WSS 454).

A24a. לשחר בן / גדיהו *lšḥr bn / gdyhw* — "Belonging to Shaḥar son of Gaddiyahu". Lentoid-form seal with a vertical strip of three pomegranates on either end (WSS 629a).

A24b. לשחר בן / גדיהו *lšḥr bn / gdyhw* — "Belonging to Shaḥar son of Gaddiyahu" (Duplicate of the previous bulla, WSS 629b).

A24c. לשחר בן / [גד]יהו *lšḥr bn / [gd]yhw* — "Belonging to Shaḥar son of Gaddiyahu" (Duplicate of the previous bulla, WSS 629c).

A24d. לשחר בן / גדי[הו] *lšḥr bn / gdy[hw]* — "Belonging to Shaḥar son of Gaddiyahu" (Duplicate of the previous bulla, WSS 629d).

A25a. לשחר [ב]/ן גדי *lšḥr [b]/n gdy* — "Belonging to Shaḥar son of Gaddi" (WSS 627a).

A25b. [לש]חר ב/[ן גדי] *[lš]ḥr b/[n gdy]* — "Belonging to Shaḥar son of Gaddi" (Duplicate of the previous bulla, WSS 627b).

A26. לשחר [ג]דיה[ו] *lšḥr [g]dyh[w]* — "Belonging to Shaḥar (son of) Gaddiyahu" (WSS 628).

A27. [ל]אליהו ב/[ן] מיכה *[l']lyhw b/[n] mykh* — "Belonging to 'Eliyahu son of Mikha" (WSS 435).

A28. לאליעז / בן הושעי[הו] *l'ly'z / bn hwš'y[hw]* — "Belonging to 'Eli'az son of Hosha'yahu" (WSS 436: 'Eli'az or 'Eli'ezer).

A29. לאלירם / שמעיהו *l'lyrm / šm'yhw* — "Belonging to 'Eliram (son of) Shema'yahu" (WSS 439).

A30. לאלנ[ת]ן / בן יאש *l'ln[t]n / bn y'š* — "Belonging to 'Elnatan son of Ya'ush". Register divider terminating at either end in a lily design (WSS 442).

A31a. [ל]אמריהו / [ב]/ן / [י]הואב *[l']mryhw / [b]/n / [y]hw'b* — "Belonging to 'Amaryahu son of Yeho'ab". Register divider terminating at either end in two papyrus flowers (WSS 449a).

A31b. [ל]אמריהו / ב/ן / יהואב *[l']mryhw / b/n / yhw'b* — "Belonging to 'Amaryahu son of Yeho'ab". Register divider terminating at either end in two papyrus flower designs (Duplicate of the previous bulla, WSS 449b).

A32. לאשחר ב/[ן] עשיהו *l'šḥr b/[n]'śyhw* — "Belonging to 'Ashḥur son of 'Aśayahu" (WSS 455).

A33. לאשיהו / בן שמעיהו *lʾšyhw / bn šmʿyhw* — "Belonging to ʾAshyahu son of Shemaʿyahu" (WSS 456).

A34. [לאש]רחי / עשיהו *[lʾš]rḥy / ʿśyhw* — "Belonging to ʾAsherḥai (son of) ʿAśayahu" (WSS 457).

A35. לבניהו / עליהו *lbnyhw / ʿlyhw* — "Belonging to Benayahu (son of) ʿAliyahu" (WSS 460).

A36. לבעדיהו / ... *lbʿdyhw / ...* — "Belonging to Baʿadiyahu ..." (WSS 461).

A37. לבעדיהו / שריהו *lbʿdyhw / śryhw* — "Belonging to Baʿadiyahu (son of) Śerayahu". Register divider terminating at either end in a lily design (WSS 462).

A38. [ל]ברכיהו / [בן ש]מעיהו *[l]brkyhw / [bn š]mʿyhw* — "Belonging to Berekhyahu son of Shemaʿyahu". Lotus-bud register divider (WSS 465).

A39. לגעלי ב/ן אליסמך *lgʿly b/n ʾlysmk* — "Belonging to Gaʿali son of ʾElisamak" (WSS 471).

A40. לגעלי ב/ן אלסמך *lgʿly b/n ʾlsmk* — "Belonging to Gaʿali son of ʾEl(i)samak" (WSS 472).

A41. לגד[לי]הו / הו[ש]עיהו *lgd[ly]hw / hw[š]ʿyhw* — "Belonging to Gedalyahu (son of) Hoshaʿyahu". Ladder-pattern register divider (WSS 468).

A42a. לדמליהו / בן רפא *ldmlyhw / bn rpʾ* — "Belonging to Demalyahu son of Raphaʾ" (WSS 481a).

A42b. [ל]דמליהו / בן ר[פא] *[l]dmlyhw / bn r[pʾ]* — "Belonging to Demalyahu son of Raphaʾ" (Duplicate of the previous bulla, WSS 481b).

A42c. [ל]דמליהו / בן רפ[א] *[l]dmlyhw / bn rp[ʾ]* — "Belonging to Demalyahu son of Raphaʾ" (Duplicate of the previous bulla, not listed in WSS).

A43a לדמליהו ב/ן הושעיה[ו] *ldmlyhw b/n hwšʿyh[w]* — "Belonging to Demalyahu son of Hoshaʿyahu" (WSS 477a).

A43b. לדמליהו [ב]/ן הושעיה[ו] *ldmlyhw [b]/n hwšʿyh[w]* — "Belonging to Demalyahu son of Hoshaʿyahu" (Duplicate of the previous bulla, WSS 477b).

A44. [לד]מליהו / [בן ה]ושעיהו *[ld]mlyhw / [bn h]wšʿyhw* — "Belonging to Demalyahu son of Hoshaʿyahu" (WSS 478).

A45. לד[מליהו] / בן הו[שעיהו] *ld[mlyhw] / bn hw[šʿyhw]* — "Belonging to Demalyahu son of Hoshaʿyahu" (WSS 479: Domleyahu).

A46. לדמלי[הו] / הוש[עיהו] *ldmly[hw] / hwš[ʿyhw]* — Belonging to Demalyahu (son of) Hoshaʿyahu" (WSS 480: Domleyahu).

A47a. להושעיהו / חלציהו *lhwšʿyhw / ḥlṣyhw* — "Belonging to Hoshaʿyahu (son of) Heleṣyahu". In the upper register a Phoenician-style palmette motif is depicted (WSS 483a).

A47b. [ל]הושעיהו / [ח]לצ[י]ה[ו] *[l]hwšʿyhw / [ḥ]lṣ[y]h[w]* — "Belonging to Hoshaʿyahu (son of) Heleṣyahu". (Duplicate of the previous bulla, WSS 483b).

A48. להושעיהו / שמע *lhwšʿyhw / šmʿ* — "Belonging to Hoshaʿyahu (son of) Shemaʿ" (WSS 484).

A49a. להצליהו / בן שבניהו *lhṣlyhw / bn šbnyhw* — "Belonging to Hiṣṣilyahu son of Shebanyahu" (WSS 485a).

A49b. להצליהו / בן [ש]בניה[ו] *lhṣlyhw / bn [š]bnyh[w]* — "Belonging to Hiṣṣilyahu son of Shebanyahu" (Duplicate of the previous bulla, WSS 485b).

A50. לזכר בן / נריהו *lzkr bn / nryhw* — "Belonging to Zakkur son of Neriyahu" (WSS 487).

A51. [לז]כר בן / ..יהו *[lz]kr bn / ..yhw* — "Belonging to Zakkur son of ...yahu" (WSS 486).

A52. לחבא ב/ן מתן *lḥbʾ b/n mtn* — "Belonging to Ḥubbaʾ son of Mattan". Double linear frame containing a row of dots (WSS 488).

A53a. לחגב בן / צפניהו *lḥgb bn / ṣpnyhw* — "Belonging to Ḥagab son of Ṣephanyahu" (WSS 490a).

A53b. [לח]גב ב[ן] / צפניה[ו] *[lḥ]gb b[n] / ṣpnyh[w]* — "Belonging to Ḥagab son of Ṣephanyahu" (Duplicate of the previous bulla, WSS 490b).

A54a. לחגב בן / צפני[הו] *lḥgb bn / ṣpny[hw]* — "Belonging to Ḥagab son of Ṣephanyahu" (WSS 491a)

A54b. לחגב בן / [צ]פני[הו] *lḥgb bn / [ṣ]pny[hw]* — "Belonging to Ḥagab son of Ṣephanyahu" (Duplicate of the previous bulla, WSS 491b).

A55. [ל]חגי בן / הודויהו *[l]ḥgy bn / hwdwyhw* — "Belonging to Ḥaggai son of Hoduyahu". Ladder-pattern register divider (WSS 492).

A56a. לחטש / שפטיהו *lḥṭš / špṭyhw* — "Belonging to Ḥaṭṭush (son of) Shephaṭyahu" (WSS 493a).

A56b. לחטש / שפט[יהו] *lḥṭš / špṭ[yhw]* — "Belonging to Ḥaṭṭush (son of) Ṣhephatyahu" (Duplicate of the previous bulla, WSS 493b).

A56c. [ל]חטש / [שפטיהו] *[l]ḥṭš / [špṭyhw]* — "Belonging to Ḥaṭṭush (son of) Ṣhephatyahu" (Duplicate of the previous bulla, WSS 493c).

A57. לחלק ב/ן עזר *lḥlq b/n ʿzr* — "Belonging to Ḥeleq son of ʿEzer". Register divider made of two curved lines (WSS 495).

A58. לחלקיהו ב/[ן] ..יהו *lḥlqyhw b/[n]..yhw* — "Belonging to Ḥilqiyahu son of ...yahu". In the upper register a Phoenician-style palmette motif is depicted (WSS 497).

A59. לחלקיהו / בן ... *lḥlqyhw / bn ...* — "Belonging to Ḥilqiyahu son of ..." (WSS 496).

A60. [ל]חלץ [בן] / אחאב *[l]ḥlṣ [bn] / ʾḥʾb* — "Belonging to Ḥeleṣ son of ʾAḥʾab" (WSS 494).

A61. לחנניהו / נחמי[הו] *lḥnnyhw / nḥmy[hw]* — "Belonging to Ḥananyahu (son of) Neḥemyahu" (WSS 506: Naḥem or Neḥenyahu).

A62. חנניהו / זרח *ḥnnyhw / zrḥ* — "Belonging to Ḥananyahu (son of) Zeraḥ" (WSS 505: Ḥananyahu or ʿAnaniyahu).

A63. [לח]נן בן / [ע]זיהו בן / ... *[lḥ]nn bn / [ʿ]zyhw bn / ...* — "Belonging to Ḥanan son of ʿUzziyahu son of ..." (WSS 501).

A64. [ל]חנן בן / שמעיהו *[l]ḥnn bn / šmʿyhw* — "Belonging to Ḥanan son of Shemaʿyahu" (WSS 502).

A65. לטבי[הו] / עבדא *lṭby[hw] / ʿbdʾ* — "Belonging to Ṭobiyahu (son of) ʿAbdaʾ" (WSS 507: Ṭobiyahu or Ṭobi).

A66. ליאש בן / אלשמע *lyʾš bn / ʾlšmʿ* — "Belonging to Yaʾush son of ʾElishamaʿ" (WSS 512).

A67. ליאש / [ב]ן פדיהו *lyʾš [b]n pdyhw* — "Belonging to Yaʾush son of Pedayahu" (WSS 513).

A68a. [לידָ[עיהו] / בן כ[רמי] *lyd[ʿyhw]/ bn k[rmy]* — "Belonging to Yedaʿyahu son of Karmi" (WSS 514b).

A68b. [ל]ידעיהו / [בן] כרמי *[l]ydʿyhw / [bn] krmy* — "Belonging to Yedaʿyahu son of Karmi" (Duplicate of the previous bulla, WSS 514a).

A69. לידעיהו / בן שעל *lydʿyhw / bn šʿl* — "Belonging to Yedaʿyahu son of Shuʿal". Double linear frame containing a row of dots (WSS 517).

A70. ליהוא / ב/ן / משמש *lyhwʾ / b/n / mšmš* — "Belonging to Yehuʾ son of *Mšmš*". Register divider made of two arched, double lines which terminate in pomegranates (WSS 519).

A71. ליהואח / אליעז *lyhwʾḥ / ʾlyʿz* - "Belonging to Yehoʾaḥ (son of) ʾEliʿaz" (WSS 520).

A72. [ל]יהואח / אלעז *[l]yhwʾḥ / ʾlʿz* — "Belonging to Yehoʾaḥ (son of) ʾEl(i)ʿaz" (WSS 521).

A73. [ליה]ואח ב/[ן] אלעז *[lyh]wʾḥ b/[n] ʾlʿz* — "Belonging to Yehoʾaḥ (son of) ʾEl(i)ʿaz" (WSS 522).

A74a. ליהועז / בן מתן *lyhwʿz / bn mtn* — "Belonging to Yehoʿaz son of Mattan" (WSS 525a).

A74b. [ל]יהועז / בן מתן *[l]yhwʿz / bn mtn* — "Belonging to Yehoʿaz son of Mattan" (Duplicate of the previous bulla, WSS 525b).

A75a. ליקמיהו / בן משלם *lyqmyhw / bn mšlm* — "Belonging to Yeqamyahu son of Meshullam". In the lower register a Phoenician-style palmette motif is depicted (WSS 526a).

A75b. ליקמיהו / בן משלם *lyqmyhw / bn mšlm* — "Belonging to Yeqamyahu son of Meshullam" (Duplicate of the previous bulla, WSS 526b).

A75c. ליקמיה[ו / בן משלם] *lyqmyh[w / bn mšlm]* — "Belonging to Yeqamyahu son of Meshullam" (Duplicate of the previous bulla, WSS 526c).

A76. ליקמ[יהו] / ס.. *lyqm[yhw] / s..* — "Belonging to Yeqamyahu (son of) S.." (WSS 528).

A77. ליקמיהו / בן נחם *lyqmyhw / bn nḥm* — "Belonging to Yeqamyahu son of Naḥum". Figure of a man with one arm stretched out before him (WSS 527).

A78. לירמ[יהו] / ישמעא[ל] *lyrm[yhw] / yšmʿʾ[l]* — "Belonging to Yirmeyahu (son of) Yishmaʿʾel" (WSS 529: Yirm... or Yirp...).

A79. לישמעאל / [ב]ן שעל בן / [חל]ציה[ו] *lyšmʿʾl / [b]n šʿl bn / [ḥl]ṣyh[w]* — "Belonging to Yishmaʿʾel son of Shuʿal son of Ḥeleṣyahu" (WSS 534).

A80. לישמ[עאל] / [ב]ן מחסי[הו] *lyšm[ʿʾl] / [b]n mḥsy[hw]* "Belonging to Yishmaʿʾel son of Maḥseyahu". Ladder-pattern register divider (WSS 533).

A81. לישמ[עאל] / ... *lyšm[ʿʾl] / ...* — "Belonging to Yishmaʿʾel / ..." (WSS 531).

A82. לישמ[עאל] / ... *lyšm[ʿʾl] / ...* — "Belonging to Yishmaʿʾel / ..." (WSS 532).

A83. לישעיהו / בן חמל *lyšʿyhw / bn ḥml* — "Belonging to Yishaʿyahu son of Ḥamal". Double linear frame containing a row of dots (WSS 535).

A84. [לי]שעיהו / [א]לצד[ק] *[ly]šʿyhw / [ʾ]lṣd[q]* — "Belonging to Yishaʿyahu (son of) ʾEliṣedeq" (Damaged fragment not listed in WSS).

A85. למחסיהו / אליהו *lmḥsyhw / ʾlyhw* — "Belonging to Maḥseyahu (son of) ʾEliyahu" (WSS 537).

A86. למח[סי]הו / בן פלטיהו *lmḥ[sy]hw / bn plṭyhw* — "Belonging to Maḥseyahu son of Pelaṭyahu" (WSS 538).

A87. [למע]שיהו / מיאמן *[lmʿ]śyhw / myʾmn* — "Belonging to Maʿaśeyahu (son of) Miʾamen" (WSS 647).

A88. [למ]יאמן / [בן] עפי *[lm]yʾmn / [bn]ʿpy* — "Belonging to Miʿamen son of ʿEphai" (WSS 539).

A89. למיר[ב] / ישמעאל *lmyr[b] / yšmʿʾl* — "Belonging to Merab (son of) Yishmaʿʾel" (WSS 540).

A90. למכיהו / בן אלעז *lmkyhw / bn ʾlʿz* — "Belonging to Mikhayahu son of ʾEl(i)ʿaz" (WSS 542).

A91. למכיה[ו] / ישעי[הו] *lmkyh[w] / yšʿy[hw]* — "Belonging to Mikhayahu (son of) Yeshaʿyahu" (WSS 543).

A92. למכיהו / בן משלם *lmkyhw / bn mšlm* — "Belonging to Mikhayahu son of Meshullam" (WSS 544).

A93. [לס]מכי[הו] / בן עמדיה[ו] *[ls]mky[hw] / bn ʿmdyh[w]* — "Belonging to Semakhyahu son of ʿImmadiyahu" (WSS 590).

A94. למכי[הו] / פלטיהו *lmky[hw] / plṭyhw* — "Belonging to Mikhayahu (son of) Pelaṭyahu" (WSS 545).

A95. למכי[הו] ב/ן שח[ר] *lmky[hw] b/n šḥ[r]* — "Belonging to Mikhayahu son of Shaḥar" (WSS 548).

A96. למכיהו / שבניהו *lmkyhw / šbnyhw* — "Belonging to Mikhayahu (son of) Shebanyahu" (WSS 546).

A97. למכיהו / שבניהו *lmkyhw / šbnyhw* - "Belonging to Mikhayahu (son of) Shebanyahu" (WSS 547).

A98. [ל]מלכיהו / חלק *[l]mlkyhw / ḥlq* — "Belonging to Malkiyayahu (son of) Ḥeleq". In the upper register a fish is depicted (WSS 549).

A99. למלכיהו / בן פדיהו *lmlkyhw / bn pdyhw* — "Belonging to Malkiyayahu son of Pedayahu" (WSS 550).

A100. [ל]מנחם / חנניהו *[l]mnḥm / ḥnnyhw* — "Belonging to Menaḥem (son of) Ḥananyahu" (WSS 648).

A101. למנחם בן / ישמעאל *lmnḥm bn / yšmʿʾl* — "Belonging to Menaḥem son of Yishmaʿʾel" (WSS 551).

A102. למנ[חם בן] / יש[מעאל] *lmn[ḥm bn] / yš[mʿʾl]* — "Belonging to Menaḥem son of Yishmaʿʾel" (Fragmentary bulla not listed in WSS).

A103. למנחם ב/ן מנש *lmnḥm b/n mnš* — "Belonging to Menaḥem son of *Mnš*" (WSS 552).

A104. למנחם / פגי *lmnḥm / pgy* — "Belonging to Menaḥem (son of) Pagi". In the upper register a fish is depicted (WSS 553: *pgy* or *ppy*).

A105a. למעשי[הו] / אשיה[ו] *lmʿśy[hw] / ʾšyh[w]* — "Belonging to Maʿaśeyahu (son of) ʾAshyahu". Dots as register divider (WSS 554a: Maʿasi).

A105b. [ל]מעשי[הו] / אשיהו *[l]mʿśy[hw] / ʾšyhw* — "Belonging to Maʿaśeyahu (son of) ʾAshyahu" (Duplicate of the previous bulla, WSS 554b: Maʿasi).

A106. למספר בן / ..יוע.. *lmspr bn / ..ywʿ..* — "Belonging to Mispar son of *..ywʿ..*" (Not listed in WSS).

A107. חלקיהו / למעשי[הו] *lmᶜśy[hw]* / *ḥlqyhw* — "Belonging to Maᶜaśeyahu (son of) Ḥilqiyahu" (WSS 555).

A108. (ל)מצר [ב]ן שלם *(l)mṣr [b]/n šlm* — "Belonging to *Mṣr* son of Shallum" (WSS 556: or *Mṣry* / *Mšlm*).

A109. ... / למקנמלך *lmqnmlk* / ... — "Belonging to Miqnemelekh / ..." (WSS 557).

A110. למשלם / אשיהו *lmšlm* / *ʾšyhw* — "Belonging to Meshullam (son of) ʾAshyahu" (WSS 558).

A111. למשלם [ב/ן] רפאיהו *lmšlm [b/n] rpʾyhw* — "Belonging to Meshullam son of Rephaʾyahu" (WSS 560).

A112. למשען ב[ן] / שחר *lmšᶜn b[n]* / *šḥr* — "Belonging to Mishᶜan son of Shaḥar" (WSS 561: *lmšᶜn* / *šḥr*).

A113. למתן בן / [א]דניחי / [בן ש]חר *lmtn bn* / *[ʾ]dnyhy* / *[bn š]ḥr* — "Belonging to Mattan son of ʾAdonihai son of Shaḥar" (WSS 562: *mtn* or *ntn*).

A114. למתן בן / פלטיהו *lmtn bn* / *plṭyhw* — "Belonging to Mattan son of Pelaṭyahu" (WSS 565).

A115. למתן בן / [פ]לטיהו *lmtn bn* / *[p]lṭyhw* — "Belonging to Mattan son of Pelaṭyahu" (WSS 566).

A116a. למתן ב[ן] / פלטיה[ו] *lmtn b[n]* / *plṭyh[w]* — "Belonging to Mattan son of Pelaṭyahu". In the center is depicted a pillar with a proto-Aeolic capital of the Phoenician type (WSS 567a).

A116b. למתן ב[ן] / [פ]לטי[הו] *lmtn b[n]* / *[p]lṭy[hw]* — "Belonging to Mattan son of Pelaṭyahu" (Duplicate of the previous bulla, WSS 567b).

A117. למתן בן / הודויהו *lmtn bn* / *hwdwyhw* — "Belonging to Mattan son of Hoduyahu" (WSS 563).

A118. למתן ב[ן] / יהוזרח *lmtn b[n]* / *yhwzrḥ* — "Belonging to Mattan son of Yehozeraḥ" (WSS 564).

A119. למתניהו ב/ן סמכיהו *lmtnyhw b/n smkyhw* — "Belonging to Mattanyahu son of Semakhyahu" (WSS 569).

A120. לנגבי ב/ן מלכיהו *lngby b/n mlkyhw* — "Belonging to Negbi son of Malkiyahu" (WSS 570).

A121. לנ[ח]ם בן / רפא[יהו] *ln[ḥ]m bn* / *rpʾ[yhw]* — "Belonging to Naḥum son of Rephaʾyahu" (WSS 572).

A122. לנמש ב[ן] / נריהו *lnmš b[n]* / *nryhw* — "Belonging to *Nmš* son of Neriyahu" (WSS 574).

A123. לנמשר / בן שעל *lnmšr* / *bn šᶜl* — "Belonging to *Nmšr* son of Shuᶜal". Thunderbolt-like register divider (WSS 576).

A124. לנמשר בן / שבניהו *lnmšr bn* / *šbnyhw* — "Belonging to *Nmšr* son of Shebanyahu" (WSS 575).

A125. לנריהו / אדנ[יהו] *lnryhw* / *ʾdn[yhw]* — "Belonging to Neriyahu (son of) ʾAdoniyahu". In the upper register the figure of a quadruped is depicted (WSS 578).

A126a. לנריהו / אשרחי *lnryhw* / *ʾšrḥy* — "Belonging to Neriyahu (son of) ʾAsherḥai" (WSS 579a).

A126b. לנריהו / אשרחי *lnryhw* / *ʾšrḥy* — "Belonging to Neriyahu (son of) ʾAsherḥai" (Duplicate of the previous bulla, WSS 579b).

A126c. לנריהו / אשרחי *lnryhw* / *ʾšrḥy* — "Belonging to Neriyahu (son of) ʾAsherḥai" (Duplicate of the previous bulla, WSS 579c).

A126d. לנריהו / אשרחי *lnryhw* / *ʾšrḥy* — "Belonging to Neriyahu (son of) ʾAsherḥai" (Duplicate of the previous bulla WSS 579d).

A126e. לנריהו / אשרחי *lnryhw* / *ʾšrḥy* — "Belonging to Neriyahu (son of) ʾAsherḥai" (Duplicate of the previous bulla, WSS 579e).

A126f. לנריהו / אשרחי *lnryhw* / *ʾšrḥy* — "Belonging to Neriyahu (son of) ʾAsherḥai" (Duplicate of the previous bulla, WSS 579f).

A126g. לנריהו / אשרחי *lnryhw* / *ʾšrḥy* — "Belonging to Neriyahu (son of) ʾAsherḥai" (Duplicate of the previous bulla, WSS 579g).

A126h. לנריהו / אשרחי *lnryhw* / *ʾšrḥy* — "Belonging to Neriyahu (son of) ʾAsherḥai" (Duplicate of the previous bulla, WSS 579h).

A126i. לנריהו / [א]שרחי *lnryhw* / *[ʾ]šrḥy* — "Belonging to Neriyahu (son of) ʾAsherḥai" (Duplicate of the previous bulla, WSS 579i).

A126j. לנריהו / [אש]רחי *lnryhw* / *[ʾš]rḥy* — "Belonging to Neriyahu (son of) ʾAsherḥai" (Duplicate of the previous bulla, WSS 579j).

A126k. לנרי[הו] / אשרח[י] *lnry[hw]* / *ʾšrḥ[y]* — "Belonging to Neriyahu (son of) ʾAsherḥai" (Duplicate of the previous bulla, WSS 579k).

A126l. [ל]נריהו / [א]שרחי *[l]nryhw* / *[ʾ]šrḥy* — "Belonging to Neriyahu (son of) ʾAsherḥai" (Duplicate of the previous bulla, WSS 579l).

A126m. לנריהו / אשרחי *lnryhw* / *ʾšrḥy* — "Belonging to Neriyahu (son of) ʾAsherḥai" (Duplicate of the previous bulla, WSS 579m).

A126n. [לנר]יהו / [אש]רחי *[lnr]yhw* / *[ʾš]rḥy* — "Belonging to Neriyahu (son of) ʾAsherḥai" (Duplicate of the previous bulla, WSS 579n).

A127. לנריהו / [א]שריחת *lnryhw* / *[ʾ]šryḥt* — "Belonging to Neriyahu (son of) ʾAsheryaḥat" (WSS 580).

A128. לנריהו ב/ן הצליהו *lnryhw b/n hṣlyhw* — "Belonging to Neriyahu son of Hiṣṣilyahu" (WSS 582).

A129. לנתן אח/מלך *lntn ʾḥ/mlk* — "Belonging to Natan (son of) ʾAḥimelek". In the upper register a Phoenician-style palmette motif is depicted (WSS 584a).

A130. לנתן / פדיהו *lntn* / *pdyhw* — "Belonging to Natan (son of) Pedayahu" (WSS 585).

A131. לסאל ב/ן יסף *lsʾl b/n ysp* — "Belonging to *Sʾl* son of Yasaph" (WSS 587).

A132. [ל]סלא ב/ן כסלא *[l]slʾ b/n kslʾ* — "Belonging to *Slʾ* son of *Kslʾ*". In the upper register a fish is depicted (WSS 589).

A133a. לסעדיה[ו] / ... *lsʿdyh[w]* / ... — "Belonging to Saʿadyahu son of ..." (WSS 591a).

A133b. לסעד[יהו] / [ב]ן ז.. *lsʿd[yhw]* / *[b]n z...* — "Belonging to Saʿadyahu son of Z..." (Duplicate of the previous bulla, WSS 591b).

A134. לעבדיהו / בן מתן *lʿbdyhw* / *bn mtn* — "Belonging to ʿObadyahu son of Mattan" (WSS 592).

A135a. לעזר / פלטיהו *lʿzr / plṭyhw* — “Belonging to ʿEzer (son of) Pelaṭyahu”. Impressed with a square seal (WSS 594a).

A135b. לעזר / פלטיה *lʿzr / plṭyhw* — “Belonging to ʿEzer (son of) Pelaṭyahu” (Duplicate of the previous bulla, WSS 594b).

A136. לעזריה[ו] / בן ס[מך] *lʿzryh[w] / bn s[mk]* — “Belonging to ʿAzaryahu son of Samakh”. Thunderbolt-like register divider (WSS 597).

A137. לעזריהו / [ב]ן פדיהו *lʿzryhw / [b]n pdyhw* — “Belonging to ʿAzaryahu son of Pedayahu”. In the center is depicted a pillar supporting a proto-Aeolic capital of the Phoenician palmette type (WSS 598).

A138a. לעזרקם / בן פרפר *lʿzrqm / bn prpr* — “Belonging to ʿAzriqam son of Parpar”. Thunderbolt-like register divider (WSS 600a).

A138b. לעזרקם / בן פרפר *lʿzrqm / bn prpr* — “Belonging to ʿAzriqam son of Parpar” (Duplicate of the previous bulla, WSS 600b).

A139. לעזרקם / [בן] צדקא *lʿzrqm / [bn] ṣdqʾ* — “Belonging to ʿAzriqam son of Ṣidqaʾ” (WSS 601).

A140. לעכב[ר בן / צפניהו] *lʿkb[r bn / ṣpnyhw]* — “Belonging to ʿAkhbor son of Ṣephanyahu”. The completion of the inscription is based on a complete duplicate bulla, in Deutsch and Heltzer 1995, no. 55 (WSS 602).

A141. לעליהו / רפא *lʿlyhw / rpʾ* — “Belonging to ʿAliyahu (son of) Raphaʾ”. The seal was a palimpsest (WSS 604).

A142. לעליהו / חלץ *lʿlyhw / ḥlṣ* — “Belonging to ʿAliyahu (son of) Ḥeleṣ” (WSS 603).

A143a. לפלטיהו ב/ן הושעיהו *lplṭyhw b/n hwšʿyhw* — “Belonging to Pelaṭyahu son of Hoshaʿyahu” (WSS 610a).

A143b. לפלטיהו ב/ן הושעיהו *lplṭyhw b/n hwšʿyhw* — “Belonging to Pelaṭyahu son of Hoshaʿyahu” (Duplicate of the previous bulla, WSS 610b).

A144a. לפלטי[הו] / הושעיה[ו] *lplṭy[hw] / hwšʿyh[w]* — “Belonging to Pelaṭyahu (son of) Hoshaʿyahu” (WSS 611a).

A144b. לפלטי[הו] / הושעי[הו] *lplṭy[hw] / hwšʿy[hw]* — “Belonging to Pelaṭyahu (son of) Hoshaʿyahu” (Duplicate of the previous bulla, WSS 611b).

A145a. [ל]פלטיהו / הושעיהו *[l]plṭyhw / hwšʿyhw* — “Belonging to Pelaṭyahu (son of) Hoshaʿyahu” (WSS 612a).

A145b. [ל]פלטיהו / הוש[ע]יה[ו] *[l]plṭyhw / hwš[ʿ]yh[w]* — “Belonging to Pelaṭyahu (son of) Hoshaʿyahu” (Duplicate of the previous bulla, WSS 612b).

A146. לפלטיהו / ..יהו *lplṭyhw / ...yhw* — “Belonging to Pelaṭyahu (son of) ...yahu” (WSS 609).

A147. לפלטיהו / הושעיהו *lplṭyhw / hwšʿyhw* — “Belonging to Pelaṭyahu (son of) Hoshaʿyahu”. Lotus-bud register divider (WSS 613).

A148. לפלטיהו / בן הושעיהו *lplṭyhw / bn hwšʿyhw* — “Belonging to Pelaṭyahu son of Hoshaʿyahu” (WSS 614).

A149. לפלטיהו / בן חלק *lplṭyhw / bn ḥlq* — “Belonging to Pelaṭyahu son of Ḥeleq” (WSS 615).

A150. לפנ.ב. / חנני *lpn.b.* / *ḥnny* — "Belonging to Pn.b. (son of) Ḥanani". Ladder-pattern register divider and dentated line above (WSS 617).

A151. לפשחר בן / אחאמה *lpšḥr bn* / *ʾḥʾmh* — "Belonging to Pashḥur son of ʾAḥiʾimoh" (WSS 618).

A152. לפשחר בן / מנחם *lpšḥr bn* / *mnḥm* — "Belonging to Pashḥur son of Menaḥem". Lentoid-shaped seal, lotus-bud register divider (WSS 619).

A153. לפתח ב/ן נחם *lptḥ b/n* / *nḥm* — "Belonging to Pataḥ son of Naḥum". Ladder-pattern register divider (WSS 620).

A154. לצפן (בן) / מקניהו *lṣpn (bn)* / *mqnyhw* — "Belonging to Ṣaphan (son of) Miqneyahu" (WSS 621: or *ṣpnyhw*).

A155. לצפניהו / שאלה *lṣpnyhw* / *šʾlh* — "Belonging to Ṣephanyahu (son of) Sheʾila" (WSS 622).

A156. לקרבאר / [ב]ן עזראל *lqrbʾr* / *[b]n ʿzrʾl* — "Belonging to *Qrbʾr* son of ʿAzarʾel" (WSS 623).

A157a. לראיהו / חלציהו *lrʾyhw* / *ḥlṣyhw* — "Belonging to Reʾayahu (son of) Ḥeleṣyahu". Ladder-pattern register divider, WSS 624a).

A157b. [ל]ראיהו / [חל]ציהו *[l]rʾyhw* / *[ḥl]ṣyhw* — "Belonging to Reʾayahu (son of) Ḥeleṣyahu" (Duplicate of the previous bulla, WSS 624b).

A158. לשלם ב/ן אלשמ[ע] *lšlm b/n ʾlšmʿ* — "Belonging to Shallum son of ʾElishamaʿ" (WSS 632).

A159. [לשל]ם בן / [אל]שמע *[lšl]m bn* / *[ʾl]šmʿ* — "Belonging to Shallum son of ʾElishamaʿ" (Not listed in WSS).

A160. לשל[ם בן] / א[ל]ש[מע] *lšl[m bn]* / *ʾ[l]š[mʿ]* — "Belonging to Shallum son of ʾElishamaʿ" (Fragmentary bulla not listed in WSS).

A161. לשלם ב[ן] / הושעיהו *lšlm b[n]* / *hwšʿyhw* — "Belonging to Shallum son of Hoshaʿyahu" (WSS 633).

A162. [ל]שמעיהו / יאזן *[l]šmʿyhw* / *yʾzn* — "Belonging to Shemaʿyahu (son of) Yaʾazan" (WSS 162).

A163. לשמעיהו / ... *lšmʿyhw* / ... — "Belonging to Shemaʿyahu ..." (WSS 634).

A164. לשעל בן / ישמעאל *lšʿl bn* / *yšmʿʾl* — "Belonging to Shuʿal son of Yishmaʿʾel" (WSS 640).

A165. לשפטי[הו] / אדניהו *lšpṭy[hw]* / *ʾdnyhw* — "Belonging to Shephaṭyahu (son of) ʾAdoniyahu". Thunderbolt-like register divider (WSS 642).

A166. לשפט ב[ן] / אחיהו *lšpṭ b[n]* / *ʾḥyhw* — "Belonging to Shaphaṭ son of ʾAḥiyahu" (WSS 641).

A167. לשבני[הו] / שריהו *lšbny[hw]* / *śryhw* — "Belonging to Shebanyahu (son of) Śerayahu" (WSS 645: *lšpṭyhw* / *šryhw*).

A168. לתנח[ם] / הצל[יהו] *ltnḥ[m]* / *hṣl[yhw]* — "Belonging to Tanḥum (son of) Hiṣṣilyahu" (WSS 646).

A169. .... / בן / גדיהו ... / *bn* / *gdyhw* - "(Belonging to ...) son of Gaddiyahu". The middle register depicts a grazing doe facing left (WSS 649).

A170. ... / [ד]מליהו בן / ... ... / [d]mlyhw bn / ... — "(Belonging to ... son of) Demalyahu son of ..." (Not listed in WSS).

A171. יהוק[ם] / ... ... / yhwq[m] — "(Belonging to ... son of) Yehoqam" (WSS 650).

A172. יקמיה[ו] / ... ... / yqmyh[w] — "(Belonging to ... son of) Yeqamyahu" (WSS 651).

A173. ישמעאל / ... ... / yšm'l — "(Belonging to ... son of) Yishma'el" (WSS 652).

A174. לש[ע]ל ב[ן] / מל[כ]יה[ו] lš[ʿ]l b[n] / ml[k]yh[w] — "Belonging to Shuʿal son of Malkiyahu" (WSS 653).

A175. מלכ[יהו] / ... ... / mlk[yhw] — "(Belonging to ... son of) Malkiyahu" (Not listed in WSS).

A176. בן נחם / ... ... / bn nḥm — "(Belonging to ... son of) Naḥum" (Not listed in WSS).

A177. עזיה[ו] / ... ... / ʿzyh[w] — "(Belonging to ... son of) ʿUzziyahu" (WSS 654).

A178. פדיהו / ... ... / pdyhw — "(Belonging to ... son of) Pedayahu" Thunderbolt-like register divider (WSS 655).

A179. ל..יהו / שמעיה[ו] l..yhw / šmʿyh[w] — "Belonging to ..yahu (son of) Shemaʿyahu" (WSS 656).

A180a. בן שפט[יהו] / ... ... / bn špṭ[yhw] — "(Belonging to) ... son of Shephaṭyahu" (WSS 657a).

A180b. [בן שפ]טיהו / ... ... [bn šp]ṭyhw — "(Belonging to ...) son of Shephaṭyahu" (Duplicate of the previous bulla, WSS 657b).

A181. ..מ ב/[ן].. יאל ..m b/[n]..yʾl — (Not listed in WSS).

A182. ..שע / ..יה ..šʿ / ..yh — Ladder-pattern register divider (Not listed in WSS).

A183. ..יהו / [פש]חר ..yhw / [pš]ḥr — "(Belonging to) ..yhw (son of) Pashḥur" (Not listed in WSS).

A184. ..למ / בן .. lm.. / bn ... — (Not listed in WSS).

A185. ..עיהו / ..שיהו ..ʿyhw / š..yhw — (Not listed in WSS).

A186. ..יהו / ..יהו ..yhw / ..yhw — (Not listed in WSS).

A187. ..יהו / ..ליה ..yhw / ..lyh — Thunderbolt-like register divider (Not listed in WSS).

A188. ..ניהו / ..הו ..nyhw / ..hw — (Not listed in WSS).

A189. ליהו.. / ... lyhw.. / ... — (Not listed in WSS).

A190. ליהו.. / עיה.. lyhw.. / ʿyh.. — (Not listed in WSS).

A191. ..איהו / ... ..ʾyhw / ... — Floral register divider (Not listed in WSS).

A192. ..ליהו / ..יהו ..lyhw / ..yhw — (Not listed in WSS).

A193. ..יה[ו] / ... ... / ..yh[w] — (Not listed in WSS).

A194. ..יהו ב[ן] / ..עי.. ..yhw b[n] / ..ʿy.. — (Not listed in WSS).

A195. ..עמל.. / ... ..ʿml.. / ... — (Not listed in WSS).

A196. לשל.. / ... lšl.. / ... — (Not listed in WSS).

A197. ..ליהו / ... ..lyhw / ... — Branch as space filler at the end of inscription (Not listed in WSS).

A198. ... / ... — (Not listed in WSS).

A199. ..ניהו ..nyhw — (Avigad states: "This is apparently to be restored as the name ʾAdoniyahu". The new reading based on a well-preserved duplicate should be: [לחז]קיהו אחז

[מ]לך / י[הדה] *[lḥz]qyhw ʾ[ḥz m]lk / y[hdh]* — "Belonging to Hezekiah (son of) ʾAḥaz, King of Judah". In the middle of the bulla, a royal two-winged beetle is depicted (Not listed in WSS).[6]

A200. ..ר.. *..r..* — In the middle of the bulla a four-winged *uraeus* is depicted (Not listed in WSS).

A201. ... / ... — In the middle of the bulla a four-winged *uraeus* is depicted (Not listed in WSS).

A202. ..בע / ..חם *..ḥm / ..bʿ* — In the middle of the bulla a bird is depicted (Not listed in WSS).

A203. ...י *...y* — A horned quadruped looking back is depicted in the middle of the bulla (Not listed in WSS).

A204. Unepigraphic. A thin and tall quadruped, with a palm branch in front, is depicted in the center of the bulla (Not listed in WSS).

A205. Unepigraphic, with a palm tree (Not listed in WSS).

A206. Unepigraphic, with a Phoenician-style palmette (Not listed in WSS).

A207-A211. Illegible bullae (Not listed in WSS).

9. Two Hebrew fiscal bullae

Two bullae which belong to the group presented in Chapter Three (below, nos. 101, 102; Avigad 1990).

1. ב 26 / שנה / אלתלד / למלך *b 26 / šnh / ʾltld / lmlk* — "In the 26th year, ʾEltolad, belonging to the king (for the king)" (WSS 421).

2. לתחת ב|ן בסי *ltḥt b|n bsy* — "Belonging to Taḥat son of Besai" (WSS 424: *ʾḥʾ bn bsy*). New reading: לאחאב / אבסי *lʾḥʾb / ʾbsy* — "Belonging to ʾAḥʾab (son of) *ʾbsy*".

10. The Josef Samel Collection

In the 1993 exhibition catalogue, "Das Heilige Land", of the Samel Collection from München, fourteen bullae are presented (Overbeck and Meshorer 1993). They are numbered in the catalogue from 31 to 44, of which seven were previously published (Avigad 1986, 29, 60, 68, 73, 114, 126j, 136). This publication suffers from several errors:

a) The photographs are given at life size (1:1), and only two samples are reproduced at a magnification of 5:1 (nos. 32, 34). This fact makes reading and examination difficult.

b) Three photographs are printed upside down.

c) Only three out of the seven bullae are mentioned that were previously published by Avigad.

d) Bulla no. 31, has been impressed with the same seal which impressed the bulla A83 (Avigad 1986). This fact was omitted.

e) Seven bullae were incorrectly deciphered. The list of the bullae with new suggested readings, based on the bullae themselves, follows:

---

6. The bulla has been partly impressed; therefore, the complete inscription can be restored based only on the well-preserved duplicate which is kept in the private collection of Mr. Shlomo Moussaieff (Cross 1999) (See enlarged color picture x7 on p. 204).

1. (no. 31) לישעיהו / בן חמל *lyšʿyhw / bn ḥml* — "Belonging to Yishaʿyahu son of Ḥamal". Double linear frame containing a row of dots. The photograph has been printed upside down. Former reading: *lyšʿyhw bn ʾlmlk* (WSS 535).

2. (no. 32) למיפלל / בן משלם *lmypll / bn mšlm* — "Belonging to Mipilel son of Meshullam" (Not listed in WSS).

3. (no. 33) [לח]גי בן / הושעיהו *[lḥ]gy bn / hwšʿyhw* — "Belonging to Ḥaggi son of Hoshaʿyahu". Former reading: *gy bn / hwšʿyhw* (Not listed in WSS).

4. (no. 34) לעמדי[הו ב]/ן פלטיה[ו] *lʿmdy[hw b]/n plṭyh[w]* — "Belonging to ʿImadiyahu son of Pelaṭyahu". Former reading: *lʿmdy.. bt plṭyhw* (Not listed in WSS).

5. (no. 35) לנריהו / [אשר]חי *lnryhw / [ʾšr]ḥy* — "Belonging to Neriyahu (son of) Asherḥai". Former reading: *lnryhw ʾḥy[ʾh].* The photograph was printed upside down (A 126j; WSS 579j).

6. (no. 36) לשלם בן / עזריהו *lšlm bn / ʿzryhw* — "Belonging to Shallum son of ʿAzaryahu". Former reading: *llm bn ʿzryhw*. The photograph was printed upside down (Not listed in WSS).

7. (no. 37) למתן בן / [פ]לטיה[ו] *lmtn bn / [p]lṭyh[w]* — "Belonging to Mattan son of Pelaṭyahu". Former reading: *lmgn bt plṭyhw* (A 114; WSS 565).

8. (no. 38) לי[דעיהו] / בן כ[רמי] *ly[dʿyhw] / bn k[rmy]* — "Belonging to Yedaʿyahu son of Karmi". Former reading: *ly.. bn k...* The reading, based on another fragmentary bulla, has been completed and published by Avigad (A 68a,b; WSS 514b).

9. (no. 39) לחמטל ב(ת) / ..צ.. *lḥmṭl b(t) / ..ṣ..* — "Belonging to Ḥamuṭal daughter of? ..ṣ..". Former reading: *lḥmṭ bn ḥgb* (Not listed in WSS).

10. (no. 40) [ל]חלץ ב[ן] / אחאב *[l]ḥlṣ b[n] / ʾḥʾb* — "Belonging to Ḥeleṣ son of ʾAḥʾab" (A 60; WSS 494).

11. (no. 41) לעזריה[ו] / בן ס[מך] *lʿzryh[w] / bn s[mk]* — "Belonging to ʿAzaryahu son of Samakh" (A 136; WSS 597).

12. (no. 42) [ל]אלנתן / יקמיהו *[l]ʾlntn / yqmyhw* — "Belonging to ʾElnatan son of Yeqamyahu" (Not listed in WSS).

13. (no. 43) לאלירם / שמעיה[ו] *lʾlyrm / šmʿyhw* — "Belonging to ʾEliram (son of) Shemaʿyahu" (A 29; WSS 439).

14. (no. 44) [ליה]ואח ב/[ן] אלעז *[lyh]wʾḥ b/[n]ʾlʿz* — "Belonging to Yehoʾaḥ son of ʾEl(i)ʿaz" (A 73; WSS 522).

11. Thirty-five Hebrew bullae from private collections

(Deutsch and Heltzer 1994, nos. 11–20; 1995, nos. 54–62b; 1997 nos. 85–96)

1. (no. 11) לברכיהו / בן נריהו / הספר *lbrkyhw / bn nryhw / hspr* — "Belonging to Berekhyahu son of Neriyahu, the scribe" (WSS 417b).

2. (no. 12) לשמעיהו / עבד המלך *lšmʿyhw / ʿbd hmlk* — "Belonging to Shemaʿyahu, servant of the king" (Not listed in WSS).

3. (no. 13) למבטחיהו / עבד המלך *lmbṭḥyhw / ʿbd hmlk* — "Belonging to Mibṭaḥyahu, servant of the king" (WSS 410).

4. (no. 14) לעזריהו ש/ער המסגר *lʿzryhw š/ʿr hmsgr* — "Belonging to ʿAzaryahu, the gate-keeper of the prison" (WSS 418).

5. (no. 15) לאדניהו *l'dnyhw* — "Belonging to ʾAdoniyahu". In the center of the bulla a four-winged *uraeus* is depicted (Not listed in WSS).

6. (no. 16) לשכני/ה/ו / אלעשה *lškny/h/w* / *ʾlʿśh* — "Belonging to Shekanyahu (son of) ʾElʿaśa". In the central register a four-winged *uraeus* is depicted (Not listed in WSS).

7. (no. 17) לעבדא בן / ידעיהו *lʿbdʾ bn* / *ydʿyhw* — "Belonging to ʿAbdaʾ son of Yedaʿyahu" (Not listed in WSS).

8. (no. 18) [ל]זכר בן / שלמיהו *[l]zkr bn* / *šlmyhw* — "Belonging to Zakkur son of Shelemyahu" (WSS 658).

9. (no. 19) לאלשמע בן / מעשיהו *lʾlšmʿ bn* / *mʿśyhw* — "Belonging to ʾElshamaʿ son of Maʿaśeyahu". The upper register depicts a bird and a palm branch (Not listed in WSS).

10. (no. 20) למלכיהו ב/ן יועליהו *lmlkyhw b/n ywʿlyhw* — "Belonging to Malkiyahu son of Yoʿaliyahu". Double lotus-bud register divider (Not listed in WSS).

11. (no. 54) לחזדא / נחם *lḥzdʾ* / *nḥm* — "Belonging to Ḥizdʾa (son of) Naḥum" (Not listed in WSS).

12. (no. 55) לעכבר בנ[ן] / צפניהו *lʿkbr b[n]* / *ṣpnyhw* — "Belonging to ʿAkhbor son of Ṣephanyahu". Two arched double lines as register divider, terminating in pomegranates. The completion of the inscription on bulla A140 (WSS 602), is based on this bulla.

13. (no. 56) לעזר ב/ן תנחם *lʿzr b/n tnḥm* — "Belonging to ʿAzar son of Tanḥum". Lotus-bud register divider (Not listed in WSS).

14. (no. 57) לשלם בן / פלטיהו *lšlm bn* / *plṭyhw* — "Belonging to Shallum son of Palṭiyahu" (Not listed in WSS).

15. (no. 58) לרפאיהו / מתניהו *lrpʾyhw* / *mtnyhw* — "Belonging to Rapʾayahu (son of) Mattanyahu" (Not listed in WSS).

16. (no. 59) [ל]מחסיהו / [ב]ן יהושע *[l]mḥsyhw* / *[b]n yhwšʿ* — "Belonging to Maḥseyahu son of Yehoshuʿa" (Not listed in WSS).

17. (no. 60) למיאמן / בניהו *lmyʾmn* / *bnyhw* — "Belonging to Miʾamen (son of) Benayahu" (Not listed in WSS).

18. (no. 61) ליחץ *lyḥṣ* — "Belonging to Yaḥaṣ". In the upper register there is a net pattern, and in the lower register a winged feature resting on a horizontal ladder (Possibly Moabite or Edomite, Lemaire 1999:172; not listed in WSS).

19. (no. 62a) ליאש בן / אלשמע *lyʾš bn* / *ʾlšmʿ* — "Belonging to Yaʾush son of ʾElishamaʿ". A duplicate of this bulla has been published by Avigad (A66; WSS 512a, and another, the next no. 20).

20. (no. 62b) ליאש בן / אלשמע *lyʾš bn* / *ʾlšmʿ* — "Belonging to Yaʾush son of ʾElishamaʿ". Duplicate of the previous bulla.

21. (no. 85) לנרא בן / מלכיהו *lnrʾ bn* / *mlkyhw* — "Belonging to Neraʾ son of Malkiyahu". Two arched lines as register divider, terminating in papyrus flowers (Not listed in WSS).

22. (no. 86) לנרא / מלכיהו *lnrʾ* / *mlkyhw* — "Belonging to Neraʾ (son of) Malkiyahu". The inscription is surrounded by an elliptic double framing line, (cartouche), all surrounded by a chain of pomegranates. A duplicate of this bulla has been published by Avigad (WSS 583; no.

66a below). A second duplicate is no. 66b (below), and a third one is kept in a private collection in Tel Aviv.

23. (no. 87) לישעיהו / חלקיהו *lyšʿyhw / ḥlqyhw* — "Belonging to Yeshaʿyahu (son of) Ḥilqiyahu" (Not listed in WSS).

24. (no. 88) [ל]רפאיהו / [מ]תניהו *[l]rpyhw / [m]tnyhw* — "Belonging to Rapaʾyahu (son of) Mattanyahu". In the upper register a four-winged *uraeus* is depicted (Not listed in WSS).

25. (no. 89) לצפן בן / ישעיהו *lṣpn bn / yšʿyhw* — "Belonging to Ṣapan son of Yeshaʿyahu". In the upper register a two-winged *uraeus* is depicted (Not listed in WSS).

26. (no. 90) ליהאר / [ב]ן הושעיהו *lyhʾr / [b]n hwšʿyhw* — "Belonging to *Yhʾr* son of Hoshaʿyahu" (Not listed in WSS).

27. (no. 91) לאשנא *lʾš/nʾ* — "Belonging to ʾUshnaʾ" (Not listed in WSS).

28. (no. 92) [ל]בקש ב/[ן] בניהו *[l]bqš b/[n] bnyhw* — "Belonging to Baqqesh son of Benayahu" (Not listed in WSS).

29. (no. 93a) לאלשמ[ע] / בן אפרח *lʾlšm[ʿ] / bn ʾprḥ* — "Belonging to ʾEishamaʿ son of ʾEpraḥ". The next bulla is a duplicate of this one (Not listed in WSS).

30. (no. 93b) [ל]אלשמ[ע] / [ב]ן אפר[ח] *[l]ʾlšm[ʿ] / [b]n ʾprḥ* — "Belonging to ʾEishamaʿ son of ʾEpraḥ". This is a duplicate of the previous bulla (Not listed in WSS).

31. (no. 94a) לאחיק[ם] / בן ח[בי] *lʾḥyq[m] / bn ḥ[by]* - "Belonging to ʾAḥiqam son of Ḥaby". Seven fragmentary duplicates are displayed in the Hecht Museum (below), (WSS 430a-g, "Ḥubbi").

32. (no. 94b) [לאח]יקם / בן חבי *[lʾḥ]yqm / bn ḥby* — "Belonging to ʾAḥiqam son of Ḥaby" (Duplicate of the previous bulla).

33. (no. 94c) [לאחיקם] / בן חבי *[lʾḥyqm] / bn ḥby* — "Belonging to ʾAḥiqam son of Ḥaby" (Duplicate of the previous bulla).

34. (no. 95) לבלבל / ... *lblbl / ...* — "Belonging to *Blbl* ..." (Not listed in WSS).

35. (no. 96) להושע / עכבר אל/שמע הו/שע | *lhwšʿ / ʿkbr ʾl/šmʿ hw/šʿ |* — "Belonging to Hosheaʿ (son of) ʿAkhbor (son of) ʾElishamaʿ (son of) Hosheaʿ" (Not listed in WSS).

12. Five Hebrew bullae in the Israel Museum

(Hestrin and Dayagi-Mendels 1979, nos. 4, 7, 26, 27, 47, formerly published).

1. (no. 4) ליהוזר/ח בן חלק/[י]הו עבד ח/זקיהו *lyhwzr/ḥ bn ḥlq/[y]hw ʿbd ḥ/zqyhw* — "Belonging to Yehozaraḥ son of Ḥilqiyahu, servant of Ḥizqiyahu". Unknown provenance, Israel Museum no. 74.16.45. A duplicate of this bulla is presented in Chapter Three, no. 2 (WSS 407).

2. (no. 7) לגאליהו / בן המלך *lgʾlyhw / bn hmlk* — "Belonging to Geʾalyahu the son of the king". IAA 31.68, Beth Zur excavations (WSS 412).

3. (no. 26) לאליקם / בן מעשיה *lʾlyqm / bn mʿśyh* — "Belonging to ʾElyaqim son of Maʿaśeyah". Cable-design register divider surmounted with three dots. Unknown provenance, Israel Museum no. 73.19.37 (WSS 438).

4. (no. 27) לחלקיהו / בן מאס *lḥlqyhw / bn mʾs* — "Belonging to Ḥilqiyahu son of *Mʾs*". Lachish excavations, IAA 36.2258 (WSS 498).

5. (no. 47) לדמלא *ldml'* — "Belonging to Domla'". In the center of the bulla a four-winged beetle is depicted. Unknown provenance, Israel Museum no. 73.19.38 (WSS 475).

13. A Hebrew bulla from the Victor Barakat Gallery Collection
(Lemaire 1983:19, no. 3)

1. לרפא בן / חלקיהו *lrp' bn / ḥlqyhw* — "Belonging to Rapa' son of Ḥilqiyahu". Unknown provenance, present location: Shlomo Moussaieff collection (WSS 625).

14. A Hebrew bulla in the W. Stern Collection
(Barkay 1993)

1. לישמעאל / בן המלך *lyšm''l / bn hmlk* — "Belonging to Yshma''el, the son of the king". Unknown provenance (Not listed in WSS).

15. Three Hebrew bulla from the Bible Lands Museum, Jerusalem

1. למש/לם מקנ/יהו *lmš/lm mqn/yhw* — "Belonging to Meshullam (son of) Miqneyahu" (BLM no. 846). Jerusalem antiquities market, unknown provenance (WSS 559).
2. לנריהו / אשרחי *lnryhw / 'šrḥy* — "Belonging to Neriyahu (son of) Asherḥai" (BLM no. 828). Unknown provenance (A 126a; WSS 579a).
3. לנריהו / [א]שריחת *lnryhw / ['] šryḥt* — "Belonging to Neriyahu (son of) Asheryaḥat" (BLM no. 850). Unknown provenance (A 127; WSS 580).

16. A Hebrew bulla from the Jerusalem antiquities market
(Lemaire 1985:31)

1. לאלשמע / חלציהו *l'lšm' / ḥlṣyhw* — "Belonging to 'Elishama' (son of) Ḥalaṣyahu". Unknown provenance (WSS 446).

Unpublished Hebrew bullae of unknown provenance

17. Two Hebrew bullae from the private collection of Dr. Elie Borowski

1. (no. 201) לצדקיה[ו] / בן חנני[הו] *lṣdqyh[w] / bn ḥnny[hw]* — "Belonging to Ṣidqiyahu son of Ḥananyahu". Unknown provenance (To be published by A. Lemaire, *lṣdqyhw / bn ḥnny*, no. 22 in: *Eretz Israel* 26, *F.M. Cross* Vol.).
2. (no. 202) ... [ל]נחמיהו *[l]nḥmyhw* ... — "Belonging to Neḥemyahu ...." In the upper register a fish is depicted. Unknown provenance (To be published by A. Lemaire, no. 19 in: *Eretz Israel* 26, *F.M. Cross* Vol.[7]).

---

7. Lemaire suggest that this bulla and bulla no. 65 below are identical, and were sealed with the same seal.

18. Twenty Hebrew Bullae from the Hecht Museum, Haifa

(Avigad, Heltzer and Lemaire, in print)

1. (no. 5) ... / לאחא[ב] *lʾḥʾ[b] / ...* — "Belonging to ʾAḥaʾb ...". HM no. 2458 (WSS 425). HM nos. H-2445-2452:

2. (no. 7a) [לאחי]ק[ם] / בן חבי *[lʾḥy]q[m] / bn ḥby* — "Belonging to ʾAḥiqam son of Ḥaby". Lotus-bud register divider (WSS 430e).

3. (no. 7b) לאחי[קם / בן חבי] *lʾḥy[qm / bn ḥby]* — "Belonging to ʾAḥiqam son of Ḥaby" (Duplicate of the previous bulla, WSS 430c).

4. (no. 7c) לאחי[קם / בן חבי] *lʾḥy[qm / bn ḥby]* — "Belonging to ʾAḥiqam son of Ḥaby" (Duplicate of the previous bulla, WSS 430f).

5. (no. 7d) לאחי[קם / בן חבי] *lʾḥy[qm / bn ḥby]* — "Belonging to ʾAḥiqam son of Ḥaby" (Duplicate of the previous bulla, WSS 430).

6. (no. 7e) [לאחי]קם / [בן חבי] *[lʾḥy]qm / [bn ḥby]* — "Belonging to ʾAḥiqam son of Ḥaby" (Duplicate of the previous bulla, WSS 430a).

7. (no. 7f) [לאחיקם] / בן ח[בי] *[lʾḥyqm] / bn ḥ[by]* — "Belonging to ʾAḥiqam son of Ḥaby" (Duplicate of the previous bulla, WSS 430).

8. (no. 7g) [לאחיקם / בן חב]י *[lʾḥyqm / bn ḥb]y* — "Belonging to ʾAḥiqam son of Ḥaby" (Duplicate of the previous bulla, WSS 430).

9. (no. 13) ... לאלנתן ב/ן שמעיהו [ב]/ן *lʾlntn b/n šmʿyhw [b]/n ...* — "Belonging to ʾElnatan son of Shemaʿyahu son of ...". HM no. H-2452 (WSS 443).

10. (no. 27) דלה *dlh* — "(Belonging to) Dalah?". HM no. K-124. In the center of the bulla, a falcon is depicted (Avigad 1989:12, no. 10; WSS 473).

11. (no. 33) חגב / כלכל *ḥgb / klkl* — "Belonging to Ḥagab (son of) Kalkol". HM no. H-1984. On the left side of the upper register a branch is depicted (WSS 489).

12. (no. 39) [ל]ידעיהו / בן שכניהו *[l]ydʿyhw / bn šknyhw* — "Belonging to Yedaʿyahu son of Shekanyahu". HM no. H-2458. Unknown provenance (WSS 516).

13. (no. 58) לנתן אח/מלך *lntn ʾḥ/mlk* — "Belonging to Natan (son of) ʾAḥimelek". HM no. H-1985. In the upper register, a Phoenician-style palmette motif is depicted (A 129; WSS 584b).

14. (no. 81) לשחר בן / גדיהו *lšḥr bn / gdyhw* - "Belonging to Shaḥar son of Gaddiyahu" HM no. H-1983. Lentoid-form seal with a vertical strip of three pomegranates on either end (A 24a). Another four replicas of this bulla are known. (WSS 629e).

15. (no. 94) [ל]שלם or [למ]שלם בן / ...יהו *[l]šlm or [lm]šlm bn / ...yhw* — "Belonging to Shallum or Meshullam son of ...yahu". HM no. H-2456 (WSS 631).

16. (no. 95) ... / [ק]רבאור *... / [q]rbʾwr* — "(Belonging to ... son of) *Qrbʾwr*". HM no. H-2457 (WSS 659).

17. ..לס / ..פא *ls.. / pʾ....* HM no. H-2460 (Not listed in WSS).

18. ... / ל[א]לר[ם] *l[ʾ]lr[m]* — "Belonging to ʾEliram ...". HM no. H-2454 (Not listed in WSS).

19. ..טיה / ..הו *..ṭyh / ..hw.* HM no. H-2459 (Not listed in WSS).

20. ... / ..א *..ʾ / ....* HM no. H-2470 (Not listed in WSS).

Iron Age bullae from the neighboring states

These bullae are presented here as evidence for the existence of the phenomena in the neighboring states.

1. Two Ammonite bullae

1. לברכאל / המלך *lbrkʾl / hmlk* — "Belonging to Barakʾel the king". Unknown provenance, London antiquities market (Deutsch 1999).

2. למלכמאור / ע/ב/ד בעלישע *lmlkmʾwr / ʿ/b/d bʿlyšʿ* — "Belonging to Milkomʾur, servant of Baʿalyisha". In the middle register a four-winged beetle is depicted. Found at Tell el-ʿUmeiri (Geraty 1985:98–100; WSS 860).

2. A Moabite bulla

1. כמשעז / הספר *kmšʿz / hspr* — "Belonging to Kemoshʿaz the scribe". Jerusalem antiquities market, unknown provenance (Avigad 1992; WSS 1009).

3. Two Edomite bullae

1. לקוסג[בר] / מלך א[דום] *lqwsg[br] / mlk ʾ[dwm]* — "Belonging to Qausgabr(i), king of ʾEdom". In the central register a sphinx is depicted. Found at Umm el-Biyara (Herr 1978:162, no. 1; WSS 1049).

2. למלכל/בע עבד / המלך *lmlkl/bʿ ʿbd / hmlk* — "Belonging to *Mlklbʿ* (Malkibaʿal), the servant of the king". In the upper register three structures are depicted. Found at Buseirah (Bennett 1974, 19; WSS 1050).

4. Eleven Assyrian Aramaic bullae

1. [ל]פנאסר/[ל]מר סרס ז/[י] סרגן *[l]pnʾsr / [l]mr srs z / [y]srgn* — "Belonging to Panʾaššurlamur eunuch of Sargon". Found at Khorsabad (Bordreuil 1992:111, fig. 28; WSS 755).

Ten bullae found at Nineveh. Each bears two different seal-impressions:

2–11. חנן *ḥnn* — "(Belonging to) Ḥanan". In the center a four-winged *uraeus* is depicted (Layard 1853, 155 in the middle and inverted; WSS 796).

2a–11a. לעתרעזר *lʿtrʿzr* — "Belonging to ʿAtarʿazar". In the center a four-winged beetle is depicted (Layard 1853, 155 on the left; WSS 837).

5. A bulla from Zenjirli (Samʾal)

1. לבררכב / בר פנמו *lbrrkb / br pnmw* — "Belonging to Barrakab son of Panamuwa" (Vattioni 1971, 129; WSS 750).

6. The "Marzeaḥ" papyrus

Moabite or Edomite bulla.

1. למלכא/ כת(ב) *lmlk/ʾ kt(b)* — "Belonging to Malkaʾ, (the scribe)" (Bordreuil and Pardee 1988:50–52 *lmlk / ʾkt.* — "Belonging to the King of Iktanu" (Cross 1996:316 *lmlk/ʾ kt.?* —

"Belonging to Malka', *kt.?*"; Hanan Eshel *lmlk/' kt(b)* personal communication; not listed in WSS).

7. A Phoenician bulla from Tell el-Ḥeres

1. בעליסף / ... ... / *bʿlysp* — "(Belonging to) Baʿalyasop". Chance find (Avigad 1964:193; WSS 732).

Persian Period bullae

The Persian Period bullae (586 — 330 B.C.E.), are presented here as evidence for the continuation of the phenomenon after the destruction of the First Temple:

1. A hoard of 65 Aramaic bullae from Judah (Avigad 1976).

1. יהד *yhd* — "Yehud" (Three identical bullae).
2. יהד *yhd* — "Yehud" (Three identical bullae, impressed with a different seal).
3. יהוד / חננה *yhwd / ḥnnh* — "Yehud Ḥanana" (Three identical bullae). According to Naveh (1996:45–46), Hanuna is a name of a woman.
4. יהוד / ..נ.. *yhwd / ..n..* — "Yehud ..n.."
5. לאלנתן / פחוא *l'lntn / pḥw'* — "Belonging to 'Elnathan the Governor".
6. לירמי / הספר *lyrmy / hspr* — "Belonging to Jeremai the Scribe" (Ten identical bullae).
7. לברוך / בן שמעי *lbrwk / bn šmʿy* — "Belonging to Baruch son of Shimʿe" (Eleven identical bullae).
8. ליגאל / בן זכרי *lyg'l / bn zkry* — "Belonging to Yg'al son of Zichri" (Eleven identical bullae).
9. לאלעזר / בן נחם *l'lʿzr / bn nḥm* — "Belonging to 'Eleʿazar son of Naḥum" (Nine identical bullae).
10. לשאל / בן נחם *lš'l / bn nḥm* — "Belonging to Sa'ul son of Naḥum" (Four identical bullae).
11. אלעזר *'lʿzr* — "(Belonging to) 'Eleʿazar" (Two identical bullae).
12. למיכה *lmykh* — "Belonging to Micah" (Seven identical bullae).

2. An Aramaic bulla of unknown provenance

1. ליוהש [ע]/בד נתן *l?whš [ʿ]/bd ntn* — "Belonging to *?whš*, servant of Nathan" (Lemaire 1991).

Summary and conclusions for chapters One and Two

In the corpus presented above are all the Hebrew inscribed seal-impressions on bullae from the First Temple period, published to date or in print. The find is divided into two categories: a) bullae with known provenance, from controlled excavations, b) bullae with unknown provenance, from uncontrolled excavations and chance finds. The published bullae from controlled excavations originate from six sites: Tell el-Judeideh, Beth-Zur, Lachish, Beer-Sheba, Tell el-Ḥesi and the City of David in Jerusalem. The total number of bullae from these sites is 61, while the number of bullae published from unprovenanced sources is 316. The total amount of published Hebrew bullae up to date is 377. Several worn out or unepigraphic bullae were not included here. Only 16.2% from the published bullae originate from controlled excavations.

Nine titles are known from 25 samples: One of the "King of Judah" (A 199), one mentioning "The servant of Hezekiah", six of "Son of the King", five of "Servant of the King", six of "Who is over the house", two identical bullae of "The Scribe", two identical bullae of "Governor of the City", a bulla of "The gate-keeper of the prison" and one of "The healer". These are only 6.63% of the total. All titles are known from the Old Testament except "The gate-keeper of the prison". Several bullae are impressed with seals belonging to officials known from the Bible (Avigad 1978a). These are: "Berekhyahu the son of Neriyahu, the scribe" (A 9; WSS 417a-b), who was the personal secretary of Jeremiah the prophet (Jer. 36:4–6, 32) and "Yerahmeʾel the son of the king" (A 8; WSS 414), both of whom lived in the time of Yehoyaqim, the king of Judah (Jer. 36:26). Two personal bullae found at the City of David excavations, bearing no titles, are probably also of biblical figures (Schneider 1994:62). These are: "Gemaryahu the son of Shafan" (S 2, WSS 470), (Jer. 36:10), and "ʿAzaryahu son of Ḥilqiyahu" (S 27, WSS 596), (I Chr. 5:39). Two sites are also mentioned. The first is the biblical town of "ʾEltolad" (Avigad 1990:262–265; WSS 421), (Josh. 15:30, 19:4). This is also the only bulla on which a date appears: "the 26st year" of a nameless king. The second town "The City", which is probably Jerusalem, appears on two bullae belonging to the "Governor of the City" (WSS 402a-b).

The onomastic list includes a total number of 193 names and hypocoristica. In 73 names the theophoric element appears: *yhw*, which is 37.8%, in three names we find the shortened theophoric form: *yh*, which is only 1.55% and in 14 names the theophoric suffix is preserved: *y*, which forms 7.25% of the total. Therefore, 46.6% of the names include the Judean theophoric element *yhw* or its shortened forms. In 16 names the theophoric element *ʾl* is to be found, and in another 10 names the suffix ʾ has been preserved. Surprisingly, not one of the names carry the northern Israelite theophoric form *yw*, despite the fact that a few dozen such seals were published.

Iconographic Hebrew bullae are rare and only 17 such samples were published. These barely constitute 4.5%. Among them we find winged scarabs, winged snakes, birds, fish, does, and on three bullae, human figures. More common are the floral and the geometric motifs which were usually used as register dividers. The new reading of the royal bulla belonging to "Hezekiah the King of Judah" (A 199, p. 42 above), reveals to us that the Egypto-Phoenician two-winged scarab had been adopted as the Judean royal emblem by the end of the 8th century B.C.E. The four- or two-winged scarab (beetle), is among the most popular motifs in the Hebrew glyptic, yet, it is common also in the neighboring states, especially in Ammon (Sass 1993:214–217). Nevertheless, here for the first time, the emblem appears together with the king's name. Therefore, we can now interpret the two-winged scarab motif which appears in the upper register of the seal belonging to "Menashe the son of the king" as a royal emblem, since Manasseh was the son of Hezekiah (Avigad 1987, fig. 7; WSS 16). It is noteworthy, that this emblem also appears on the so-called *lmlk* jar handles of the same period. All this now confirms what was assumed in the past (Yadin 1967), that the winged scarab which is depicted on the *lmlk* jar handles, is indeed the royal emblem of Hezekiah. Moreover, this proves that the prefix *l* at the beginning of the word *mlk* "King", was meant to represent the king's ownership on the sealed jars, i.e. *lmlk* means: "Belonging to the King".

In 1849–1850 Layard excavated Nimrud and found in the North-west Palace, a hoard of bronze and copper objects. Among them are Phoenician and Aramaic inscribed bowls and copper weights. Two of these bowls are decorated with two-winged scarabs, while two copper weights have gold-inlaid scarab motifs, similar to the royal emblem of Hezekiah (Layard, 1853:177–196). These items are not Assyrian and it has been suggested that they are booty brought from Phoenicia or Israel (Reade 1995; Barnett 1967:6*). The appearance of the two-winged scarabs on the objects found at Nimrud led Yadin to suggest that they originated from a Judean palace (Yadin 1967). The appearance of the winged scarab as the royal emblem of Hezekiah and of his son Manasseh supports Yadin's assumption.

Indexes for chapters One and Two

Personal names

אביהו	*ʾbyhw* — A13
אדניהו	*ʾdnyhw* — A1, A2a-b, A11, A125, A165, DH5
אדניחי	*ʾdnyḥy* — A113
אוהל	*ʾwhl* — J4, J5
אחא	*ʾḥʾ* — J23, J35
אחאב	*ʾḥʾb* — A16, A17, A18a-c, A19, A60, H1
אחאמה	*ʾḥʾmh* — A151
אחז	*ʾḥz* (sic) — A199
אחזיהו	*ʾḥzyhw* — J1?
אחיאב	*ʾḥyʾb* — J2
אחיהו	*ʾḥyhw* — J10, J11, A13, A166
אחימה	*ʾḥymh* — J3
אחמלך	*ʾḥmlk* — A129
אחקם	*ʾḥqm* — A14, A15, A16
אחיקם	*ʾḥyqm* — DH29a-c, H2a-g
אליהו	*ʾlyhw* — A27, A85
אליסמך	*ʾlysmk* — A39
אליעז	*ʾlyʿz* — A28, A71
אליקם	*ʾlyqm* — J4, J5
אלירם	*ʾlyrm* — A29
אלנתן	*ʾlntn* — J6, J7, A30, S12, H3
אלסמך	*ʾlsmk* — A40
אלעז	*ʾlʿz* — A17, A18a-c, A72, A73, A90
אלעשה	*ʾlʿśh* — DH6
אלצדק	*ʾlṣdq* — A84
אלרם	*ʾlrm* — H12
אלשמע	*ʾlšmʿ* — J1?, J8, J9, J34, A4, A66, A158, A159, A160, DH9, DH19a-b, DH28a-b, DH31, AM1
אמריהו	*ʾmryhw* — A31a-b
אפרח	*ʾprḥ* — J10, J11, J39, A19, A20, A21, A22, A23, DH28a-b
אשחר	*ʾšḥr* — A32
אשיהו	*ʾšyhw* — J38, A33, A105a-b, A110
אשנא	*ʾšnʾ* — DH26
אשרחי	*ʾšrḥy* — A34, A126a-n
אשריחת	*ʾšryḥt* — A127
בלבל	*blbl* — DH95
בלגי	*blgy* — J6, J7, J12
בנזכר	*bnzkr* — J25
בניהו	*bnyhw* — J13, A35, DH17, DH27
בסי	*bsy* (sic *ʾbsy*) — F2
בעדיהו	*bʿdyhw* — A36, A37

בקש	*bqš* — DH27
ברכיהו	*brkyhw* — J14, J15, A9, A38, DH1
גאליהו	*gʾlyhw* — BZ1, J16?, A6
גדי	*gdy* — A25a-b
גדיהו	*gdyhw* — J17, A23, A24a-d, A26, A169
גדליהו	*gdlyhw* — BM1, A5, A41, L1
גמריה	*gmryh* — J18
גמריהו	*gmryhw* — J19
געלי	*gʿly* — A39, A40
דלא	*dlʾ* — H4
דליה	*dlyh* — J20
דליהו	*dlyhw* — J12
דמליהו	*dmlyhw* — J32, J43, A42a-c, A43a-b, A44, A45, A46, A170
הודויהו	*hwdwyhw* — A55, A117
הושע	*hwšʿ* — A45, DH31 twice
הושעיהו	*hwšʿyhw* — J13, J20, J21, A28, A41, A43a-b, A44, A45, A46, A47a-b, A48, A143a-b, A144a-b, A145a-b, A146, A147, A148, A161, S3, DH25
הצליהו	*hṣlyhw* — A49a-b, A128, A168
זכר	*zkr* — J24, J45, A50, A51, DH8
זרח	*zrḥ* — A62
חבא	*ḥbʾ* — A52
חבי	*ḥby* — DH29a-c, H2a-g
חגב	*ḥgb* — A53a-b, A54a-b, H5
חגי	*ḥgy* — A55, S3
חזדא	*ḥzdʾ* — DH11
חזקיהו	*ḥzqyhw (sic)* — A199
חטש	*ḥṭš* — A56a-c
חלץ	*ḥlṣ* — A60, A142
חלציהו	*ḥlṣyhw* — A47a-b, A79, A157a-b, AM1
חלק	*ḥlq* — A57, A98, A149
חלקיהו	*ḥlqyhw* — L2, J36, A58, A59, A107, DH22, VB1
חמטל	*ḥmṭl* — S9
חמל	*ḥml* — A83
חנמלך	*ḥnmlk* — J22
חנן	*ḥnn* — A63, A64
חנני	*ḥnny* — A150
חנניה	*ḥnnyh* — J3
חנניהו	*ḥnnyhw* — J23, BM1, A61, A62, A100, B1
חצי	*ḥṣy* — J30
טביהו	*ṭbyhw* — A14, A65
טבשלם	*ṭbšlm* — J24, J25, J45?
יאזן	*yʾzn* — A162
יאזניהו	*yʾznyhw* — J27, J40
יאש	*yʾš* — A30, A66, A67, DH19a-b
ידעיהו	*ydʿyhw* — J28, A68a-b, A69, S8, DH7, H6
יהאר	*yhʾr* — DH25
יהוא	*yhwʾ* — A70
יהואב	*yhwʾb* — J2, J8, A31a-b
יהואח	*yhwʾḥ* — A71, A72, A73
יהואל	*yhwʾl* — L6
יהוזרח	*yhwzrḥ* — A118

יהוחי *yhwḥy* — L3
יהוכל *yhwkl* — L3
יהועז *yhwʿz* — A74a-b
יהוקם *yhwqm* — A12, A171
יהורם *yhwrm* — L10
יהושמע *yhwšmʿ* — J1?
יהושע *yhwšʿ* — A20, A21, DH16
יועליהו *ywʿlyhw* — DH10
יחץ *yḥṣ* — DH18
יסף *ysp* — A131
יקמיהו *yqmyhw* — A11, A75a-c, A76, A77, A172. S12
ירחמאל *yrḥmʾl* — A8
ירמיהו *yrmyhw* — L8, L9, A78
ישמעאל *yšmʿʾl* — TH1, J22, A78, A79, A80, A81, A82, A89, A101, A102, A164, A173, SC1
ישעיהו *yšʿyhw* — A83, A84, A91, DH22, DH24
כברה *kbrh* — TJ1
כלכל *klkl?* — H5
כסלא *kslʾ* — A132
כרמי *krmy* — A68a-b, S8
מאס *mʾs* — L2
מבטחיהו *mbṭḥyhw* — DH3
מגן *mgn* — J18
מחסיהו *mhsyhw* — J41, A80, A85, A86, DH16
מיאמן *myʾmn* — L6, A87, A88, DH17
מיכה *mykh* — A27
מכיהו *mkyhw* — J30, J37, A90, A91, A92, A94, A95, A96, A97
מיפלל *mypll* — S2
מירב *myrb* — A89
מלכי *mlky* — J14
מלכיהו *mlkyhw* — A98, A99, A120, A174, A175, DH10, DH20, DH21
מנחם *mnḥm* — A100, A101, A102, A103, A104, A152
מנש *mnš* — A103
מספר *mspr* — A106
מעשיהו *mʿśyhw* — J27, A87, A105a-b, A107, DH9
מצר *mṣr* — A108
מקניהו *mqnyhw* — A154, BLM1
מקנמלך *mqnmlk* — A109
משלם *mšlm* — J28, A75a-c, A92, A110, A111, S2, BLM1, H9?
משמש *mšmš* — A70
משען *mšʿn* — A112
מתן *mtn* — A52, A74a-b, A113, A114, A115, A116a-b, A117, A118, A134, S7
מתניהו *mtnyhw* — TH1, A21, A119, DH15, DH23
נבי *nby* — L8, L9
נגבי *ngby* — A120
נחם *nḥm* — L4, J31, A77, A121, A153, A176, DH11
נחמיהו *nḥmyhw* — A61, B2
נמש *nmš* — A122
נמשר *nmšr* — A123, A124
נרא *nrʾ* — DH20, DH21
נריהו *nryhw* — BS1, L5, J32, A7, A9, A15, A50, A122, A125, A126a-n, A127, A128, DH1
נתן *ntn* — A3, A129, A130

נתניהו	*ntnyhw* — J33?
סאל	*s'l* — A131
סילא	*syl'* — J34, A132
סמך	*smk* — A136
סמכיהו	*smkyhw* — J9, A93, A119
סעדיהו	*sʿdyhw* — A133a-b
עבדא	*ʿbd'* — A65, DH7
עבדיהו	*ʿbdyhw* — BS1, A134
עזיהו	*ʿzyhw* — J1?, A63, A177
עזר	*ʿzr* — J17, A57, A135a-b, DH13
עזראל	*ʿzr'l* — A156
עזריהו	*ʿzryhw* — J26, J35, J36, A136, A137, S6, DH4
עזרקם	*ʿzrqm* — J37, A138A-B, A139
עכבר	*ʿkbr* — A140, DH12, DH31
עליהו	*ʿlyhw* — A35, A141, A142
עמדיהו	*ʿmdyhw* — J38, A93, S4
ענניהו	*ʿnnyhw* — L4
עפי	*ʿpy* — A88
עשיהו	*ʿśyhw* — A32, A34
פגי	*pgy* — A104
פדיהו	*pdyhw* — A12, A67, A99, A130, A137, A178
פלטיהו	*plṭyhw* — J42, A86, A94, A114, A115, A116a-b, A135a-b, A143a-b, 144a-b, 145a-b, A146, A147, A148, A149, S4, S7, DH14
פרעש	*prʿš* — L5
פרפר	*prpr* — A138a-b
פשחר	*pšḥr* — A151, A152, A183
פתח	*ptḥ* — A153
צדקא	*ṣdq'* — A139
צדקיהו	*ṣdqyhw* — B1
צפן	*ṣpn* — J44, DH24
צפניהו	*ṣpnyhw* — L8, L9, A53a-b, A54a-b, [A140], A154, A155, DH12
קרבאר	*qrb'r* — A156, H10
ראיהו	*r'yhw* — A157a-b
רחם	*rḥm* — J33?
רפא	*rp'* — A42a-c, A141, VB1
רפאיהו	*rp'yhw* — J39, A111, A121, DH15, DH23
שאלה	*š'lh* — J31, A155
שבניהו	*šbnyhw* — L7, A49a-b, A96, A97, A124, A167
שחר	*šḥr* — A22, A23, A24a-d, A25a-b, A26, A95, A112, A113
שכניהו	*šknyhw* — DH6, H6
שלם	*šlm* — A108, A158, A159, A160, A161, S6, DH14, H9?
שלמיהו	*šlmyhw* — DH8
שמע	*šmʿ* — A48
שמעיהו	*šmʿyhw* — J40, J41, J42, A29, A33, A38, A64, A162, A163, A179, DH2, H3
שמרנ..	*šmrn..* — TJ2
שעל	*šʿl* — A69, A79, A123, A164, A174
שפט	*špṭ* — A166
שפטיהו	*špṭyhw* — J43, J44, A56a-c, A165, A180a-b
שפן	*špn* — J19
שריהו	*śryhw* — A37, A167
תחת	*tḥt* (sic *'ḥ'b)* — F2

תנחם	*tnḥm* — A168, DH13
ב...	*b...* — J29
ז...	*z...* — A133b
י...	*y...* — J26
יה...	*yh...* — J29
יהו...	*yhw...* — L11, A189, A190
מ...	*m...* — A184
ס...	*s...* — A76, H11
ע...	*ʿ...* — J15
פא...	*pʾ...* — H11
פנ.ב..	*pn.b..* — A150
של...	*šl...* — A196
..יוע..	*..ywʿ..* — A106
..עי..	*..ʿy..* — A194
..עיה..	*..ʿyh..* — A190
..עמל..	*..ʿml..* — A195
...א	*...ʾ* — H14
..איהו	*..ʾyhw* — A191a
..בע	*..bʿ* — A202
..הו	*..hw* — A182, H13
..חם	*..ḥm* — A202
..טיה	*..ṭyh* — H13
..יאל	*..yʾl* — A181
..יה	*..yh* — A182
..יהו	*..yhw* — J21, A51, A58, A179, A183, A186 twice, A187, A192, A193, A194, A197
..ליהו	*..lyhw* — A187
..ניהו	*..nyhw* — A188
..עיהו	*..ʾyhw* — A185
..שיהו	*..šyhw* — A185
..שע	*..šʿ* — A182
..ם	*..m* — A181

Titles and professions

אשר על הבית	*ʾšr ʿl hbyt* "Who is over the House" — L1, A1, A2a-b, A3
בן המלך	*bn hmlk* "The son of the King" — BZ1, L7?, A6, A7, A8, SC1
הספר	*hspr* "The Scribe" — A9, DH1
הרפא	*hrpʾ* "The Healer" — J45
למלך	*lmlk* "Belonging to the King" — F1
מלך יהדה	*mlk yhdh* "King of Judah" — A199 (sic)
עבד המלך	*ʿbd hmlk* "The Servant of the King" — L7?, A4, A5, DH2, DH3
שער המסגר	*šʿr hmsgr* "The Gate-keeper of the Prison" — DH4
שר הער	*śr hʿr* "Governor of the City" — A10a-b

Toponyms, words and numerals

אלתלד	*ʾltld* — F1
שנה	*šnh* — F1
26	26 — F1

A = Avigad, 1986; **AM** = Antiquities Market; **B** = Dr. Elie Borowski private collection; **BLM** = Bible Land Museum; **BM** = British Museum; **BS** = Beer-Sheba; **BZ** = Beth-Zur; **DH** = Deutsch and Heltzer, 1994, 1995, 1997; **F** = Avigad, 1990, fiscal bullae; **H** = Reüben Hecht Museum; **J** = Jerusalem, City of David; **L** = Lachish; **S** = Josef Samel collection; **SC** = Stern collection; **TH** = Tell el-Ḥesi; **TJ** = Tell el-Judeideh; **VB** = Victor Barakat gallery.

Chapter Three

109 Hebrew Bullae from the Time of Isaiah Through the Destruction of the First Temple in the Shlomo Moussaieff Collection

Yeshayahu 1:1[1]

"The vision of Yeshayahu the son of Amoz, which he saw concerning Yehuda and Yerushalayim in the days of ʿUzziyyahu, Yotam, Ahaz, Yehizqiyyahu, kings of Yehuda"

1. Four kings are mentioned in this verse. Three of them are mentioned in the bullae presented below.

A Royal Bulla

1. ʾAḥaz (son of) Yehotam, King of Judah

A complete bulla of elliptic shape, made of reddish-brown clay in an excellent state of preservation, it measures 14.7x12.5 mm. On its left edge, a fingerprint is visible, possibly the fingerprint of Ahaz the King of Judah himself. On the reverse of the bulla, the imprint of the texture of the papyrus to which the bulla was affixed is visible, along with two grooves where the cord which tied the papyrus ran. The elliptical seal impression measures 10.5x8.2 mm. Around the seal impression, a 1 mm. thick groove is present. This indicates that the seal was set in a metal bezel, probably of a signet ring or a pendant, while it served to impress the bulla. The craftsman encircled the seal surface with a triple framing circular line and engraved the legend in it in three lines.

The Hebrew inscription reads:

לאחז.י/הותם.מלך./ יהדה

lʾḥz.y/hwtm.mlk./ yhdh

"Belonging to ʾAḥaz (son of) Yehotam, King of Judah"

The inscription, composed of small letters, is notable for its high calligraphic quality. Divider-dots are placed between the words, yet register divider-lines are missing. The inscription is clear and complete. The letters *lamed*, *mem* and *kaf* are ca. 45° inclined rightward and the letters *he* and *dalet* are ca. 45° inclined leftward. The vertical line with the horizontal stroke at the top of the letters *he* forms an angle, yet the rightward extension of the upper horizontal line is present at the third letter *he*. The upright letter *ḥet* has three horizontal bars and the letter *zayin* bears a long cursive tail. A unique phenomenon of this script are the letters *mem* and *kaf* which have an prominent curved leftward leg forming a semicircle. No special features are detected at the letters *alef*, *taw*, *waw* and *yod*. Surprisingly, the seal is aniconic and a royal emblem is absent. Yet, the emblem could be present on the back of the seal.

ʾḥz — The name of the twelfth king of Judah. Ahaz was the son of king Yehotam (II Kgs.

15:38; II Chr. 27:9) and the father of king Hezekiah (II Kgs. 29:20; II Chr. 28:27). According to the biblical record: "Twenty years old was Ahaz when he began to reign, and he reigned sixteen years in Jerusalem" (II Kgs. 16:2; II Chr. 28:1). Ahaz reigned between 732/1–716/5 B.C.E.[2] The name of Ahaz the King of Judah also appears on the iconic seal of one of his officials: *lʾšnʾ ʿbd ʾḥz* "Belonging to ʾUšnaʾ, servant of ʾAḥaz" (Torrey 1940; WSS 5). The name Ahaz is a hypocoristicon, a shortened name which lost its theophoric element. Such theophoric names are: Yehoahaz, Ahzay and Ahazyahu which are known from the Hebrew Bible (I Kgs. 22:40; II Kgs. 8:25, 10:35; Neh. 11:13). Four other kings are called Ahazyahu or Yehoahaz: Ahazyahu the son of Ahab, the ninth Israelite king who reigned between 853 — 852 B.C.E. (I Kgs. 22:40); Yehoahaz the son of Yehu, the twelfth king of Israel who reigned seventeen years between 814/3–798 B.C.E. (II Kgs. 13:1); Ahazyahu (called Yehoahaz) the son of Yehoram, the sixth king of Judah, who reigned only one year in 841 B.C.E.; and Yehoahaz the son of Yoshiyahu, the seventeenth king of Judah who reign only three months in 609 B.C.E. Ahaz was the name of another biblical personage, Ahaz son of Mikha (I Chr. 8:35). In the annals of the Assyrian king Tiglath-pileser III (744–727 B.C.E.), which has been found at Nimrud and recounts the names of the kings from whom he received tribute, the name of Ahaz is spelled *Ia-ú-ḫa-zi* (ANET 282).

yhwtm — The name of Ahaz' father, Yehotam was the eleventh king of Judah, the son of ʿUzziyyahu from his wife Yerusha, the daughter of Zadok (II Kgs. 15:32–33). He reigned from 750 to 732/1 B.C.E. although the period between 750–740/39 B.C.E. was conjointly with his father. Within the inscription: *lʾḥz.y/hwtm.mlk./yhdh* the word *bn* "son" is missing, probably due to the lack of space on the surface of the minute seal (10.5x8.2 mm.). However, this is a common feature on other seals, including the seal of King Hezekiah (above p. 42) and the missing word creates no problem. The name of Yehotam appears nineteen times in the Bible and the spelling of the name is always *ywtm* "Yotam" (Even-Shoshan 1990:462). Yet, according to the inscription on the bulla, which is a contemporary document from the time of Ahaz, the correct spelling of the King's name is *yhwtm* "Yehotam". This spelling contains the Judean theophoric type element *yhw* in contrast to the northern Israelite type element *yw*. Therefore the omission of the letter *he* from the theophoric element of the name in the Bible is puzzling. Yotam was the name of another two biblical individuals: Yotam, son of Yerubbaal (Judg. 9:5) and Yotam son of Yohday of the Kalev clan (I Chr. 2:47). The name Yehotam or Yotam does not appear in other Hebrew epigraphic material. The name *ytm* "Yatom", however, does appear on a seal which has been found at Ezion-Geber (Glueck 1940:13–15), but its meaning is "orphan" similar to the name with the same spelling found on 5th century B.C.E. Aramaic papyri from Elephantine (Kornfeld 1978:55).[3]

mlk yhdh — "King of Judah". The name of the Kingdom of Judah has been written on the royal seal of Ahaz without the consonant *waw*, in contrast with eight hundred biblical records

---

2. The dates according to Thiele (1983)
3. Elephantine is an island in the Nile, in southern Egypt, between the first and second cataracts, west of Aswan. In the Persian period, 5th century B.C.E., a Jewish community existed on the island and a temple to *Yhwh* was built. The Aramaic papyri found on the island are dated between 495–399 B.C.E.

of the name with its full spelling *yhwdh* (Even-Shoshan, 1990:437–439). It is noteworthy that spellings such as: *yhd*, *yhwd* and *yhdh* are common two hundred years later in the Persian period on seals, sealings and sealed jar handles (Avigad 1976) and also on minute silver coins from the 4th and 3rd century B.C.E., which were struck in Judah (Meshorer 1982).

Two biblical accounts, II Kgs. chapter 16 and II Chr. chapter 28, are reports concerning the history of Ahaz, the King of Judah. Both texts are very similar in many sections, with some additions and omission. This points toward a common source for both books. This fact was pointed out by both scribes which identified the source with: "The rest of the acts of Ahaz which he did, are they not written in the book of the chronicles of the kings of Yehuda?" (II Kgs. 16:19) and "The rest of his acts and all his ways, first and last, behold, they are written in the book of the kings of Yehuda and Yisrael" (II Chr. 28:26).

According to the Bible, Ahaz was a negative king: "And did not do that which was right in the sight of the Lord his God, like David his father" (II Kgs. 16:2; II Chr.28:1).

Iron Age royal seal impressions from the neighboring states are very rare and only three are known. The first bulla belonged to an Ammonite king: *lbrkʾl / hmlk* "Belonging to Barakʾel the King" (Deutsch 1999), the second bulla was found at Umm el-Biyara in 1965: *lqwsg[br] / mlk ʾ[dwm]* "Belonging to Qausgabri King of ʾEdom" (Bennett 1966, pl. 22,b; WSS 1049) and the third found at Zinjirli in 1913: *lbrrkb / br pnmw* "Belonging to Barrakkab son of Panamuwa (the King)" (Sendschirli V, pl.38.b; WSS 750).

Three Bullae Bearing the Title "Servant of Hezekiah"

2. Yehozaraḥ son of Ḥilqiyahu, servant of Ḥizqiyahu

A damaged black clay bulla, with the upper part missing, it measures 11.0x10.3 mm. Around the seal impression a groove is present. This indicates that the seal was set in a metal bezel, probably of a signet ring or a pendant, while it served to impress the bulla. The seal impression, if restored, measures 9.7x 7.8 mm. On the reverse of the bulla the imprint of the texture of the papyrus to which the bulla was affixed is visible. The inscription which is composed of small letters is notable for its high calligraphic quality. The legend is divided into four lines without register dividers, but divider-dots are placed between some words. Only remnants of the first line have survived, nevertheless, the completion of the legend is certain, due to the fact that another bulla sealed from the same seal has been published in the past (Hestrin and Dayagi-Mendels 1974).

The Hebrew inscription reads:

[ליה]וֹזֹ[ר]/ח בן חלק/יהו עבד חֹ/זקיהו

[lyh]ẇż[r]/ḥ bn ḥlq/yhw ʿbd ḥ̇ /żqyhw

"Belonging to Yehozaraḥ son of Ḥilqiyahu, servant of Ḥizqiyahu"

yhwzrḥ — Yehozaraḥ, a theophoric name similar to the biblical name Zeraḥiah (I Chr. 5:32), meaning "The God Yahweh distributes its light". Note also the hypocoristicon Zeraḥ (I Chr. 6:6). The name appears on another bulla from the 7th century B.C.E.: *lmtn bn yhwzrḥ* "Belonging to Mattan son of Yehozaraḥ" (Avigad 1986, 118).

ḥlqyhw — Ḥilqiyahu is a biblical theophoric personal name (II Kgs. 18:18, 26; 22:4, 8, 14), meaning "The God Yahweh is my share, portion". Ḥilqiyahu is the name of several important figures in the Bible, such as the high priest in the time of Yoshiyyahu (II Kgs. 22:4), the father of Elyaqim, who was "over the house" during the siege of Sennacherib (II Kgs. 18:18), etc. The name is common on Hebrew epigraphic material and has been recorded 16 times on seals and bullae (Davies 1991:352) and once on an ostraca (Deutsch and Heltzer 1995:83). The name appears also on the bulla *[lʾ]lyqm / ḥlqyhw* "Belonging to ʾElyaqim (son of) Ḥilqiyahu", no. 30 below.

ʿbd ḥzqyhw — "servant of Hezekiah", a high official in the royal administration, connected directly to king Hezekiah, the thirteenth king of Judah (II Kgs. 16:20; II Chr. 28:27). He reigned for a relatively long period between ca. 716/5–687/6 B.C.E. Establishing an exact date to his reign presents difficulties because of two contradictory biblical traditions in the book of II Kings, chapter 18. According to verse 10, Samaria, the capital of the kingdom of Israel, was conquered by the Assyrians in the sixth year of Hezekiah. Samaria was destroyed in ca. 720 B.C.E., which means that Hezekiah ascended to the throne in ca. 726 B.C.E. Yet, according to verse 13, Sennacherib conquered the fortified towns of Judah in the 14th year of Hezekiah. This campaign took place in ca. 701 B.C.E. which means that Hezekiah ascend the throne in ca. 715 B.C.E. In addition, verse 2 tells us that the reign of Hezekiah lasted 29 years. Therefore, according to the Bible there are two possible options to date his reign: a) 726–697/6 B.C.E., a high date as adopted by Galil (1996), b) 716/5–687/6 B.C.E., a low date as adopted by Thiele (1983). We will follow the second lower option as adopted by Thiele. The title: *ʿbd ḥzqyhw* "Servant of Hezekiah", is present also on bullae nos. 3 and 4.

3. ʿAzaryahu son of Yehoʾaḥ, servant of Ḥizqiyahu

A complete bulla of elliptic shape, made of reddish-brown clay, broken in three parts and glued, it measures 13.0x10.2 mm. Around the seal impression, which measures 10.3x7.4 mm., a groove is present. This indicates that the seal was set in a metal bezel, probably of a signet ring or a pendant, while it served to impress the bulla. On the reverse of the bulla, the imprint of the texture of the papyrus to which the bulla was affixed is visible.

The Hebrew inscription reads:

לעזריה̊/ו.בן.י̊הו/[א]ח.עבד.חז/קיהו.

lʿzryh̊/w.bn.ẙhw/[ʾ]ḥ.ʿbd.ḥz/qyhw

"Belonging to ʿAzaryahu son of Yehoʾaḥ, servant of Ḥizqiyahu"

The four-line inscription, composed of small letters, is encircled by a framing line of which only the lower part has survived. Divider-dots are placed between the words, yet register divider-lines are missing. The second line is damaged, but the inscription is clear and complete.

ʿzryhw — ʿAzaryahu is a theophoric name meaning "Yahweh has helped". This is the name of one of the Judean kings: "ʿAzaryah the son of ʾAmazyah and Yekholyahu the Jerusalemite" (II Kgs. 15:1). "ʿAzaryah" and "ʿAzaryahu" are the names of other biblical high officials: "ʿAzaryah son of Yeroham, captain of hundreds" (II Chr. 23:1), "ʿAzaryah the son of Yohanan, priest in the Temple built by Solomon in Jerusalem" (I Chr. 5:36), "ʿAzaryah the son of Ḥilqiyyah, the ruler of the house of God" (I Chr. 9:11), "ʿAzaryah the son of Zadok the priest, high official in the time of Solomon (I Kgs. 4:2), "ʿAzaryahu the son of Natan, who was over the officers" (I Kgs. 4:5), "ʿAzaryahu the son of ʿOded, the prophet" (II Chr. 15:1), "ʿAzaryahu the son of ʿOved, captain of hundreds" (II Chr. 23:1), "ʿAzaryahu the high priest" (II Chr. 26:17), "ʿAzaryahu the chief priest" (II Chr. 31:10), as well as two sons of kings: "ʿAzaryah the son of king Yehoshafat" (II Chr. 21:2) and "ʿAzaryah the son of king Yoram" (II Chr. 22:6). ʿAzaryahu is also the name of the "gate keeper of the prison" as is known from his bulla (Deutsch and Heltzer 1994, 41). The name is one of the most frequent names in the Hebrew epigraphy and has been recorded thirty times by Davies (1991:459). It appears also on bullae nos. 10 and 74 (below).

yhwʾḥ — Yehoʾaḥ is a theophoric name meaning "The God Yahweh is my Brother". The name is found in the Bible only in variants such as: "ʾAḥiyah", "ʾAḥiyahu", "ʾAḥiyau" and

"Yauʾaḥ". The name is also rare in the Hebrew epigraphic material and is known only from three non-identical bullae: *yhwʾḥ (bn) ʾlyʿz* — "Belonging to Yehoʾaḥ (son of) ʾEliʿaz" (A 71) and *yhwʾḥ (bn) ʾlʿz* — "Belonging to Yehoʾaḥ (the son of) ʾEl(i)ʿaz" (A 72, 73).

ʿbd ḥzqyhw — "Servant of Hezekiah", is the title of ʿAzaryahu son of Yehoʾaḥ, a high official in the royal administration of king Hezekiah, son of Ahaz king of Judah, who reign between ca. 687/6–716/5 B.C.E. The title "Servant of Hezekiah' also appears on the previous bulla no. 2, and the next one no. 4 (see discussion on the title "Servant of the King" with bulla no. 10 below).

4. ... servant of Ḥizqiyahu

A black clay bulla, the upper edge is missing and it measures 9.5x10.2 mm. On the left side of the bulla, a groove is visible. This indicates that the seal was set in a metal bezel, probably of a signet ring or a pendant, while it served to impress the bulla. On the reverse of the bulla, the imprint of the texture of the papyrus to which the bulla was affixed is visible, along with two grooves where the cord which tied the papyrus ran. The surface of the bulla was damaged and only several letters and fragments of letters are visible. The letters are small and the inscription is divided into four lines without register dividers.

The Hebrew inscription reads:

... / ... / עבד חזק/יהו

... / .../ ʿb̊d̊.ḥzq/yh̊ẘ

"(Belonging to ... son of ...), servant of Ḥizqiyahu"

The name of the seal's owner and of his father are lost, yet his title is preserved. According to the distribution of the letters, it is clear that the seal used to impress this bulla is a different one from the two presented above (nos. 2 and 3).

Following is a list of Hebrew epigraphic seals and seal impressions containing the title *ʿbd* "Servant" together with the name of the king:

1. *lšmʿ ʿbd yrbʿm* — "Belonging to Shemaʿ, servant of Yarobʿam". This is the seal of a high

official, probably of Yarobʿam II, king of Israel (783–743 B.C.E.).[4] The seal, made of jasper, was found in 1904 at Megiddo, Level V (Schumacher and Steuernagel 1908:99; WSS 2).

2. *lʾbyw ʿbd ʿzyw* — "Belonging to ʾAbiyau, servant of ʿUzziyau". Seal made of agate (Bordreuil 1986:45, no. 40; WSS 4).

3. *lšbnyw // lšbnyw ʿbd ʿzyw* — "Belonging to Shebanyau // Belonging to Shebanyau, servant of ʿUzziyau". Bi-faceted seal made of reddish limestone (Bordreuil 1986:45, no. 41; WSS 3).

4. *lʾšnʾ ʿbd ʾḥz* — "Belonging to ʾUshnaʾ, servant of ʾAḥaz". Seal made of carnelian (Torrey 1940; WSS 5).

5. *lʿbdy ʿbd hwšʿ* — "Belonging to ʿAbday, servant of Hosheaʿ". Seal made of pink chalcedony (Lemaire 1995; not listed in WSS).

6. *lyhwzrḥ bn ḥlqyhw ʿbd ḥzqyhw* — "Belonging to Yehozaraḥ son of Ḥilqiyahu, servant of Ḥizqiyahu". Clay bulla (Hestrin and Dayagi-Mendels 1979, no. 4; WSS 407).

7. *lyhwzrḥ bn ḥlqyhw ʿbd ḥzqyhw* — "Belonging to Yehozaraḥ son of Ḥilqiyahu, servant of Ḥizqiyahu". Clay bulla, duplicate of the previous one (bulla no. 2 above, not listed in WSS).

8. *lʿzryhw bn yhwʾḥ ʿbd ḥzqyhw* — "Belonging to ʿAzaryahu son of Yehoʾaḥ, servant of Ḥizqiyahu". Clay bulla (no. 3 above, not listed in WSS).

9. ... *ʿbd ḥzqyhw* — "Belonging to ... son of ..., servant of Ḥizqiyahu". Clay bulla (no. 4 above, not listed in WSS).

It is noteworthy that the above three high official bullae of the "servants of Hezekiah", have several common features:

a) The seals used to impress these bullae were very small in size.
b) All three seals were set in metal bezels.
c) All three are aniconic.
d) Register divider are missing.
e) The inscriptions are inscribed widthwise in four lines.
f) The letters are minute and paleographically similar (See Pl. I).
g) Chronologically, all three belonged to the reign of king Hezekiah.

Therefore, we can assume that all three seals were made in the same workshop, or even by the same craftsman.

4. For a different dating of the seal to Yarobʿam I, see: Ahlström 1993 and Ussishkin 1994.

Two Bullae Bearing the Title "Who is Over the House"

5. **ʾAdoniyahu, who is over the house**

A complete bulla made of brown clay in a good state of preservation, it measures 12.3x11.5 mm. On the reverse of the bulla, the imprint of the texture of the papyrus to which the bulla was affixed is visible, along with grooves where the cord which tied the papyrus ran. The lump of clay on which the seal has been impressed was too small, therefore the edges are missing. The surface of the bulla is divided into two registers by a double parallel line. The two-line inscription lacks the word-divider dots. Three letters at the left side of the bulla are damaged and the letter *taw*, at the end of the lower register is missing. Even so, the reading is certain.

The Hebrew inscription reads:

לאדניהו / אשר על הבי[ת]

lʾdnyhw / ʾšr ʿl hby[t]

"Belonging to ʾAdoniyahu who is over the house"

Three bullae impressed with two different seals, belonging to ʾAdoniyahu "who is over the house", were previously published by Avigad (1986, 1, 2a, 2b), yet the above-presented bulla was impressed with a third, different seal. The comparison of this bulla with the three bullae published by Avigad reveals a paleographic similarity. Therefore we can assume that all four seals belonged to the same minister.[5]

ʾdnyhw — ʾAdoniyahu is a theophoric name meaning "My lord is Yahweh". Three persons in the Bible bear this name: one of the sons of King David with Haggit (II Sam. 3:4), a Levite in the time of King Jehoshaphat (II Chr. 17:8) and one of the leaders of the people in the time of Nehemiah (Neh. 10:16).

5. See also the three different seals of "ʾElyashib son of ʾAshyahu" found at Arad (Aharoni, 1981:119, 105–107; WSS 70–72).

The name is known from other Hebrew epigraphic seals and sealings: the above-mentioned three bullae: *l'dnyhw 'šr 'l hbyt* "Belonging to 'Adoniyahu who is over the house" (Avigad 1986, 1, 2a-b; WSS 403, 404a-b), on four personal bullae: 1) *l'dnyhw bn yqmyhw* "Belonging to 'Adoniyahu son of Yeqamyahu", 2) *lnryhw 'dnyhw* "Belonging to Neriyahu (son of) 'Adoniyahu", 3) *lšpṭyhw 'dnyhw* "Belonging to Shephaṭyahu (son of) 'Adoniyahu" (Avigad 1986, 11, 125, 165; WSS 423, 578, 642), 4) on a bulla depicting a four-winged ***uraeus***: *l'dnyhw* "Belonging to 'Adoniyahu" (Deutsch and Heltzer 1994:42, no. 15), as well as on a bronze seal: *l'dnyhw šm'* "Belonging to 'Adoniyahu (son of) Shema'" (Avigad 1989a, 9; WSS 50). It appears also on bulla no. 29 below.

'šr 'l hbyt — "Who is over the house", lit. in charge over the house, is the title of a high official, probably in charge over the king's property, the Minister of Finance (Avishur and Heltzer 1996:55–58). Six officials bearing this title are known from the Bible:

1. אחישר — "'Aḥishar" in the time of King Solomon (I Kgs. 4:6).
2. יותם — "Yotam" in the time of his father King 'Uzziah, before he became king himself (II Kgs. 15:5).
3. שבנא — "Shebna'" in the time of King Hezekiah (Isa. 22:15).
4. אליקים בן חלקיהו — "'Elyaqim son of Ḥilqiyahu" in the time of King Hezekiah (II Kgs. 18:18).
5. ארצא — "'Arza'" in the time of King Elah (I Kgs. 16:8–9).
6. עבדיהו — "'Ovadyahu" in the time of King 'Aḥ'ab (I Kgs. 18:3).

Five officials bearing this title are known from the Hebrew epigraphy published to date:

1. *...]yhw 'šr 'l hbyt* — "...yahu who is over the house". Siloam tomb inscription: *z't [qbrt ...]yhw 'šr 'l hbyt. 'yn (ph) ksp wzhb ky 'm ('ṣmtw) w'ṣmt 'mtw 'th. 'rwr h'dm 'šr ypth 't z't* — "This is the [sepulchre of ...]yahu who is over the house. There is no silver and no gold here but [his bones] and the bones of his slave-wife with him. Cursed be the man who will open this" (Avigad 1953). This is probably the burial of "Shebna who is over the house" whose tomb is mentioned in the Bible (Isa. 22:15–16): "Thus says the Lord God of hosts, Go, get thee to this steward, to Shebna, who is over the house. Say to him, What hast thou here?, and whom hast thou here, that thou hast hewn thee out a tomb here, hewing out a tomb on high, carving a habitation for himself in a rock"
2. *l'dnyhw 'šr 'l hbyt* — "Belonging to 'Adoniyahu who is over the house". Three bullae impressed with two different seals (Avigad 1986, 1, 2a-b; WSS 403, 404a-b).
3. *lntn 'šr 'l hbyt* — "Belonging to Natan who is over (the) house". Clay bulla (Avigad 1986, 3; WSS 406).
4. *ldlyhw 'šr 'l hbyt* — "Belonging to Gedalyahu who is over the house". Clay bulla found at Lachish (Lachish III:348, Pl. 44–45, no. 173; WSS 405).
5. *[l]ydw 'šr ['] l hbyt* — "Belonging to Yiddo who is over the house". Seal in the Hecht Museum (Avigad 1979:119f, no. 1; WSS 1).
6. *lmbṭ[ḥyhw] 'šr '[l hbyt]* — "Belonging to Mibṭaḥyahu who is over the house" (The next bulla no. 6).

7. *lmbṭḥyhw ʾšr ʿl hbyt* — "Belonging to Mibṭaḥyahu who is over the house". Unpublished bulla.[6]

6. Mibṭaḥyahu who is over the house

A fragmentary bulla made of reddish clay, it measures 12.4x11.5 mm. On the reverse of the bulla, the imprint of the texture of the papyrus to which the bulla was affixed is visible. The surface of the bulla is divided into two registers by a double line. The left side of the bulla is missing.

The Hebrew inscription reads:

[ל]מבט̇[חיהו] / אשר ע̇[ל הבית]

[l] mbṭ̇[ḥyhw] / ʾšr ʿ[l hbyt]

"Belonging to Mibṭaḥyahu who is over the house"

In the upper register only three letters from the owner's name survive: ...מבט *mbṭ...* and the completion of the name to: *mbṭḥyhw* is self-evident. In the lower register the first four letters of the title have survived. These can form several titles such as: *ʾšr ʿ[l hbyt]* — "who is over the house", *ʾšr ʿ[l hʿr]* — "who is over the city", *ʾšr ʿ[l hms]* — who is over the tax", etc. However, the first possibility is to be preferred because there is another bulla bearing the same inscription: "Belonging to Mibṭaḥyahu who is over the house", impressed with a similar, but not identical seal.[7] A third bulla bears the inscription: "Belonging to Mibṭaḥyahu, servant of the king" (Deutsch and Heltzer 1994, 13). This is possibly the same person, due to the fact that the title "servant of the king" is a general title of a high official, as is the title: "who is over the house".

mbṭḥyhw — Mibṭaḥyahu is a rare Hebrew theophoric personal name meaning "My

6. The bulla, without provenance, was seen on the antiquities market in Jerusalem. It was examined by the author in December 1996. It is a complete and well-preserved bulla, with its inscription of high calligraphic style (Sh. Moussaieff collection, to be published by the author).

7. See note no. 6.

confidence is Yahweh". The name does not occur in the Bible. It appears on a bulla of another official (which is probably the same person): *lmbṭḥyhw ʿbd hmlk* "Belonging to Mibṭaḥyahu, servant of the king" (Deutsch and Heltzer 1994, 13; WSS 410), and on an ostracon from Lachish: *mbṭḥyhw bn yrmyhw* "Mibṭaḥyahu son of Yirmiyahu" (Lachish III:331, 1:4).

ʾšr ʿl hbyt — "Who is over the house", lit. in charge over the house, is the title of a high official, probably in charge over the king's property. About this title see bulla no. 5 above.

Four Bullae Bearing the Title "Servant of the King"

7. ʾAbiyahu servant of the king

A complete bulla of elliptic shape, made of reddish-brown clay in a good state of preservation, it measures 13.3x9.9 mm. On the reverse of the bulla, the imprint of the texture of the papyrus to which the bulla was affixed is visible, along with two grooves where the cord which tied the papyrus ran. Around the seal impression, a 1 mm. thick groove is present. This indicates that the seal was set in a metal bezel, probably of a signet ring or a pendant, while it served to impress the bulla. The surface of the bulla has been divided into two registers by a lotus-bud motif. The inscription, composed of small letters, is notable for its high calligraphic quality.

The Hebrew inscription reads:

לאביהו / עבד המלך

lʾbyhw / ʿbd hmlk

"Belonging to ʾAbiyahu servant of the king"

ʾbyhw — ʾAbiyahu is a theophoric name meaning "My father is Yahweh". "ʾAbiyahu" was also the name of a Judean King: "ʾAbiyahu the son of Rehoboam" who reign between 913–911/10 B.C.E. (II Chr. 13:20). The name in its shortened form "ʾAbiyah" is common in the Bible. It is scarce in the Hebrew epigraphy and appears only twice, on an ostracon from Arad: ...... בן אביהו *bn ʾbyhw* — "... son of ʾAbiyahu" (Aharoni 1981, 27:6) and on a bulla: [לא]חיהו [בן א]ביהו *[lʾ]ḥyhw [bn ʾ]byhw* — "Belonging to ʾAḥiyahu son of ʾAbiyahu" (Avigad 1986, 13).

ʿbd hmlk — "servant of the king", is the title of a high official in the royal administration, related to the king, but in contrast to the other three bullae presented above (nos. 2–4), the name of the king is not mentioned. This title also appears on three other bullae, nos. 8–10 below (see the discussion on the title "servant of the king", with bulla no. 10 below).

8. Gedalyahu servant of the king

A complete bulla of elliptic shape, made of light-brown clay in a good state of preservation, it measures 14.5x13.3 mm. On the reverse of the bulla, the imprint of the texture of the papyrus to which the bulla was affixed is visible, along with grooves where the cord which tied the papyrus ran. The field is divided into two registers by a lotus-bud motif.

The Hebrew inscription reads:

לׄגׄדליהו / עׄבד המלך

l̇ġdlyhw / ʿbd hmlk

"Belonging to Gedalyahu servant of the king"

This is the second bulla bearing this inscription. The previous one, published by Avigad (1986, 5), was impressed with a different seal. Yet, a very close paleographical similarity between these two bullae points toward a common source, and they probably belonged to the same person.

gdlyhw — Gedalyahu is a theophoric name meaning "Great is Yahweh". The name "Gedalyahu" and its shortened form "Gedalyah", occurs five times in the Bible, and two of them could have held the title "servant of the king": גדליהו בן אחיקם בן שפן — "Gedalyahu son of Aḥikam son of Shaphan" (Jer. 40:5). His father Aḥikam son of Shaphan, together with four other officials, were sent by King Yoshiyyahu to Ḥulda the prophetess to "inquire of the Lord for the people and Judah" (II Kgs. 22:12–14). Aḥikam son of Shaphan also rescued Jeremiah from death (Jer. 26:24). Shaphan, the grandfather of Gedalyahu, was the scribe of King Yoshiyyahu (II Kgs. 22:3). The other biblical official was גדליהו בן פשחור — "Gedalyahu son of

Pashḥor" (Jer. 38:1), a minister in the time of King Zedekiah who urged the king to let Jeremiah be killed (Jer. 38:4).

ʿbd hmlk — "servant of the king", is the title of a high official in the royal administration, at the court, but in contrast to the other three bullae presented above (nos. 2–4), the name of the king is not mentioned. This title appears also on three other bullae, nos. 7, 9–10 (see the discussion on the title "servant of the king", with bulla no. 10 below).

9. Nethanmelekh servant of the king

A complete bulla of elliptic shape, made of brown clay in a good state of preservation, it measures 12.5x11.5 mm. On the reverse of the bulla, the imprint of the texture of the papyrus to which the bulla was affixed is visible, along with grooves where the cord which tied the papyrus ran. The surface of the bulla is divided into two registers by a double line. The script is of high calligraphic quality.

The Hebrew inscription reads:

לנתנמלך / עבד המלך

lntnmlk / ʿbd hmlk

"Belonging to Nethanmelekh servant of the king"

lntnmlk — Nethanmelekh is a very rare name meaning "The King (epithet of the God) has given". This is the first appearance of the name in the Hebrew epigraphy and it occurs only once in the Bible. The owner of this seal is probably the biblical "Nathan-melekh the chamberlain", called הסריס *hsrys*, lit. "eunuch", under King Josiah (II Kgs. 23:11). Josiah removed the horses dedicated to the sun-god Šamaš to the chamber of Nathan-melekh which was in the suburbs, and burned the chariots of the sun with fire. The suggested identification of "Nethanmelekh servant of the king", from our bulla, with the biblical "Nathan-melekh the chamberlain", is based on four arguments:

1. The name is very rare and it appears only once in the Hebrew epigraphy on our bulla and again only once in the Bible.

2. There is a chronological resemblance between the biblical account, the time of King Josiah

(641/40–609 B.C.E.) and the date of the bulla on a paleographical basis to the second half of the 7th century B.C.E.

3. The title "servant of the king", is an unspecific title of a high official in the royal administration and the "chamberlain" or the "eunuch" was such a status.

4. The name of the biblical כושי איש סריס — "Kushi, eunuch man, or chamberlain", was עבד־מלך "Eved-melekh", meaning "servant of king" (Jer. 38:7). Therefore, his nickname "Eved-melekh", was probably given to him in accordance with his position in the royal court.

ʿbd hmlk — "servant of the king". In contrast to the other three bullae presented above (nos. 2-4), the name of the king is not mentioned. This title also appears on the three bullae, nos. 7–8, 10 (see the next bulla for a discussion on the title "servant of the king").

10. ʿAzaryahu servant of the king

A fragmentary bulla made of brown clay, it measures 9.0x9.8 mm. On the reverse of the bulla, the imprint of the texture of the papyrus to which the bulla was affixed is visible, along with grooves where the cord which tied the papyrus ran. The surface of the bulla is divided into two registers by a double line.[8]

The Hebrew inscription reads:

לעזריה[ו] / עבד המל[ך]

l̇ʿzrẏh[w] / ʿbd hml̇[k]

"Belonging to ʿAzaryahu servant of the king"

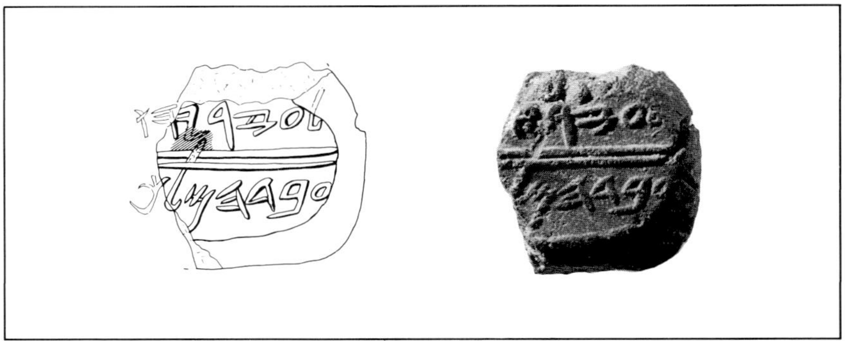

ʿzryhw — ʿAzaryahu is a theophoric name meaning "Yahweh has helped". This is the name of one of the Judean kings: "ʿAzaryah the son of ʾAmazyah and Yekholyahu the Jerusalemite" (II Kgs. 15:1). "ʿAzaryah" and "ʿAzaryahu" are the names of other biblical high officials: "ʿAzaryah son of Yeroham, captain of hundreds" (II Chr. 23:1), "ʿAzaryah the son of Yohanan, priest in the Temple built by Solomon in Jerusalem" (I Chr. 5:36), "ʿAzaryah the son of Ḥilqiyyah, the

8. The bulla was published in 1997 (WSS 411), with erroneous reading and measurements, based on a poor quality photograph: *ʿzrʾl or ʿzrqm.*

ruler of the house of God" (I Chr. 9:11), "ᶜAzaryah the son of Zadok the priest, high official in the time of Solomon (I Kgs. 4:2), "ᶜAzaryahu the son of Natan, who was over the officers" (I Kgs. 4:5), "ᶜAzaryahu the son of ᶜOded, the prophet" (II Chr. 15:1), "ᶜAzaryahu the son of ᶜOved, captain of hundreds" (II Chr. 23:1), "ᶜAzaryahu the high priest" (II Chr. 26:17), "ᶜAzaryahu the chief priest" (II Chr. 31:10), as well as two sons of kings: "ᶜAzaryah the son of king Yehoshafat" (II Chr. 21:2) and "ᶜAzaryah the son of king Yoram" (II Chr. 22:6). ᶜAzaryahu is also the name of the "gate keeper of the prison" as is known from his bulla (Deutsch and Heltzer 1994, 41). The name is one of the most frequent names in the Hebrew epigraphy and has been recorded thirty times by Davies (1991:459). It also appears on bullae nos. 3 (above) and 74 (below).

ᶜbd hmlk — "servant of the king", is the title of a high official in the royal administration, at the court, but in contrast to the other three bullae presented above (nos. 2–4), the name of the king is not mentioned. This title also appears on other three bullae (nos. 7–9 above). Literally, the term *ᶜbd hmlk* means: "slave of the king", however, this is a general title, "self-named" by all the king's officials (Avishur and Heltzer 1996:74–80). Four "servants of kings" are recorded in the Bible: 1) "ᶜAśayah servant of the king" (II Kgs. 22:12, II Chr. 34:20), 2) "Yoʾab son of Zeruya, servant of the king" (I Sam. 26:6; II Sam. 18:29), 3) "Yarobᶜam servant of Solomon" (I Kgs. 11:26), 4) "Nevuzaradan, captain of the guard, servant of the king of Babylon" (II Kgs. 25:8). The title also occurs on an ostracon from Lachish: *ṭbyhw ᶜbd hmlk* "Ṭobyahu servant of the king" (Lachish III:333, 3:19). The following is an updated list of Hebrew seals and bullae which belonged to servants of kings:

1. *lyʾznyhw ᶜbd hmlk* — "Belonging to Yaʾazanyahu servant of the king". Banded agate seal depicting a fighting cock, found in 1932 at Tell en-Naṣbeh, the biblical Mizpah (Naṣbeh I, p. 163; WSS 8).
2. *lᶜbdyhw ᶜbd hmlk* — "Belonging to ᶜObadyahu servant of the king". Hematite seal (Schroder 1880; WSS 9).
3. *lgʾlyhw ᶜbd hmlk* — "Belonging to Geʾalyahu servant of the king". White quartz seal, found in 1978 at Umm el-Qanafid in Jordan (Fulco 1979; WSS 7).
4. *ᶜśnyhw ᶜbd hmlk* — "(Belonging to) ᶜAśaniyahu servant of the king". Limestone seal, chance find at Tell Qasile, Persian period? (Vattioni 1969, no. 125; WSS 1206 questionable).
5. *lšmᶜ ᶜbd hmlk* — "Belonging to Shemaᶜ servant of the king". Red carnelian seal bought in Jerusalem (Vincent 1903; WSS 10).
6. *lʾlyqm ᶜbd hmlk* — "Belonging to ʾElyaqim servant of the king". Carnelian seal (Bordreuil 1992, 122; WSS 6).
7. *lᶜśyhw ᶜbd hmlk* — "Belonging to ᶜAśayahu servant of the king". Reddish limestone seal, depicting a galloping horse (Deutsch and Heltzer 1994:50, no. 21; not listed in WSS).
8. *lʾlšmᶜ ᶜbd hmlk* — "Belonging to ʾElishamaᶜ servant of the king". Clay bulla (Avigad 1986, 4; WSS 408).
9. *lgdlyhw ᶜbd hmlk* — "Belonging to Gedalyahu servant of the king". Clay bulla (Avigad 1986, 5; WSS 409).
10. *lšbnyhw [ᶜbd/bn] hmlk* — "Belonging to Shebanyahu [servant/son] of the king". Clay bulla with missing fragment on which was the title. According to the space which exists before

the word *hmlk*, there is room for the three letters *ʿbd* (Aharoni 1975:21, no. 5; WSS 416).

11. *lšmʿyhw ʿbd hmlk* — "Belonging to Shemaʿyahu servant of the king". Clay bulla from the Jerusalem antiquities market (Deutsch and Heltzer 1994:38, 12; not listed in WSS).

12. *lmbṭḥyhw ʿbd hmlk* — "Belonging to Mibṭaḥyahu servant of the king". Clay bulla from the Jerusalem antiquities market (Deutsch and Heltzer 1994:39, 13; WSS 410).

13. *lʾbyhw ʿbd hmlk* — "Belonging to ʾAbiyahu servant of the king". Clay bulla (no. 7 above).

14. *lgdlyhw ʿbd hmlk* — "Belonging to Gedalyahu servant of the king". Clay bulla (no. 8 above).

15. *lntnmlk ʿbd hmlk* — "Belonging to Nethanmelekh servant of the king". Clay bulla (no. 9 above).

16. *lʿzryh[w]ʿbd hml[k]* — "Belonging to ʿAzaryahu servant of the king". Clay bulla (no. 10 above; WSS 411).[9]

Three Bullae Bearing the Title "Governor of the City"

11. Ṭobshalem governor of the city

A fragmentary bulla, made of grey-brown clay, it measures 14.5x10.9 mm. On the reverse of the bulla, fingerprints are visible. The surface of the bulla is divided into two registers by a lotus-bud motif and surrounded by a framing circle.

The Hebrew inscription reads:

לטבשל[ם] / שר ה̇[ער]
lṭbšl[m] / śr ḣ[ʿr]
"Belonging to Ṭobshalem governor of the city"

9. See also "servants", with the specific names of the kings (bullae no. 2–4 above).

ṭbšlm — Ṭobshalem is a rare personal name meaning "Well recompensed (by God)", probably according to the biblical verse: ויהוה ישלמך טובה תחת היום הזה — "so may the Lord reward thee good for what thou hast done to me this day" (I Sam. 24:19). The name does not occur in the Bible but is found three times in the Hebrew epigraphy: on an ostracon from Lachish: *yʾznyhw bn ṭbšlm* — "Yaʾazanyahu son of Ṭobshalem" (Lachish III:331, 1:2), on a seal from En Goren, ancient En Gedi: *ṭbšlm* — "(Belonging to) Ṭobshalem" (Herr 1978:95, no. 28, 6th century B.C.E.; WSS 172) and on two bullae found at the City of David in Jerusalem: *lṭbšlm bn zkr* — "Belonging to Ṭobshalem son of Zakkur" and *lṭbšlm bn bnzkr* — "Belonging to Ṭobshalem son of Benzakar" (Shoham 1994:57, no. 4–5; WSS 508, 509).

śr hʿr — "Governor of the city", is a biblical title of a senior official appointed by the king, responsible for the city administration and its civil affairs, similar to a mayor. This is an archaic title and appears before the kingship in Israel. Governors of cities were appointed in large towns and provinces. Several biblical personalities have this title:

1. "Zebul governor of the city", the representative of Abimelekh son of Gidʿon (Jud. 9:30).

2. "Amon governor of the city", in Shomeron, in the days of King Ahab (I Kgs. 22:26; II Chr. 18:25).

3. "Yehoshua governor of the city", in the time of King Josiah (II Kgs. 23:8).

4. "Maʿaśeyahu governor of the city", in the time of King Josiah (II Chr. 34:8).

5. "Governors of the city", without mentioning the names of the governors, in the time of King Hezekiah (II Chr. 29:20).

6. "Who is over the city (of Shomeron)", without mentioning the name of the governor, in the time of King Ahab (II Chr. 10:5).

In addition to the Bible, the title *śr hʿr* "Governor of city" appears twice in the Hebrew epigraphic material of the beginning of the 8th century B.C.E., found at Kuntillet ʿAjrud (Meshel 1978, fig. 21) and on two identical bullae with Assyrian iconography (Avigad 1994; Barkay 1994; WSS 402a-b). The title "governor of the city" appears on three bullae presented here (nos. 11–13), on which, for the first time, two personal names of the officials are also mentioned. Moreover, the title "Governor of (the city of) Ekron", was found in 1996 in a royal dedicatory inscription at Ekron (Gitin, Dothan and Naveh 1997).

12. Peqadyahu governor of the city

A complete bulla of elliptic shape, made of brown clay in a good state of preservation, it measures 16.9x13.8 mm. On the reverse of the bulla, the imprint of the texture of the papyrus to which the bulla was affixed is visible, along with grooves where the cord which tied the papyrus ran. The surface of the bulla is divided into two registers by a double line. The script is of a high calligraphic style.

The Hebrew inscription reads:

[ל]פקדיהו / שׂר העׂר

[l]p̂qdyhẇ / śr hʿr̂

"Belonging to Peqadyahu governor of the city"

pqdyhw — Peqadyahu is a theophoric personal name expressing the wish "Yahweh attend". The name does not occur in the Bible and here is its first appearance in the Hebrew epigraphic material (not listed by Zadok 1988:447). The northern Israelite version of the name with the theophoric suffix *yw*, appears apparently, on a Persian period seal from Gezer: *[l]ʾbnr / [p]qdyw* — "Belonging to ʾAbner (son of) Peqadyau" (Avigad 1950; not listed in WSS).

śr hʿr — "Governor of the city", title of an official appointed by the king, responsible for the city administration and its civil affairs, similar to a mayor (for a discussion on the title and parallels, see bulla no. 11).

13. Governor of the city

A complete bulla of convex shape, made of brown-black clay, it measures 11.8x10.3 mm. On the reverse of the bulla, the imprint of the texture of the papyrus is absent, instead of which, fingerprints are visible. This points towards a different use of the bulla, probably as a receipt rather than to seal a document. This type of bullae were called "Fiscal bullae" by Avigad (1990:262). Another similar fiscal bulla belonged to: *ʿzryhw šʿr hmsgr* — "ʿAzaryahu the gate-keeper of the prison" (Deutsch and Heltzer 1994:41, 14). The inscription consists of five large angular letters arranged in one line in the center, without a word divider between the two words.

The Hebrew inscription reads:

שר הער

śr hʿr

"Governor of the city"

The letter *he* has a prominent rightward extension of the upper horizontal line, and the ends of the three horizontal parallel lines begin to converge on the left. The letter *ʿain*, has an almond shape and in the word ע(י)ר *ʿ(y)r* — "city", the letter *yod* (the *mater lectionis*), is missing.

śr hʿr — "Governor of the city". This is the third seal impression bearing this title on which the owner's name is absent (WSS 402a-b). Therefore, the seal used to impress this bulla apparently belonged to the office and not to an official bearing the title. This is also the only title recorded to date, which bears no personal names. Noteworthy is the lack of the prefix *lamed* — "belonging to" on this, and on the other two previously published such bullae (WSS 402a-b), which is the indication of ownership (see the parallels and the discussion on the title "governor of the city", with bulla no. 11 above).

Five Bullae Which Belonged to Women

14. Noiyah daughter of the king

A complete bulla made of light-brown clay, in a good state of preservation, it measures 15.8x16.0 mm. On its upper edge, fingerprints are visible. The reverse of the bulla has a conical shape and no imprint of the texture of papyrus. This indicates that the bulla served a different purpose rather than to seal a document, probably it served as a sealing plug for a vessel. The inscription is divided between two registers by a double line and surrounded by a framing circular line of which only segments are visible. The script is fully legible.

The Hebrew inscription reads:

לנויה / בת המלך

lnwyh / bt hmlk

"Belonging to Noiyah daughter of the king"

nwyh — Noiyah is a personal feminine name with a possible meaning "The dwelling place of Yahweh". An etymology with the root *nʾh* "to ornate", or with the root *nwh* "extol, praise", is also to be considered (Beit-Arieh 1986–7:35). The name is new in the Hebrew epigraphy and does not occur in the Bible. The masculine form of the name appears on an ostracon from Ḥorvat ʿUza: *hwšʿyhw bn nwy* "Hoshaʿyahu son of Nawy" (Beit-Arieh 1986–7:32). The northern Israeli variant of the name *nwyw* "Noiyaw, Noiyo", appears on a silver signet ring (Deutsch and Heltzer 1997:43–44, no. 97).[10]

bt hmlk — "daughter of the king", the filiation of Noiyah which is also her title. The name of the king is omitted. The corresponding masculine title is the "son of the king", and both the "son of the king" and the "daughter of the king" were probably children of kings, princes and princesses. The term "daughter of the king" is known in the Bible and appears four times (II Kgs. 9:34, 11:2; Ps. 45:14; Dan. 11:6). The title is rare in the Hebrew epigraphy and appears only once on a seal: *lmʿdnh bt hmlk* "Belonging to Maʿadana daughter of the King" (Avigad 1978; WSS 30). The corresponding masculine title "Son of the king", appears 17 times, on ten seals, six bullae and on one handle.[11]

15a-b. *ʾAḥmyh* daughter of Mattan

Two complete bullae impressed by the same seal, made of grey clay and in a good state of preservation, they are: a) 19x18.6, and b) 15.7x21.6 mm. in size. On the upper edge of both bullae, fingerprints are visible. On the reverse of the bullae, the imprint of the texture of the papyrus to which the bullae were affixed is visible, along with grooves where the cord which tied the papyrus ran. The script is divided into two registers by a ladder-type motif.

The Hebrew inscription reads:

לאחמיה / בת מתן

lʾḥmyh / bt mtn

"Belonging to *ʾAḥmyh* daughter of Mattan"

---

10. The signet ring was bought at the Jerusalem antiquities market and is presently kept in the private collection of Mr. Shlomo Moussaieff of London.
11. See an updated list of the title "son of the king" owners, in Barkay, 1993:111. There no. 1 has to be: *lhllyhw bn hmlk* (Overbeck and Meshorer, 1993:3, no.A4).

ʾḥmyh — A hitherto unrecorded feminine personal name in the Hebrew epigraphy, missing also in the Hebrew Bible. A close parallel is the name: *ʾḥmʾ* "ʾAḥimʾo" which appears four times in the eighth century B.C.E. Samaria ostraca (Samaria I, 32, 37–39). Another close form is the name: *ʾḥmh* "ʾAḥimo" which appears on an eighth century B.C.E. Aramaic seal (Levy, 1869, 20) and on an ostracon from Gezer (Rosenbaum and Seger 1986, 52). In addition, we find the forms: *ʾḥymh* "ʾAḥiymo", on a bulla from the City of David (Shoham 1994, no. 28; WSS 429), and *ʾḥʾmh* "ʾAḥiʾimmo" on a seal and a bulla of the sixth century B.C.E (WSS 54, 618).

mtn — Mattan is a hypocoristic personal name, the shortened form of the biblical name "Mattanyahu" meaning "Gift of (the God) Yahweh". The name is known from the Bible (II Kgs. 11:18; Jer. 38:1) and is common in the Hebrew epigraphy (listed 18 times by Davies 1991:436). The name "Mattanyahu" appears on three other bullae in this chapter, nos. 20, 62 and 63 below.

Hebrew seals of women bearing the filiation "daughter" are rare and only twelve are known to date. This is the first time that women's seal impressions on bullae have been found (nos. 14, 15a-b, 16 and 17 in this chapter). These raise their number to a total of seventeen.[12] Following is an updated alphabetic listing of the Hebrew women's seals and sealings bearing the filiation "daughter":

Princesses

1. *lmʿdnh / bt hmlk* — "Belonging to Maʿadanah daughter of the king" (Avigad 1978; WSS 30).
2. *lnwyh / bt hmlk* — "Belonging to Noiyah daughter of the king" (no. 14 above).

12. See the bulla *lʿmdy.. bt pltyh* in the Samel collection (DHL A34). There the reading of the word *bt* (daughter) instead of the word *bn* (son), is based on the upper part of the damaged letter *nun* as *taw*. Therefore, the correct reading should be *lʿmdy[hw] bn pltyh[w]*.

Personal seals:

3. *l'bgyl b/t 'lḥnn* — "Belonging to ʾAbigayil daughter of ʾElḥanan" (Avigad 1979, no. 8; WSS 32).

4. *l'ḥmyh / bt mtn* — "Belonging to *ʾḥmyh* daughter of Mattan" (no. 15a above).

5. *l'ḥmyh / bt mtn* — "Belonging to *ʾḥmyh* daughter of Mattan" (no. 15b above, duplicate of the previous bulla).

6. *lḥmyʾhl bt / mnḥm* — "Belonging to Ḥamiʾohel daughter of Menaḥem" (Hestrin and Dayagi-Mendels 1979, 34; WSS 35).

7. *lḥmyʿdn / bt ʾḥmlk* — "Belonging to Ḥamiʿadan daughter of ʾAḥimelek" (Hestrin and Dayagi-Mendels 1979, 33; WSS 36).

8. *lyhwʿdn / bt ʾryhw* — "Belonging to Yehoʿadan daughter of ʾUriyahu" (Avigad 1987, 13; WSS 38).

9. *lyph b/t šmʿ/yhw* — "Belonging to Yaffa daughter of Shemaʿayahu" (Deutsch and Heltzer 1995:61, no. 64; not listed in WSS).

10. *lnʾhbt b/t dmlyhw* — "Belonging to Neʾehebet daughter of Domleyahu" (Diringer, 1934, no. 60; WSS 39).

11. *lnʿmh / bt šʿl* — "Belonging to Naʿama daughter of Shuʿal" (DHL A9; WSS p. 610).

12. *lʿmd / bt yqmyhw* — "Belonging to ʿAmad daughter of Yeqamyahu" (Deutsch and Heltzer 1994:58, no. 26; not listed in WSS).

13. *lʿmd/yhw bt / ʿz/ryhw* — "Belonging to ʿImmadiyahu daughter of ʿAzaryahu" (AHL 68; WSS 40).

14. *lʿmdyhw / bt šbnyhw* — "Belonging to ʿImmadiyahu daughter of Shebanyahu" (Diringer 1934, no. 61; WSS 41).

15. *lʿmnwyhw / bt gdl* — "Belonging to ʿImmanuyahu daughter of Giddel" (Avigad 1989:90, no. 1; WSS 42).

16. *lšlmh b/t šbnyhw* — "Belonging to Shalomeh daughter of Shebanyahu" (bulla no. 16 below).

17. ... */ bt pqḥ* — "(Belonging to ...) daughter of Peqaḥ" (bulla no. 17 below).

Another daughter appears on an ostracon from Judea: *mšlmt bt ʾlkn* — "Meshullemet daughter of ʾElikon" (Deutsch and Heltzer 1995:83, 77:6).

16. Shalomeh daughter of Shebanyahu

A brown clay bulla, it measures 20.6x14.1 mm. and the impression measures 12.5x12.5 mm. Its upper part is missing but the inscription is complete. The script is divided into two registers by a ladder-type motif and surrounded by a double circular line.

The Hebrew inscription reads:

לשלמה ב/ת שבניהו

lšlmh b/t šbnyhw

"Belonging to Shalomeh daughter of Shebanyahu"

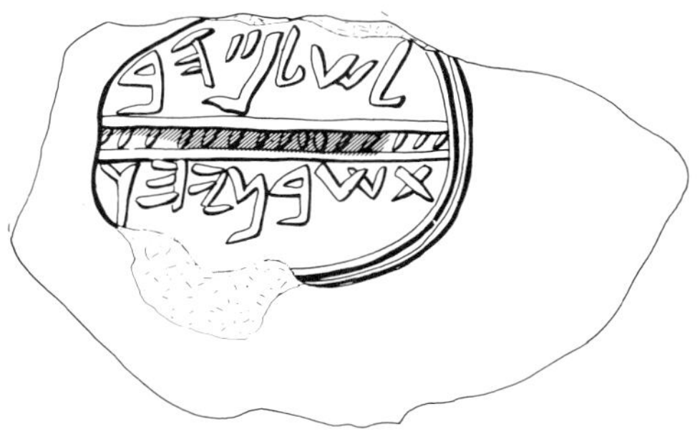

šlmh — Shalomeh, the name means "The God has completed", or "The God is entire". A third possibility is the adjectives "entire, complete, perfect", similar to names like Yaffa "beautiful", Neʾehebet "loved" and Maʿadanah "delight". The name does not appear as the name of a woman in the Hebrew Bible, but is the name of the third king of the United Kingdom, the son of David with Bath-Sheba (II Sam. 5:14). Likewise, the name is absent from the First Temple period Hebrew epigraphy. It does appears on another bulla in this chapter: *lšlmh / yšʿyhw* (no. 88 below), on which the filiation was not mentioned and it could have belonged to a woman. Nevertheless, names such as: *šlm*, *šlmy*, *šlmyh* and *šlmyhw*, are very common in the Hebrew epigraphy and are recorded 32 times by Davies (1991:495–497).

šbnyhw — Shebanyahu is a theophoric personal name meaning "God Yahweh, return" (Avigad 1986:48, no. 49). The name appears in the Bible (I Chr. 15:24), as well as in the Hebrew epigraphy, recorded eighteen times by Davies (1991:490).

This is also the name of ʿImmadiyahu's father which appears on her personal seal: "ʿImmadiyahu daughter of Shebanyahu" (Clermont-Ganneau 1902:264; WSS 41). The name occurs again on bullae nos. 61a-b and 85 below.

17. Daughter of Peqaḥ

The lower part of a black clay bulla, it measures 14.5x8.5 mm. On the back of the bulla, the fibrous imprint of wood, to which the bulla had been attached, is visible. The fragmentary inscription appears under a double line in the remaining lower register. The script is fine and clear.

The Hebrew inscription reads:

... / בת פקח

... / *bt pqḥ*

"(Belonging to ...) daughter of Peqaḥ"

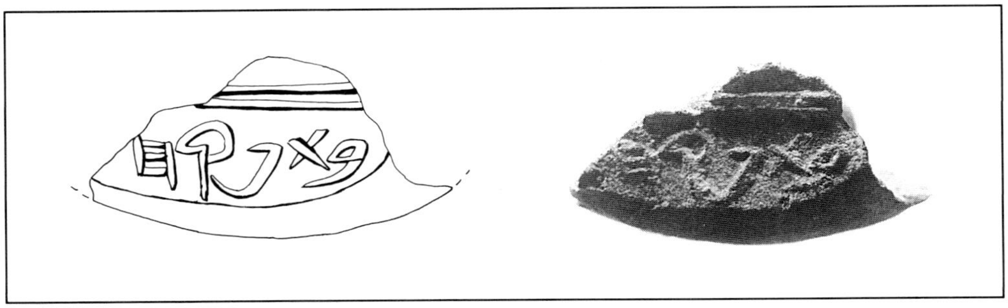

pqḥ — Peqaḥ is a hypocoristicon of the name "Peqaḥyahu" which means "The God Yahweh has opened my eyes". Peqaḥ, and Peqaḥya are the names of two kings in the Bible: Peqaḥ, the son of Ramalyahu (II Kgs. 15:27) and Peqaḥya, the son of Menaḥem (II Kgs. 15:22), both kings of Israel. In the Hebrew epigraphy, the name appears on the seal: *pqḥ* "(Belonging to) Peqaḥ" (Diringer 1934:167, no. 4; WSS 1170 undefined), on an ostracon from Lachish (Lachish III:338, 19:2) and on a jar body-sherd from Ḥazor: *lpqḥ smdr* "Belonging to Peqaḥ, *smdr*" (Ḥazor II, Pl. CLXXI). The name appears again on bulla no. 39 below.

The name of the seal owner, the daughter of Peqaḥ, is missing.

Personal Bullae

18a-b. ʾAḥab son of ʾAḥimelek

Two identical bullae impressed by the same seal, the first one is made of grey clay and measures 20.5x20.4 mm., and the second is made of brown-black clay and measures 15.5x14.2 mm. On the left edge of the second bulla a fingerprint is visible. On the reverse of both bullae, the imprint of the texture of the papyrus to which the bullae were affixed is visible, along with grooves where the cord which tied the papyrus ran. Despite this fact, these two bullae did not seal the same document. The Hebrew script is divided into two registers by two parallel lines.

The Hebrew inscription reads:

a) לאחאב / בן אחמלך
b) לאחאב / בן אחמל[ך]
lʾḥʾb / bn ʾḥmlk
"Belonging to ʾAḥʾab son of ʾAḥimelek"

ʾḥʾb — ʾAḥʾab is a Hebrew theophoric personal name meaning "The Brother (which is a divine epithet of the God), is the father". ʾAḥʾab is the name of the seventh king of Israel, the son and successor of ʿOmry in the 9th century B.C.E. (I Kgs. 16:28). Another biblical figure bearing this name is ʾAḥʾab son of Kolaiah, who was condemned by Jeremiah for prophesying false things in the Babylonian exilic period (Jer. 29:21–23). The name is very common in the Hebrew epigraphy. It appears on seven bullae (Avigad 1986, 16–19, 60), on a seal found in Lachish: *lšbnʾ (bn) ʾḥʾb* "Belonging to Shebnʾa (son of) ʾAḥʾab" (Lachish III, 348, no. 171; WSS 350), on another seal found at Tell eṣ-Ṣafi: *lyhwʿz ʾḥʾb* "Belonging to Yehoʿaz (son of) ʾAḥʾab" (WSS 178) and on a seal in the Hecht Museum: *lmtn (bn) ʾḥʾb* "Belonging to Mattan (son of) ʾAḥʾab" (Avigad 1989:10, no. 5; WSS 257). In addition, the name is incised on a handle found at Tell el-Ḥamme (Gophna and Porat 1972:214). The name ʾAḥʾab occurs on two other bullae in this chapter, nos. 19 and 72.

ʾḥmlk — ʾAḥimelek is a theophoric personal name meaning "The Brother (which is a divine epithet of the God), is the king". The name occurs in the Bible in its full spelling: *ʾḥymlk* (I Sam. 21:2, 26:6; II Sam. 8:17). The name is very common in the Hebrew epigraphy and it is recorded twenty times by Davies (1991:274–275), once in a seal impression on a jar handle: *ʾḥmlk ʿmdyhw* "ʾAḥimelek (son of) ʿImmadiyahu" (Deutsch and Heltzer 1994, no. 8) and on bulla no. 26 below.

19. ʾAḥʾab (son of ...)

A brown clay bulla, it measures 16.5x14.2 mm. On the back of the bulla, the fibrous imprint of wood, to which the bulla had been attached, is visible along with grooves where the cord ran. The inscription is divided between two registers by a double parallel line and surrounded by a circular framing line. The lower register is damaged and therefore the patronymic is lost.

The Hebrew inscription reads:

לאחאב / ...
lʾḥʾb / ...
"Belonging to ʾAḥʾab ...

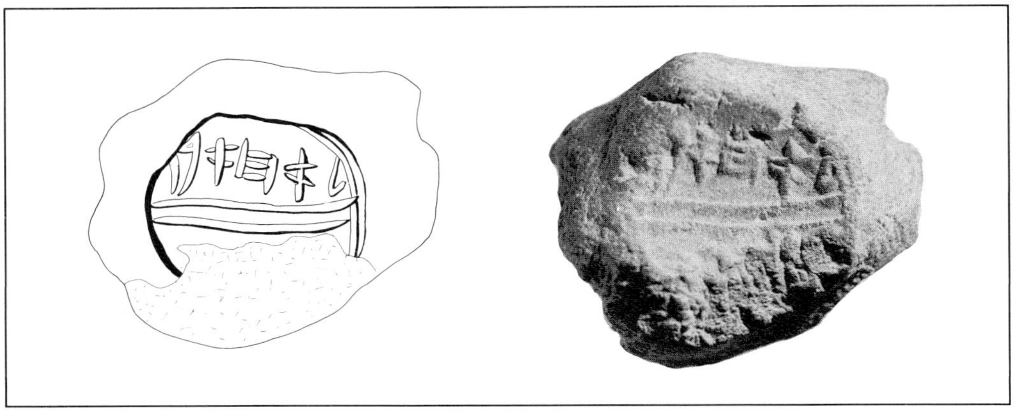

ʾḥʾb — ʾAḥʾab is a theophoric personal name meaning "The Brother (which is a divine epithet of the God), is the father". ʾAḥʾab is the name of the seventh king of Israel, the son and successor of ʿOmri in the 9th century B.C.E. (I Kgs. 16:28). For the name and parallels see the previous bullae, nos. 18a-b or bulla no. 72 below.

20. ʾAḥyʾa son of Mattanyahu

The right part of a light-brown clay bulla, measuring 15.5 x18.5 mm. On the reverse of the bulla, the fibrous imprint of wood, to which the bulla had been attached, is visible along with grooves where the cord ran. On the edge, a finger print is present. The inscription is divided between two registers by two parallel lines and surrounded by a circular framing line.

The Hebrew inscription reads:

אחיא [ב]/ן מת[ניהו]
ʾḥyʾ [b]/n mt[nyhw]
"(Belonging to) ʾAḥyʾa son of Mattanyahu"

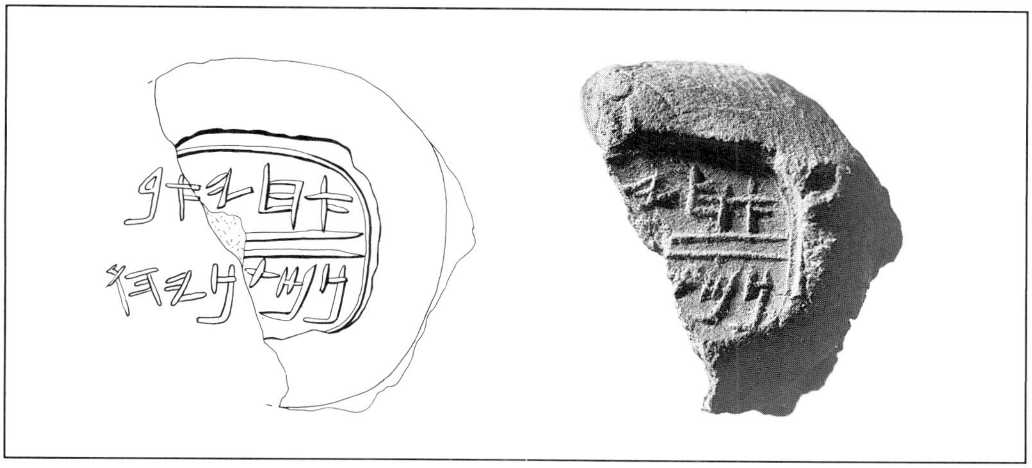

In the upper register the three letters *ʾḥy* are entirely preserved and a fourth letter, probably an *alef*, is only partly visible. The name can be completed to *ʾḥyʾm*, *ʾḥyʾb* etc. Yet, considering the lack of space, it is preferable to suppose that the upper register contained the name *ʾḥyʾ* after which appeared the letter *bet* belonging to the word *bn* "son" which is divided between the two registers, since the first sign in the lower register is the letter *nun*.

ʾḥyʾ — ʾAḥyʾa is a theophoric personal name which means "My Brother (which is a divine epithet) is the God". The name is known from the Bible in a different spelling: *ʾḥyh* "ʾAḥiyah" (I Chr. 2:25 etc.). The name is rare in the Hebrew epigraphy and it occurs only on the next bulla, no. 21.

Only the first two letters, *mem* and *taw*, are preserved from the patronym. Therefore, the name "Mattanyahu" or its shortened form is to be considered.

mt[nyhw] — Mattanyahu is a theophoric personal name meaning "Gift of the God Yahweh". It is a biblical name (I Chr.25:4; II Chr. 29:13), common in the Hebrew epigraphy, listed eleven times by Davies (1991:436–437) and appears on two other bullae in this chapter, nos. 62 and 63 below. The shortened form of the name: "Mattan", has been presented above, bullae nos. 15a-b.

21. ʾAḥyʾa son of Miʾamen

A complete bulla made of grey clay, in a good state of preservation, it measures 20.5x16.3 mm. in size. On the reverse of the bulla, the imprint of the texture of a fabric (a sack?), to which the bulla was affixed is visible, along with grooves where the cord ran. The script is divided into two registers by a lotus-bud motif and surrounded by a circular framing line.

The Hebrew inscription reads:

לאחיא ב/ן מאמ[ן]

lʾḥyʾ b/n mʾṁ[n]

"Belonging to ʾAḥyʾa son of M(i)ʾamen"

The left edge of the bulla has been carelessly impressed, therefore some letters are damaged or missing. In the upper register six letters are visible: *lʾḥyʾb*, and in the lower register four letters *nmʾm*... Therefore a possible reading will be: *lʾḥyʾ[b]b/n m(i)ʾm[n].* Yet, there is no room for a second letter bet at the end of the upper register. A second possibile reading: *lʾḥyʾb/n m(i)ʾm[n],* will use the letter *bet* as a double letter, as the end of the name *ʾḥyʾb*, and as the beginning of the word *bn* "son". Such a phenomena is known on a seal from Arad: *lʾlšb/n ʾšyh* "Belonging to ʾElisa$^{b}/_{s}$on of ʾAshyah". There the double use of the letter *bet* is evident, since two other seals of the same person, with a correct spelling, were found in the same locus (Aharoni 1981:119, 105–107; WSS 70–72). Nevertheless, the reading: *lʾḥyʾ b/n mʾm[n],* is preferable, assuming that the scribe did not made any mistake.

ʾḥyʾ — ʾAḥyʾa is a theophoric personal name which means "My Brother (which is a divine epithet) is the God". The name is known from the Bible in a different spelling: *ʾḥyh* "ʾAḥiyah" (I Chr. 2:25 etc.). The name is rare in the Hebrew epigraphy and it occurs only on the previous bulla, no. 20.

mʾm[n] — M(i)ʾamen is the defective spelling of the name "Miʾamen" which is according to

Avigad, an interrogative deriving from the root "faith", "Who is faithful (in god Yahweh)", such as the names Micaiah or Michael (Avigad 1986:68), or simply "Faithful". The name is mentioned both in the Bible: *mymn* (Neh. 10:8) and in the Hebrew epigraphy in its full spelling: *my'mn*. It occurs on a seal: *my'mn ..ʿdd* "Belonging to Miʾamen (son of) ..ʿdd" (Hestrin and Dayagi-Mendels 1978, 94; WSS 228) and on four bullae: 1) *[lmʿ]śyhw my'mn* "Belonging to Maʿaśeyahu (son of) Miʾamen", 2) *[lm]y'mn [bn]ʿpy* "Belonging to Miʾamen son of ʿEpai" (Avigad 1986, 87, 88; WSS 647, 539), 3) *lyhwʾl myʾmn* "Belonging to Yehoʾel (son of) Miʾamen" found at Lachish (Lachish V:21, 4; WSS 523), 4) *lmyʾmn bnyhw* "Belonging to Miʾamen (son of) Benayahu" (Deutsch and Heltzer 1995, 60). The name in its full spelling: *myʾmn*, appears on bullae nos. 57 and 84 below.

22. ʾAḥiʾem son of Shallum

A grey clay bulla, measuring 15.5 x15.5 mm. On the reverse of the bulla, the fibrous imprint of papyrus, to which the bulla has been attached, is visible along with grooves where the cord ran. The inscription is divided between two registers by a ladder-pattern and surrounded by a circular framing line which has survived only in the lower side. The left edge has been damaged by the cord while the bulla was still wet.

The Hebrew inscription reads:

[ל]אחיאם / בן שלם

[l]ʾḥyʾm / bn šlm

"Belonging to ʾAḥiʾem son of Shallum"

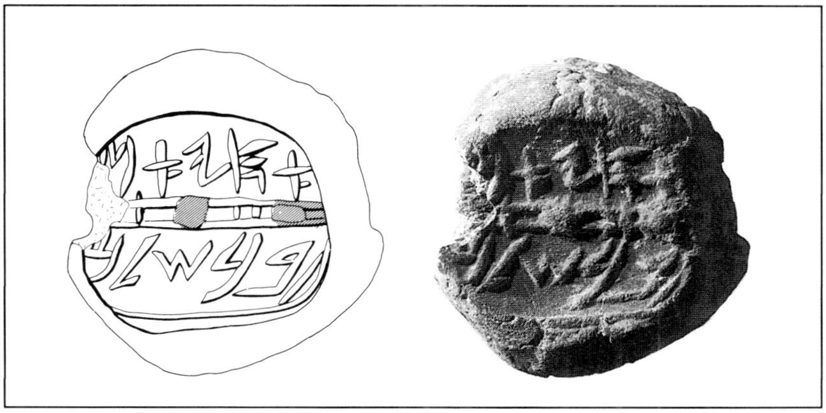

ʾḥyʾm — ʾAḥiʾem is a very rare personal name, occurs once in the Bible: "Aḥiʾem son of Sharar the Ararite" (II Sam. 23:33). Its meaning is not clear. The theophoric element *ʾḥ* "Brother" is found in several biblical names such as *ʾḥyʾb*, *ʾḥybn*, *ʾḥylwd*, *ʾḥymwt*, *ʾḥymlk*, *ʾḥyrm* etc. This is the first appearance of the name in the Hebrew epigraphy.

šlm — Shallum is a Hebrew theophoric biblical name (Gen. 46:24; I Chr. 4:25), the shortened version of Shelemyahu meaning "Yahweh has recompensed". This is a very common name in the Hebrew epigraphy and was recorded nineteen times by Davies (1991:495), twice by Deutsch and Heltzer (1995, nos. 57, 65), once in DHL (no. 36), once in WSS 366 (*editio princeps*) and once on the bulla *lšlm b/n ʾlyqm* "Belonging to Shalum son of ʾElyaqim", no. 87 below.

23. ʾAḥiʿezer son of ʾUriyahu

A reddish clay bulla, measuring 10.5 x10.5 mm. On the reverse of the bulla, the fibrous imprint of papyrus, to which the bulla has been attached, is visible along with grooves where the cord ran. The inscription is divided between two registers by two parallel lines and surrounded by two circular framing lines which survived only on the lower side. The surface of the bulla is weathered, yet the entire inscription is clear and legible.

The Hebrew inscription reads:

לאחיעזר / אריהו

lʾḥyʿzṙ / ʾryhw

"Belonging to ʾAḥiʿezer son of ʾUriyahu"

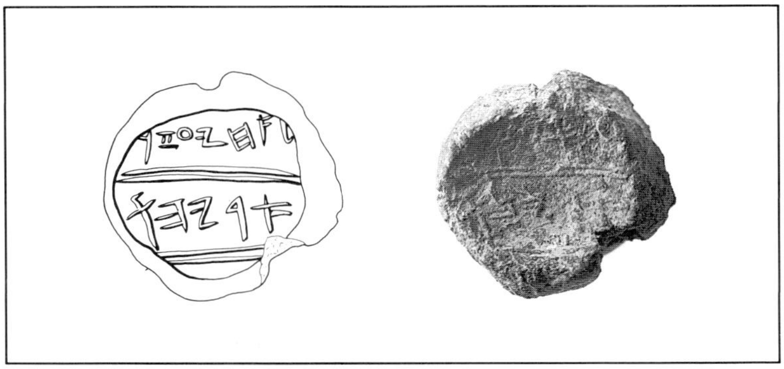

ʾḥyʿzr — ʾAḥiʿezer is a Hebrew theophoric personal name, hitherto unrecorded. It has the meaning "My Brother (which is a divine epithet) is my help". The theophoric element *ʾḥ* "Brother" is found in several biblical names such as *ʾḥyʾb*, *ʾḥybn*, *ʾḥylwd*, *ʾḥymwt*, *ʾḥymlk*, *ʾḥyrm* etc.

ʾryhw — ʾUriyahu is a theophoric personal name meaning "My light is Yahweh". In the Bible it occurs in its full spelling *ʾwryhw* (Jer. 26:20) and in its shortened form *ʾwryh* (II Sam. 11:3; II Kgs. 16:10 etc.). The name is common in the Hebrew epigraphic material and has been recorded nine times by Davies (1991:290) and appears on two other bullae in this chapter, nos. 37 and 63 below.

24. ʾAḥiqam son of ʾAḥiyahu

A light-reddish clay bulla, measuring 14.5 x 12.0 mm. On the reverse of the bulla, the fibrous imprint of papyrus, to which the bulla has been attached, is visible. The inscription is divided between two registers by a ladder-pattern and surrounded by a circular ladder-frame. The surface of the bulla is weathered and some letters, which form the patronym, are damaged, yet, the name can be completed.

The Hebrew inscription reads:

לאחיקם / בן [א]חי[הו]
l'ḥyqm / bn [']ḥy[hw]
"Belonging to ʾAḥiqam son of ʾAḥiyahu"

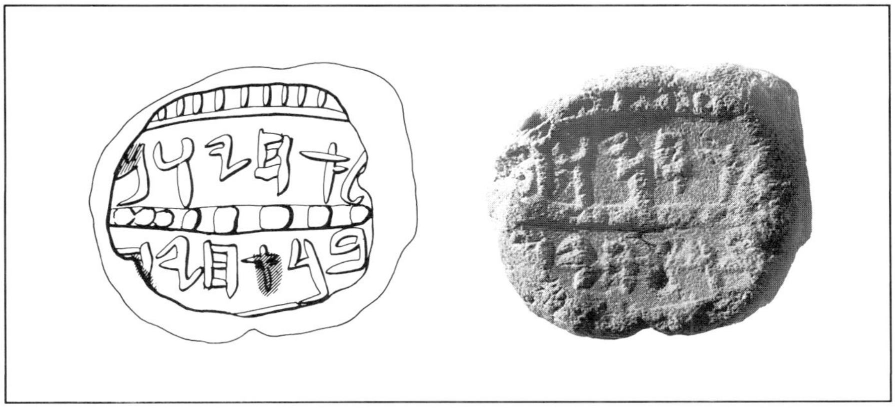

ʾḥyqm — ʾAḥiqam, theophoric personal name meaning "My Brother (which is the epithet of God), will establish". Similar names are: *yhwyqm* "Yehoyaqim", *ʾlyqm* ʾElyaqim and *ywqm* "Yoqim" etc. In the Bible (II Kgs. 22:12–13), "ʾAḥiqam" is the son of "Shaphan" (see his bulla, no. 25 below). In the Hebrew epigraphic material, the name appears four times: on an ostracon from Arad (Aharoni 1981, 31:5), on an ostracon from the city of David (Shiloh 1981:165), on the seal: *l'ḥqm / mtn* "Belonging to ʾAḥiqm (son of) Mattan" (Avigad 1979, no. 6; WSS 57) and on ten identical bullae: *l'ḥyqm bn ḥby* "Belonging to ʾAḥiqam son of Ḥubbi or Ḥaby or Ḥabay" (Deutsch and Heltzer 1997 nos. 94a-c; WSS 430a-g). The shortened form of the name *ʾḥqm*, has been recorded six times by Davies (1991:275). The name *ʾḥyqm* appears also on the next bulla, no. 25.

[']ḥy[hw] — ʾAḥiyahu. Some letters are damaged in the lower register, yet the reading of the patronym is self evident as the letters *ḥet* and *yod* are clear. This is a theophoric personal name meaning "My Brother (which is the divine epithet of God) is Yahweh". The hypocoristicon *ʾḥyh* "ʾAḥiyah" is common in the Bible (I Chr. 8:7, 26:20; I Kgs. 25:26 etc.). The name is common in the Hebrew epigraphy and has been recorded eight times by Davies (1991:273).

25. ʾAḥiqam son of Shapan

A brown clay bulla with the right edge missing, it measures 9.9x13.2 mm. On its edge, fingerprints are present. On the reverse of the bulla, the imprint of the texture of the papyrus to which the bulla was affixed is visible. The inscription is divided between two registers by a double parallel line and surrounded by two parallel circular framing lines. In the upper register the prefix *lamed* and the first letter in the owners name, the ʾ*alef*, are missing but the reading of the name *[ʾ]ḥyqm* "ʾAḥiqam" is evident and is the only possibility (WSS 431).

The Hebrew inscription reads:

[לא]חיקם / [ב]ן שפן

[lʾ]ḥyqm / [b]n špn

"Belonging to ʾAḥiqam son of Shapan"

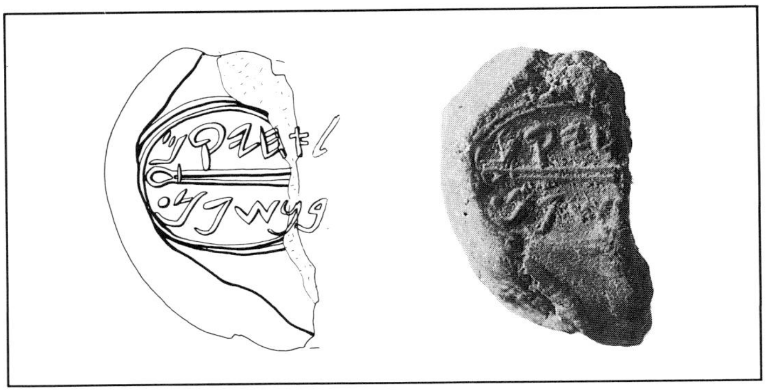

The identification of the owner on this seal impression with the biblical figure mentioned as high official in the time of Josiah and Jehoiakim is evident. King Josiah commanded five of his officials, among them ʾAḥiqam son of Shapan, to go to Hulda the prophetess, to "inquire the Lord" (II Kgs. 22:12–13). He is also mentioned as saving Jeremiah from death (Jer. 26:24).

ʾḥyqm — ʾAḥiqam is a Hebrew theophoric personal name meaning "My Brother (which is the epithet of God), will establish". Similar names are: *yhwyqm* "Yehoyaqim", *ʾlyqm* ʾElyaqim and *ywqm* "Yoqim" etc. For parallels see the previous bulla, no. 24.

špn — Shapan, lit. "rabbit", is a Hebrew personal name. Names derived from animals such as this are common and are known from the Bible and from the Hebrew epigraphic material. Such names are: "Shuʿal" (fox), "ʿAkhbor" (mouse), (II Kgs. 22:12), "ʿOreb" (crow), (WSS 693) etc. The name "Shapan" is rare and it appears only once in the Bible. He is the son of ʾAṣalyahu the scribe (II Kgs. 22:3) and the father of ʾAḥiqam. ʾAṣalyahu was the man sent by Josiah the King to Ḥilqiyahu the high priest with the command to repair the "House of the Lord" (II Kgs. 22:3–6). Shapah the high priest received the Book, the Torah, found in the Temple by Ḥilqiyahu and brought it to the king (II Kgs. 22:8–9). The name Shapan is rare also in the Hebrew epigraphy and appears on a bulla from the City of David: *lgmryhw / bn špn* "Belonging to Gemaryahu son of Shapan" (Shoham 1994:57, no. 2; WSS 470), on the seal: *lšpn / pdyhw* "Belonging to Shapan (son of) Pedayahu" (Avigad 1989:12, no. 9; WSS 388) and on a burial inscription from Jerusalem (Prignaud 1978:136). Despite the rarity of the name, it appears on another four bullae in this group, nos. 56, 92–94.

26. ʾAḥimelek (son of) Miqneyahu

A complete bulla made of light brown clay, measuring 13.9x10.5 mm. and 6.2 mm. in height. The back of the bulla has a convex shape. The inscription is divided between two registers by a double parallel line and surrounded by two parallel circular framing lines. The surface of the bulla is concave and slightly damaged, yet the letters are clear.

The Hebrew inscription reads:

לאחמלך / מקניהו

lʾḥmlk̇ / mq̇nyḣw

"Belonging to ʾAḥimelek (son of) Miqneyahu"

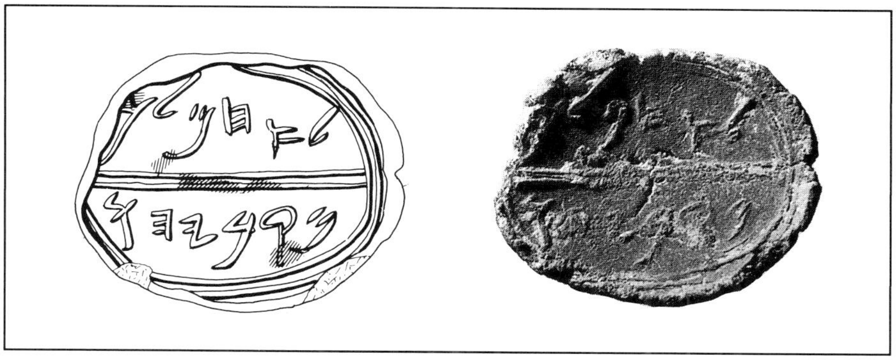

ʾḥmlk — ʾAḥimelek is a theophoric personal name meaning "The Brother (which is a divine epithet of the God), is the king". The name occurs in the Bible in its full spelling: *ʾḥymlk* (I Sam. 21:2, 26:6; II Sam. 8:17). The name is very common in the Hebrew epigraphy and it is recorded twenty times by Davies (1991:274–275), once on a seal impression on a jar handle: *ʾḥmlk ʿmdyhw* "ʾAḥimelek (son of) ʿImmadiyahu" (Deutsch and Heltzer 1994, no. 8) and on the bullae nos. 18a-b above.

mqnyhw — Miqneyahu is a theophoric personal name meaning "(The infant) is the property, or creation, of Yahweh". The name is rare and occurs only once in the Bible where it belongs to a Levite gatekeeper in the time of King David (I Chr. 15:18). In the Hebrew epigraphy the name appears only four times, on the bulla: *lspn mqnyhw* "Belonging to Ṣaphan (son of) Miqneyahu" (Avigad 1986, no. 154; WSS 621), on the seal: *lmqnyhw bn yhwkl* "Belonging to Miqneyahu son of Yehukal" (Driver 1945 *mqnyhw bn yhwmlk*; WSS 250), on the seal: *lmqnyhw bn ʾḥmlk* "Belonging to Miqneyahu son of ʾAḥimelek" (WSS 249) and on an ostracon from Arad (Aharoni 1981, 60:4).

27. ʾEliyah (son/daughter of) ʾEliʾab

A complete bulla made of brown clay, measuring 20.2x18.3 mm. On the reverse of the bulla, the imprint of wood fibres, to which the bulla has been attached, is visible along with grooves where the cord ran. The upper part of the bulla has been damaged by the cord while the clay was still wet. On the edges, fingerprints are present. The inscription is divided between two registers by a double parallel line and surrounded by a circular framing line. The surface of the bulla is slightly damaged.

The Hebrew inscription reads:

לאליה / אליאב

lʾlyh / *ʾlyʾb*

"Belonging to ʾEliyah (son/daughter of) ʾEliʾab"

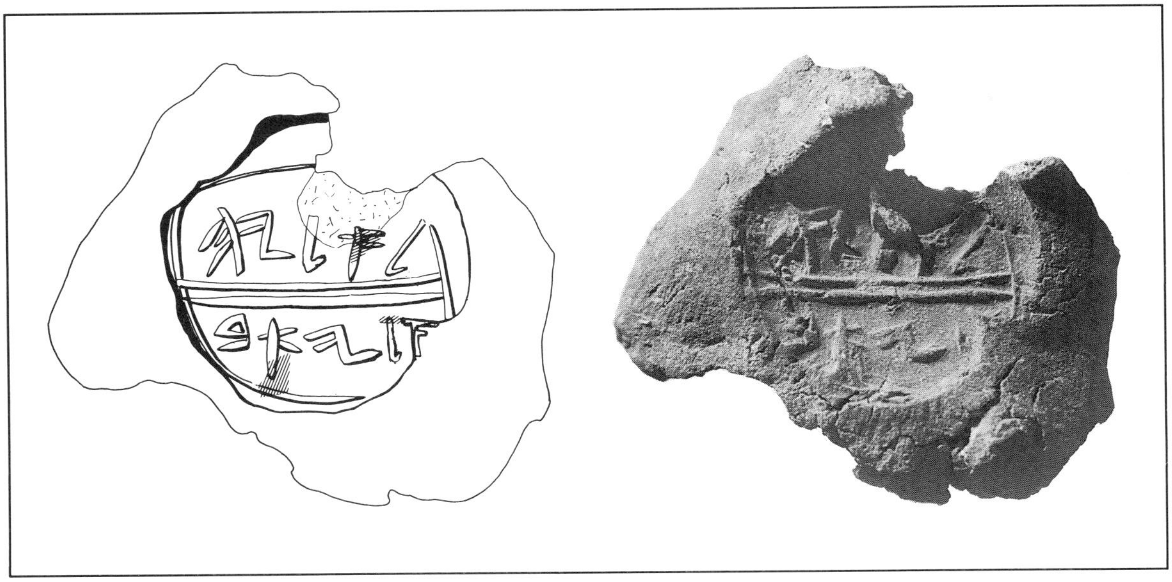

ʾlyh — ʾEliyah is a Hebrew theophoric shortened name meaning "My God is Yahweh". The name is common in the Bible (I Kgs. 17:1; I Chr. 8:27; Ezra 10:21 etc.). In the Hebrew epigraphic material the name appears only in its full spelling *ʾlyhw*, and has been recorded six times by Davies (1991:280) and twice on bullae nos. 28 and 29 below.

ʾlyʾb — ʾEliʾab is a Hebrew theophoric personal name meaning "My God is my father". It appears in the Bible in the time of Moses (Num. 1:9, 2:7, 10:16 etc.), in the time of Saul (I Chr. 6:12) and in the time of David (I Chr. 12:10, 15:18, 20). The name is absent in the Hebrew epigraphic material, but parallels are known such as: *yhwʾb* "Yehoʾab", *ʾbyw* "ʾAbiyau", *ʾbyh* "ʾAbiyah", and *ʾbyhw* "ʾAbiyahu" (Davies 1991:266, 365).

28. ʾEliyahu

A fragmentary bulla made of red clay and measuring 9.8x13.0 mm. The left side is missing. On the reverse of the bulla, the imprint of the texture of the papyrus to which the bulla was affixed is visible, along with grooves where the cord which tied the papyrus ran. In the lower area of the seal impression, a groove is present. This indicates that the seal was set in a metal bezel, while it served to impress the bulla. A bird (rooster?), executed in a very high artistic style, is depicted in the center. Four letters have survived, over and below the bird, and the corner of a fifth one.

The Hebrew inscription reads:

לאל/י/הׄ[ו]

ʾl/y/ḣ[w]

"Belonging to ʾEliyahu"

ʾlyhw — ʾEliyahu is a Hebrew theophoric name meaning "My God is Yahweh". The name is common in the Bible (I Chr. 26:7, 27:18). Eliyahu the Tishbite was a prophet in the time of Ahab and Ahaziyahu (I Kgs. 17:1). The name was recorded six times in the Hebrew epigraphy (Davies 1991:280) and it appears on the next bulla, no. 29.

29. ʾEliyahu (son of) ʾAdoniyahu

A complete bulla made of dark brown clay and measuring 15.0x17.5 mm. The back of the bulla is of conoid shape covered with fingerprints. This shows that the soft clay was impressed with the seal while it was held between the fingers. The conoid shape of the bulla indicates a use which is different than sealing a document and it probably served as a document or a receipt itself. Around the seal impression, a groove is present, indicating that the seal was set in a metal bezel. The two registers are divided by a double line.

The Hebrew inscription reads:

לׄאליהו / אדניׄהׄו

ḷʾlyhw / ʾdnẏḣw

"Belonging to ʾEliyahu (son of) ʾAdoniyahu"

ʾlyhw — ʾEliyahu is a Hebrew theophoric personal name meaning "My God is Yahweh". The name is common in the Bible (I Chr. 26:7, 27:18). Eliyahu the Tishbite was a prophet in the time of Ahab and Ahaziyahu (I Kgs. 17:1). The name was recorded six times in the Hebrew epigraphy (Davies 1991:280) and it appears on the previous bulla, no. 28.

ʾdnyhw — ʾAdoniyahu is a Hebrew theophoric personal name meaning "My lord is Yahweh". Three persons in the Bible bear this name: one of the sons of King David with Haggit (II Sam. 3:4), a Levite in the time of King Jehoshaphaṭ (II Chr. 17:8) and one of the leaders of the people in the time of Nehemiah (Neh. 10:16). The name is known from other Hebrew epigraphic seals and sealings: the above mentioned three bullae of: "ʾAdoniyahu who is over the house" (Avigad 1986, 1, 2a, 2b), on four personal bullae: 1) "ʾAdoniyahu son of Shemaʿyahu", 2) "Neriyahu (son of) ʾAdoniyahu", 3) "Shephaṭyahu (son of) ʾAdoniyahu" (Avigad 1986, 33, 125, 165) and 4) on the bulla depicting a four-winged *uraeus* "ʾAdoniyahu" (Deutsch and Heltzer 1994:42, no. 15), as well as on a bronze seal: "ʾAdoniyahu (son of) Shemaʿ" (Avigad 1989a, 9). It also appears on bulla no. 5 above.

30. ʾElyaqim (son of) Ḥilqiyahu

A complete bulla made of dark grey clay, not entirely impressed, and measuring 10.8x8.9 mm. The back of the bulla is of conoid shape, covered with fingerprints. The conoid shape of the bulla indicates a use which is different than sealing a document and it probably served as a document or a receipt itself. The surface is divided by a double line and surrounded by a circular framing line which survives only on the upper left corner. Three letters are missing at the right edge but the restoration of the inscription is evident.

The Hebrew inscription reads:

[לא]ליקם / [ח]לקיהו

[lʾ]lyqm / [ḥ]lqyhw

"Belonging to ʾElyaqim (son of) Ḥilqiyahu"

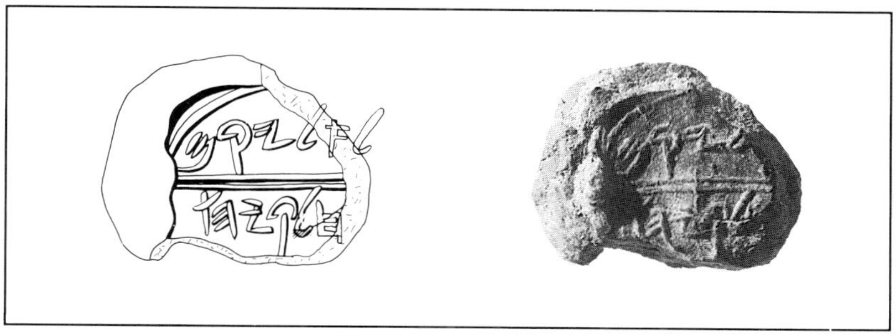

In the Bible, ʾElyaqim son of Ḥilqiyahu was a high official bearing the title "Who is over the house" (in charge of the palace), and a contemporary of King Hezekiah (II Kgs. 18:18). According to Isaiah's prophecy, ʾElyaqim son of Ḥilqiyahu will take the place of his competitor "this steward", Shebna, who is in charge of the palace (Isa. 22:15). ʾElyaqim son of Ḥilqiyahu who is over the house, together with Shebna the Scribe and Joah son of Asaph the secretary, participated in the royal delegation who meet the Assyrian royal envoys, the supreme commander Ravshaqe, Rav Saris and Tartan, during the Assyrian siege of Jerusalem (II Kgs. 18:17, 18).

ʾlyqm — ʾElyaqim is a Hebrew theophoric personal name meaning "My God will raise, establish". Similar names are Yehoyaqim and Yeqamyahu. Two other biblical figures bearing the name ʾElyaqim are recorded: ʾElyaqim son of Josiah who was made king by Pharaoh Neco and changed his name to Yehoyaqim (II Kgs. 23:34) and a priest in the time of Nehemiah who participated in the dedication ceremony of the restored temple (Neh. 12:41). The name is common in the Hebrew epigraphical material and appears on four identical seal impressions on jar handles: *lʾlyqm nʿr ywkn* "Belonging to ʾElyaqim steward of Yokin", found at Ramat Raḥel, Beth Shemesh and Tell Beth Mirsim (Hestrin and Dayagi-Mendels 1978, 8–9; WSS 663), on three bullae, two identical from Jerusalem: *lʾlyqm bn ʾwhl* "Belonging to ʾElyaqim son of ʾOhel" (Shoham 1994:58, nos. 29–30; WSS 437), and *lʾlyqm bn mʿśyh* "Belonging to ʾElyaqim son of Maʿaśeyah" (Avigad 1969:4, no. 8; WSS 438). Two seals are also recorded: *lʾlyqm ʿzʾ* "Belonging to ʾElyaqim (son of) ʿUzzaʾ" (Hestrin and Dayagi-Mendels 1978, 91; WSS 69) and *lʾlyqm ʿbd hmlk* "Belonging to ʾElyaqim servant of the king" (Bordreuil 1992, 122; WSS 6). The name appears also on the bulla *lšlm bn ʾlyqm* "Belonging to Shallum son of ʾElyaqim", no. 87 below (possibly his son).

ḥlqyhw — Ḥilqiyahu is a biblical theophoric personal name (II Kgs. 18:18, 26; 22:4, 8, 14), meaning "The God Yahweh is my share, portion". Ḥilqiyahu is the name of several important figures in the Bible, such as the high priest in the time of Yoshiyyahu (II Kgs. 22:4), the father of ʾElyaqim, who was "over the house" during the siege of Sennacherib (II Kgs. 18:18), etc. The name is common in Hebrew epigraphic material and has been recorded 16 times on seals and bullae (Davies 1991:352) and once on an ostracon (Deutsch and Heltzer 1995:83). The name also appears on the bulla *[lyh]wz[r]/ḥ bn ḥlq/yhw ʿbd ḥ/zqyhw* "Belonging to Yehozeraḥ son of Ḥilqiyahu, servant of Ḥizqiyahu", no. 2 above.

31. ʾElsamak (son of) ʾAbʾa

A dark grey clay bulla measuring 16.5x12.2 mm. On the back of the bulla the imprint of the texture of the papyrus to which the bulla was affixed is visible, along with grooves where the cord which tied the papyrus ran. The inscription is divided between two registers by a double line and surrounded by a circular framing line which survives only on the left side.

The Hebrew inscription reads:

לאלסמ̇/ך̇ אבא

lʾlsṁ/k̇ ʾbʾ

"Belonging to ʾElsamak (son of) ʾAbʾa"

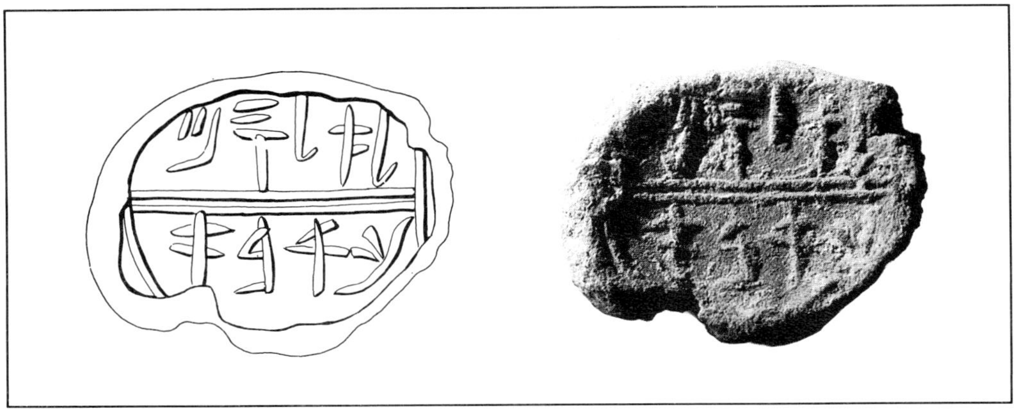

ʾlsmk — ʾElsamak is a Hebrew theophoric personal name meaning "The God is supporting, savior". The Bible provides us with a similar but inverted form: Semakyahu (I Chr. 26:7). The name is found in the Hebrew epigraphic material: in a graffito on the base of a bowl from Tell Zeror ...*bʿ lʾlsmk* (Naveh 1970:278), on the seal *sʿdyh(w)* / *ʾlsmk* (Belonging to) Saʿadyah(u son of) ʾElsamak" (Lemaire 1985:30, no. 3; WSS 285) and on two bullae belonging to the same person but differently spelled: *lgʿly b/n ʾlysmk and lgʿly b/n ʾlsmk* "Belonging to Gaʿali son of ʾElisamak" (Avigad 1986, 39–40; WSS 471–2). On a Ammonite or Aramaic seal, the name is spelled: *lʾlsmky* "Belonging to ʾElsamky" (Hestrin and Dayagi-Mendels 1979, 132; WSS 1106).

ʾbʾ — ʾAbʾa is a rare name made of two components *ʾb* "Father" and the suffix *ʾ (alef)* which serves as the theophoric element. Similar names are: *ʾby*, *ʾbyh* and *ʾbyhw*. The name is absent from the Bible and is rare in the Hebrew epigraphic material. It appears on the seal: *lʾbʾ* "Belonging to ʾAbʾa" (Galling 1941:173, no. 5; WSS 44). Two other seals, one Aramaic (Hestrin and Dayagi-Mendels 1979, 135; WSS 877) and the second probably Philistine, dated to the 12th century B.C.E., were found in the area of Tell Miqne/Ekron (Giveon 1961:38–39, Pl. III:A; WSS 1067).

32. ʾEliram N..., son of Yirmiyahu

A complete bulla made of brown clay, not entirely impressed, and measuring 14.1x9.9 mm. On the back of the bulla the imprint of the texture of the papyrus to which the bulla was affixed is visible, along with a groove where the cord which tied the papyrus ran. On the upper edge a fingerprint is visible. The surface is divided into four registers by three double lines and surrounded by a circular framing line which survives only on the right side. The upper register contains an *ankh* (the Egyptian sign symbolizing the key of life), flanked by the remnants of two quadrupeds. Based on the location of the *ankh* symbol, which was probably placed in the middle of the register, one can reconstruct the size of the entire seal. This indicates that approximately a third of the impression, the left side is missing. The inscription appears in the second and third registers. Unclear remnants in the fourth and lower register are either the end of the inscription or simply additional iconography.

The Hebrew inscription reads:

לאלרם נ.. / בן ירמי[הו] / ...

lʾlrm n.. / bn yrmẏ[hw] / ...

"Belonging to ʾEliram N... son of Yirmiyahu"

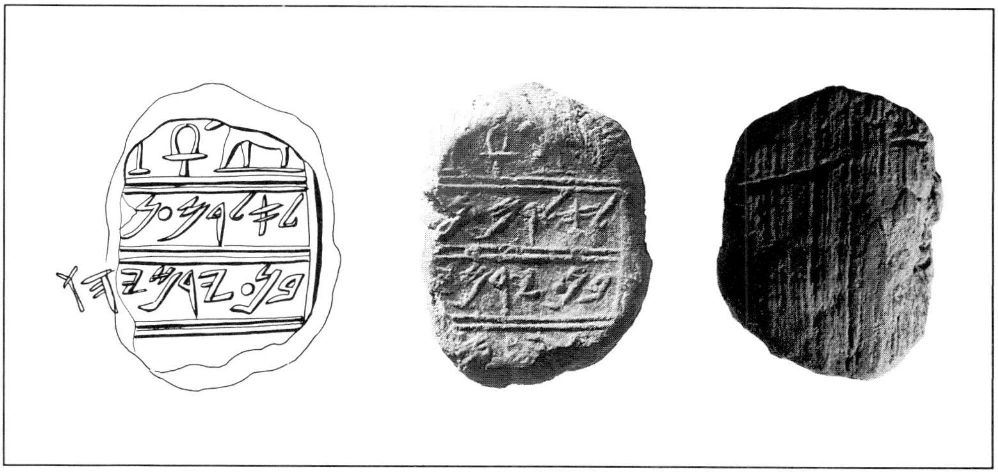

ʾlrm — ʾEliram is a Hebrew theophoric personal name meaning "My God is exalted". This is a defective spelling of the name *ʾlyrm*. The name is not found in the Bible but has a parallel, the name Yehoram (I Kgs. 22:41; II Kgs. 1:17). The name is rare in the Hebrew epigraphic material and appears only on one seal: *lʾlrm ḥsdyhw* "Belonging to ʾEliram (son of) Ḥasadyahu" (Martin 1964:208, no. 3; WSS 79). The name is more common on Ammonite seals and is found on five seals: *lʾlrm* "Belonging to ʾEliram" (Torrey 1923, no. 5; WSS 907), *lʾlrm bn bdʾl* "Belonging to ʾEliram son of Bodʾel" (Bordreuil 1986:72–3, no. 83; WSS 908), *lʾlrm ..l..š* "Belonging to ʾEliram ..l..š" (WSS 909), *lʾlrm bn tmʾ* "Belonging to ʾEliram son of Tammʾa" (Clermont-Ganneau,

1883:145, no. 25; WSS 910) and *lʿbdʾ nʿr ʾlrm* "Belonging to ʿAbdʾa, steward of ʾEliram" (Avigad 1964:192–193; WSS 864). The name *ʾlyram* in *scriptio plane* is found on the seal of a scribe: *lʾlyrm hspr* "Belonging to ʾEliram the scribe" (Deutsch and Heltzer 1997:56, no. 106).

n... — N..., is the beginning of an unclear word, maybe the prefix of the name of ʾEliram's father, and Yirmiyahu is the name of his grandfather.

yrmyhw — Yirmiyahu is a Hebrew theophoric personal name meaning "May Yahweh raise up". Ten individuals bear this name in the Bible. Among them the prophet Jeremiah son of Hilkiah (Jer. 1:1), and the father of Hamutal, mother of Jehoahaz and Zedekiah, kings of Judah (II Kgs. 23:31; Jer. 52:1). The name is very common in the Hebrew epigraphy and it is recorded 12 times by Davies (1991:379). The name occurs on another bulla in our group, no. 55, and its hypocoristicon *yrm* on bulla no. 54 below.

33. ʾElishamaʿ son of Malkiyahu

A fragmentary bulla made of brown clay and measuring 15.8x18.0 mm. The back of the bulla is concave and smooth without papyrus imprint. On the upper edge fingerprints are visible. The surface is divided into two registers by three parallel lines with a thicker central line and surrounded by a double circular framing line which survives only on the upper part. The last letter *w (waw)* is missing but the reading is evident.

The Hebrew inscription reads:

לאלשמע ב/ן מלכיה[ו]

l̇ʾlšmʿ b/ṅ mlkyḣ[w]

"Belonging to ʾElishamaʿ son of Malkiyahu"

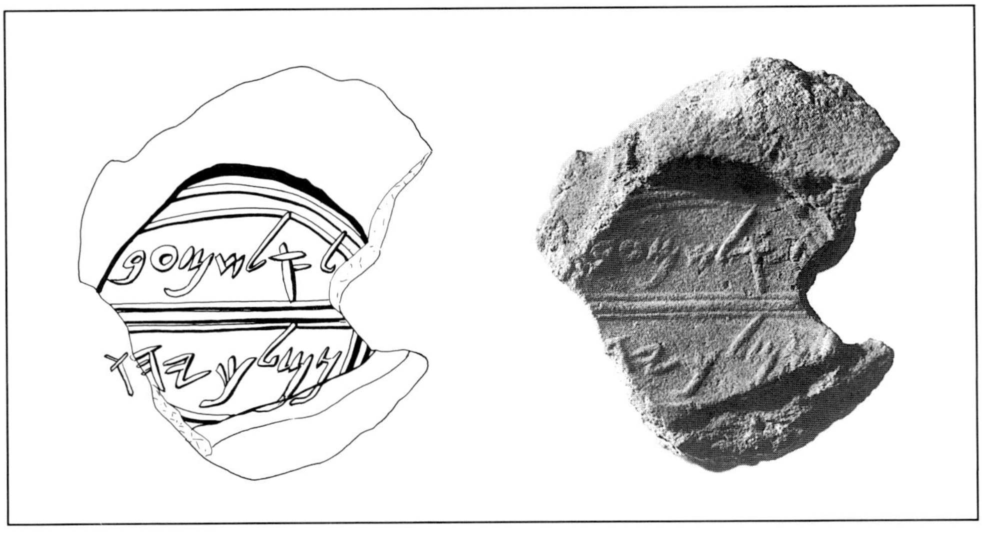

ʾlšmʿ — ʾElishamaʿ is a Hebrew theophoric personal name meaning "My God listened". The name is common in the Bible in its full spelling *ʾlyšmʿ* "ʾElyshamaʿ" (I Chr. 2:41; II Chr. 17:7–8;

II Kgs. 25:25 etc.) and is very common in the Hebrew epigraphic material. It is recorded 16 times by Davies (1991:284–5), and four times by Deutsch and Heltzer (1994, 19; 1995, 62a-b two identical; 1997, 93a-b two identical, 96). This name appears also on the next bulla, no. 34.

mlkyhw — Malkiyahu is a very common Hebrew theophoric personal name meaning "Yahweh is my King". 12 individuals bear this name in the Bible (Kimchi 1991:575–576) and it is recorded 18 times in the Hebrew epigraphic material (Davies 1991:426; Deutsch and Heltzer 1994, 20; 1977, 85, 86). The name appears on three other bullae in our group, nos. 59, 66a-b below.

34. ʾElishamaʿ son of Shuʿal

A complete bulla made of black clay and measuring 13.5x10.3 mm. On the back of the bulla the imprint of the texture of the papyrus to which the bulla was affixed is visible, along with grooves where the cord which tied the papyrus ran. Around the edges fingerprints are visible. The inscription is divided between two registers by two parallel lines which are split at the ends and surrounded by a circular framing line.

The Hebrew inscription reads:

לאלשמע / בן שעל

lʾlšmʿ / bn šʿl

"Belonging to ʾElishamaʿ son of Shuʿal"

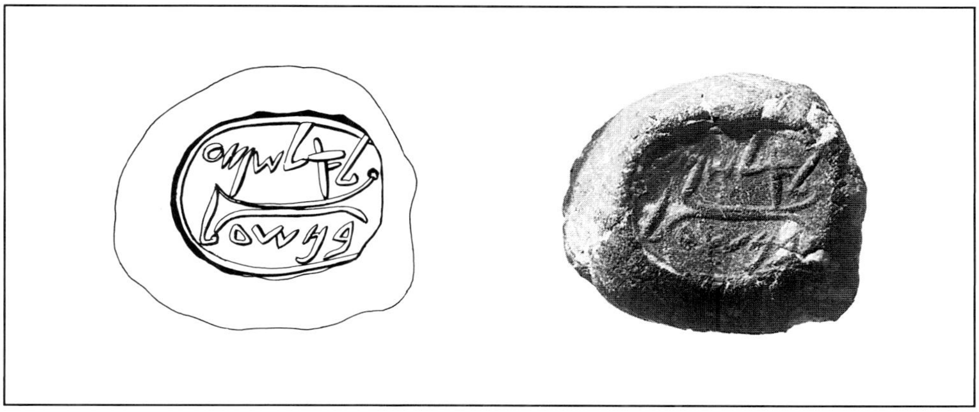

ʾlšmʿ — ʾElishamaʿ is a Hebrew biblical theophoric personal name meaning "My God listened". For the name see the previous bulla, no. 33.

šʿl — Shuʿal, literally "Fox" is a Hebrew personal name given after this animal. This is made clear by a bronze seal on which the name Shuʿal appears together with the picture of a running fox (Deutsch and Heltzer, 1994, 25). Names derived from animals such as this are common and are known from the Bible and from the Hebrew epigraphic material. Such names are: "ʿAkhbor" (mouse), (II Kgs. 22:12), "ʿOreb" (crow), (WSS 693), etc. The name appears only once in the

Bible in full spelling *šwʿl* (I Chr. 7:36), but is common in the Hebrew epigraphical material. It is mentioned on two ostraca from Arad (Aharoni 1981, 38:2, 49:14) and engraved on a jar handle of unknown provenance *hmṣh šʿl* (Avigad 1972:5–9). Seven Hebrew and three Ammonite seals and bullae bearing this name are also known (WSS p. 538), as well as bulla no. 38 in our group.

35. **ʾAmaryahu son of ʾAsap**

An intact bulla made of light brown clay, not entirely impressed and measuring 13.5x10.3 mm. On the back of the bulla the imprint of the texture of the papyrus to which the bulla was affixed is visible, along with a groove where the cord which tied the papyrus ran. The surface is divided into three registers by two double lines. The upper register contains a four-winged cobra snake *uraeus*. The inscription is divided between the two lower registers. As the seal was not fully impressed the edge around it is missing. Therefore the first letter in the lower register is missing. This should be the letter *b (bet)* of the word *bn* (son).

The Hebrew inscription reads:

לאמריהו / [ב]ן אסף
lʾmryhw / [b]ṅ ʾsṗ
"Belonging to ʾAmaryahu son of ʾAsap"

ʾmryhw — ʾAmaryahu is a Hebrew theophoric personal name meaning "Yahweh established". This name and its shortened forms *ʾmry* and *ʾmryh* are common in the Bible (I Chr. 5:33; Ezra 10:42; Neh. 10:4). An official by the name ʾAmaryahu, in the time of Hezekiah has been appointed by the king over the "freewill offerings of God" (II Chr. 31:14,15). The Hebrew epigraphic material provides us with a seal: *lyšʿyhw ʾmryhw* "Belonging to Yeshaʿyahu (son of) ʾAmaryahu (Avigad 1963:324; WSS 212), with two identical bullae: *lʾmryhw bn yhwʾb* "Belonging to ʾAmaryahu son of Yehoʾab" (Avigad 1986, 31a-b; WSS 449a-b), with two graffiti from Beer-Sheba: *lnryhw lʾmryhw* and *lʾm[ryhw]* "Belonging to Neriyahu, Belonging to ʾAmaryahu" and "Belonging to ʾAmaryahu' (Beer-Sheba I:73, 74) and several jar handles from

Gibeon: *gbʿn gdr ʾmryhw* "Gibeʿon, Gdor, ʾAmaryahu" (Pritchard 1959, 3). The name also occurs on bullae nos. 45 and 62 below.

ʾsp — ʾAsap is a hypocoristicon of the Hebrew personal name ʾAsapyahu meaning "Yahweh gathered (me)". Four individuals bear this name in the Bible (I Chr. 6:24, 26:1; II Kgs. 18:18; Neh. 2:8). The epigraphic material provides us with two seals; one found at Megiddo: *lʾsp* "Belonging to ʾAsap" (Guthe, Erman and Kautzsch 1906; WSS 85) and another without provenance: *lmšlm ʾsp* "Belonging to Meshullam (son of) ʾAsap" (Bordreuil and Lemaire 1982, no. 14; WSS 253). The name appears on another bulla in our group, no. 53 below.

36. ʾEpraḥ son of Neḥemyahu

A complete bulla made of light brown clay, measuring 15.6x12.9 mm. On the back of the bulla the imprint of the texture of the papyrus to which the bulla was affixed is visible, along with a groove where the cord which tied the papyrus ran. The surface is divided into two registers by a ladder-motif. The letters are large and eminent.

The Hebrew inscrition reads:

לאפרח / נחמיה[ו]
lʾprḥ / ṅḥmyḣ[w]
"Belonging to ʾEpraḥ son of Neḥemyahu"

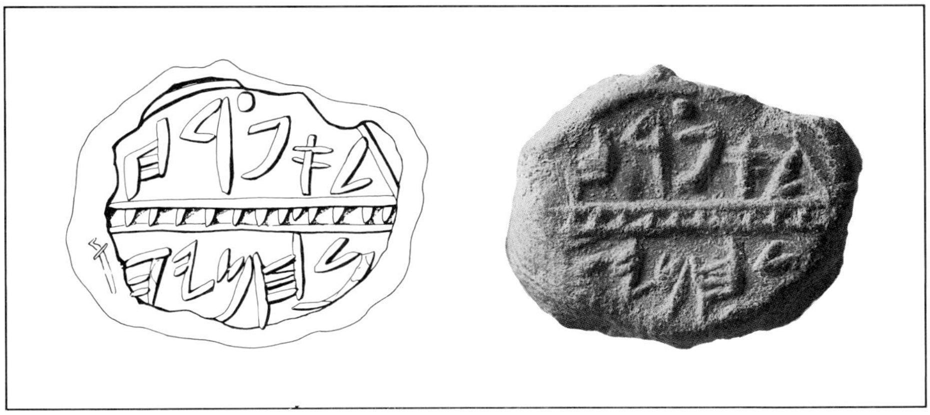

ʾprḥ — ʾEpraḥ is a Hebrew personal name deriving from the root *prḥ* "blossoming" with the meaning "to flourish" (Heltzer and Ohana 1978:138; Avigad 1986:37). The name is not found in the Bible but is very common in the Hebrew epigraphic material. It occurs on an ostracon from Ḥorvat ʿUza: *lʾlyšb bn ʾprḥ* "Belonging to ʾElyashib son of ʾEpraḥ" (Beit-Arieh 1987:56), on two seals: 1) *lʾprḥ bn ʾḥʾb* "Belonging to ʾEpraḥ son of ʾAḥʾab" (Hestrin and Dayagi-Mendels 1979, 51; WSS 87), 2) *lʾprḥ b smkyhw* "Belonging to ʾEpraḥ so(n of) Semakyahu" (Avigad 1969, 5; WSS 88), and on twelve bullae, three from Jerusalem (Shoham 1994:58, nos. 9, 10, 17; WSS

450, 626) and nine without provenance (Avigad 1986, 19–23; WSS 426, 451–454; Deutsch and Heltzer 1977, 93a-b, two identical).

nḥmyhw — Neḥemyahu is a Hebrew theophoric personal name meaning "My comfort is Yahweh". In the Bible it occurs in its shortened form *nḥmyh* (Neh. 1:1, 3:16; Ezra. 2:2). The name appears in the Hebrew epigraphic material on ostraca from Arad (Aharoni 1981 25:5, 31:3, 36:1, 40:1, 59:3), on the seal: *lnḥmyhw bn mykyhw* "Belonging to Neḥemyahu son of Mikayahu" (Wright, 1882:54, no. 1; WSS 265), on two bullae: 1) *lḥnnyhw nḥmyhw* "Belonging to Ḥananyahu (son of) Neḥemyahu" (Avigad 1986, 61; WSS 506), 2) *lnḥmyhw ...* "Belonging to Neḥemyahu ..." (no. 202 in the Borowsky collection, to by published by A. Lemaire, no. 19 in *Eretz Israel* 26, *F.M. Cross Vol.*[13]) and on another two bullae in our group, nos. 58 and 65 below. The shortened form of the name "Naḥum" appears on bulla no. 64 below.

37. ʾUriyahu (son of) ʿEzer

A fragmentary bulla made of light brown clay, measuring 13.5x14.0 mm. On the back of the bulla deep grooves are visible. The surface is divided into three registers by two double lines and surrounded by a circular framing line which survives only on the right side. In the upper register a grazing doe is depicted. In the middle register four letters have survived: *lʾry...* and the completion of the name to: *ʾryhw* is evident. In the lower register at the end of the inscription, a dot which serves as a space filler is found.

The Hebrew inscription reads:

לארי[הו] / עזר.

lʾry[hw] / ʿzr .

"Belonging to ʾUriyahu (son of) ʿEzer"

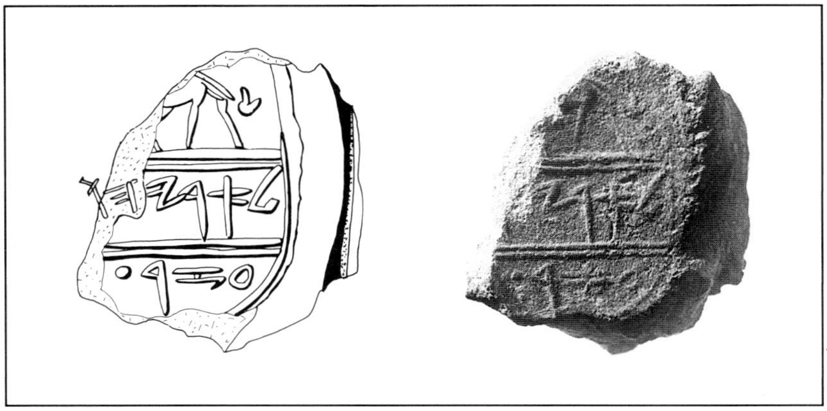

13. Lemaire suggest that this bulla and bulla no. 65 below are identical, and were sealed with the same seal.

ʾryhw — ʾUriyahu is a Hebrew theophoric personal name meaning "My light is Yahweh". In the Bible it occurs in its full spelling *ʾwryhw* (Jer. 26:20) and in its shortened form *ʾwryh* (II Sam. 11:3; II Kgs. 16:10 etc.). The name is common in the Hebrew epigraphic material and has been recorded nine times by Davies (1991:290). It appears on two other bullae in this chapter, no. 23 above and no. 63 below.

ʿzr — ʿEzer is a hypocoristicon (shortened form) of the Hebrew personal name ʿAzriʾel or ʿAzaryahu meaning "Yahweh is my help". This name and its shortened forms are very common in the Bible (Kimchi 1991:687–8, 692–5) and in the Hebrew epigraphic material. It was recorded 19 times by Davies (1991:458), three times by Deutsch and Heltzer (1994, 24, 77:3; 1995, 56) and it appears on bulla no. 73 below. The name in its full spelling occurs also on bullae nos. 3, 10 above and 74 below.

38. ʾAshyahu son of Shuʿal

A fragmentary and worn bulla made of light brown clay and measuring 17.2x15.0 mm. The back of the bulla is of conoid shape and indicates a use which is different than to seal a document. It may have functioned itself as a document similar to a receipt. The inscription is divided between two registers by a double line and surrounded by a circular framing line. Despite the poor condition of the bulla the inscription is clear. At the end of the lower register a palm branch is depicted. This probably serves as an empty space filler.

The Hebrew inscription reads:

[ל]אשיהו / שעל
[l]ʾšyhw / šʿl
"Belonging to ʾAshyahu (son of) Shuʿal"

ʾšyhw — ʾAshyahu is a Hebrew theophoric personal name not found in the Bible. Similar names are *yʾšyhw*, *ywʾš* and *yʾwš*. They all contain the component *ʾwš* which means "to give". Therefore the meaning of the name is "Yahweh has given", similar to names such as *ntnyhw* and *yhwntn* (Avigad 1986:42). The name ʾAshyahu appears on three different seals of the same person: *ʾlyšb bn ʾšyhw* "Elyashib son of ʾAshyahu", found at Arad (Aharoni 1981:119, 105–107). It has been recorded 13 times by Davies (1991:292) and once by Deutsch and Heltzer (1995:92, 79:7) on an ostracon from Judah: *nʿr ʾšyhw bn nmšr* "steward of ʾAshyahu son of Nimshar".

šʿl — Shuʿal, literally "Fox" is a Hebrew personal name given after this animal. This is made clear by a bronze seal on which the name Shuʿal appears together with the picture of a running fox (Deutsch and Heltzer 1994, 25). Names derived from animals such as this are common and are known both from the Bible and from the Hebrew epigraphic material. Such names are: "ʿAkhbor" (mouse), (II Kgs. 22:12), "ʿOreb" (crow), (WSS 693) etc. The name appears only once in the Bible in full spelling *šwʿl* (I Chr. 7:36). It is mentioned on two ostraca from Arad (Aharoni 1981, 38:2, 49:14) and is engraved on a jar handle of unknown provenance *hmṣh šʿl* (Avigad 1972:5–9). Seven Hebrew and three Ammonite seals and bullae bearing this name are also known (WSS p. 538), in addition to bulla no. 34 in our group.

39. Benayahu son of Neriyahu son of Peqaḥ

A fragmentary bulla made of light brown clay and measuring 13.5x14.8 mm. On the back of the bulla the papyrus imprint is visible. The inscription is divided between three registers by two double lines and surrounded by a double circular framing line. The name of the owner in the upper register is reconstructed based on the last three preserved letters *yhw*, and the remains of the first two letters of his name: *bn (bnyhw)*. Despite the missing right side of the bulla the names of his father and of his grandfather have survived in their entirety.

The Hebrew inscription reads:

[ל]בׄנׄיהו / בׄן נריהו / [ב]ןׄ פׄקח

[l]ḃṅyhw / ḃn nryhw / [b]ṅ ṗqḥ

"Belonging to Benayahu son of Neriyahu son of Peqaḥ"

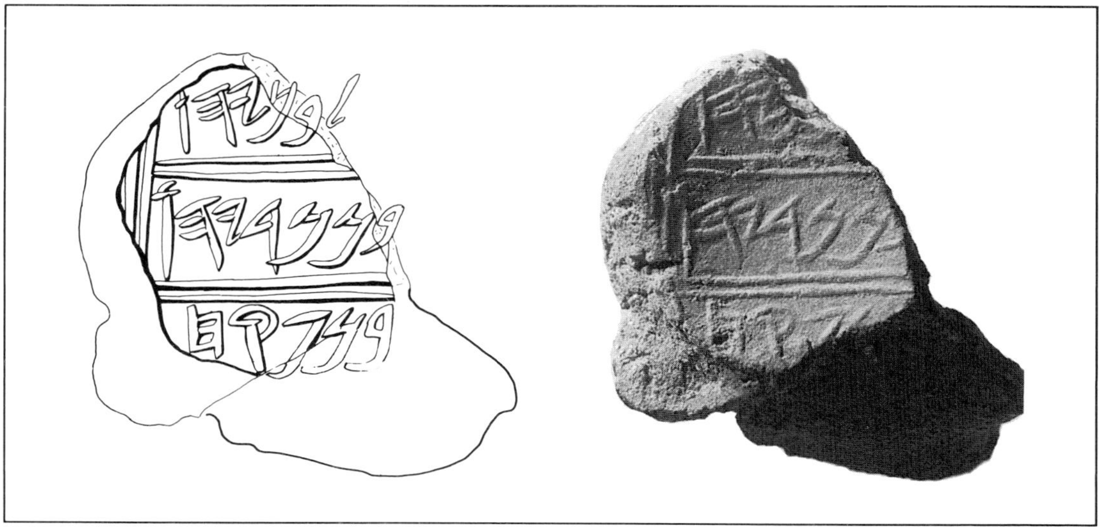

bnyhw — Benayahu is a Hebrew theophoric personal name meaning "Son of Yahweh". The name, and its shortened form *bnyh*, are very common in the Bible where we find 13 individuals bearing this name (Kimchi 1991:173–175). The Hebrew epigraphic material is also a rich source and the name was recorded nine times by Davies (1991:315), twice by Deutsch and Heltzer (1994, 25; 1997, 92) and on the next bulla, no. 40 in our group.

nryhw — Neriyahu is a Hebrew theophoric personal name meaning "My light is Yahweh". The name occurs only once in the Bible: Berekyahu son of Neriyahu the scribe (Jer. 32:12, 36:14 etc.). Two bullae of Berekyahu son of Neriyahu the scribe were published (Avigad 1986, 9; Deutsch and Heltzer 1994, 11; WSS 417). The name is very common in the Hebrew epigraphy where it is recorded 26 times (Davies 1991:444, Deutsch and Heltzer 1994:54, 23) and again on bulla no. 54 below.

pqḥ — Peqaḥ is a hypocoristicon of the Hebrew name "Peqaḥyahu" which means "The God Yahweh has opened my eyes". Peqaḥ and Peqaḥya are the names of two kings in the Bible: Peqaḥ, the son of Ramalyahu (II Kgs. 15:27) and Peqaḥya, the son of Menaḥem (II Kgs. 15:22), both kings of Israel. In the Hebrew epigraphy, the name appears on the seal: *pqḥ* "(Belonging to) Peqaḥ" (Diringer 1934:167, no. 4; WSS 1170 undefined), on an ostracon from Lachish (Lachish III:338, 19:2), and on a jar body-sherd from Ḥazor: *lpqḥ smdr* "Belonging to Peqaḥ, *smdr*" (Ḥazor II, Pl. CLXXI). The name also appears on bulla no. 17 above.

40. Baqqush son of Benayahu

A complete bulla made of brown clay, measuring 16.0x14.0 mm. On the back of the bulla the imprint of the texture of the papyrus to which the bulla was affixed is visible, along with a groove where the cord which tied the papyrus ran. On the right edge fingerprints are visible. The inscription is divided between two registers by a double line and surrounded by a double circular framing line. The letters are large and eminent.

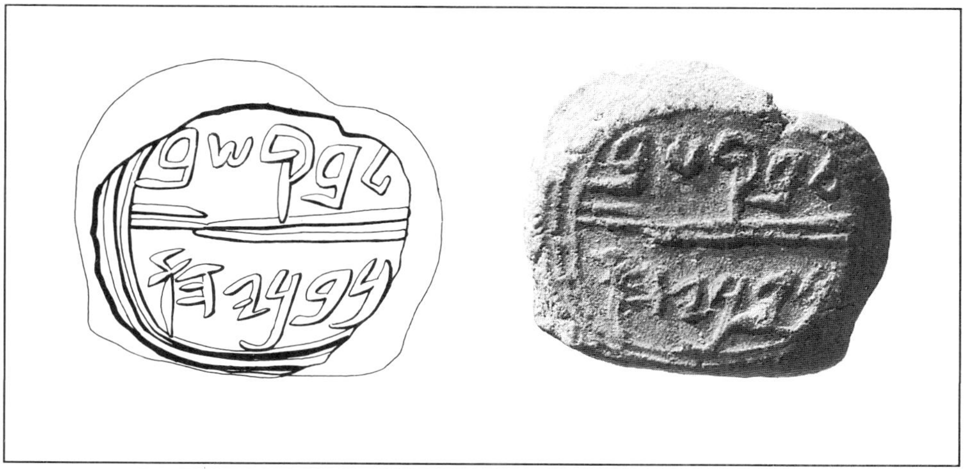

The Hebrew inscription reads:

לבקש ב/ן בניהו

lbqš b/n bnyhw

"Belonging to Baqqush son of Benayahu"

bqš — Baqqush is a hypocoristic personal name meaning "To seek the God". The name is not found in the Bible and is rare in the Hebrew epigraphic material. It occurs on a Hebrew seal: *smk bqš* "(Belonging to) Samak (son of) Baqqush" (Hestrin and Dayagi-Mendels 1979, 83; WSS 281) and on two Ammonite seals (WSS 924, 925). The feminine form of the name: *bqšt* is also known from a seal in the British Museum (WSS 34).

bnyhw — Benayahu is a Hebrew theophoric personal name meaning "Son of Yahweh". The name, and its shortened form *bnyh*, are very common in the Bible where we find 13 individuals bearing this name (Kinchi 1991:173–175). The Hebrew epigraphic material is also a rich source and the name was recorded nine times by Davies (1991:315), twice by Deutsch and Heltzer (1994, 25; 1997, 92) and on the previous bulla, no. 39 in our group.

An identical bulla sealed with the same seal was recently published (Deutsch and Heltzer 1997, 92).

41. **Hoshaᶜa[yahu] son of Raʾa(yahu)**

A fragmentary and worn bulla made of light brown clay and measuring 13.6x14.8 mm. On the back of the bulla wooden fibre impression is visible. The surface is divided into three registers by a single and a double line. Only a small section from the circular surrounding framing line is visible on the right side. In the upper register the legs of a quadruped are visible. Despite the fragmentary inscription the name of the owner is certain, however the restored patronym is only a suggestion.

The Hebrew inscription reads:

להושע[יהו] / ראֹ(יהו)
*lhwš*ʿ*[yhw] / r*ʾ*(yhw)*
"Belonging to Hoshaʿa[yahu] (son of) Raʾa(yahu)"

*hwš*ʿ*yhw* — Hoshaʿayahu is a Hebrew theophoric personal name meaning "Yahweh has saved". In the Bible it appears in its shortened form *hwš*ʿ which is also the name of the last king of Israel: Hoshea son of Elah (II Kgs. 15:30). The nickname of Joshuah son of Nun was also Hoshea (Num. 13:8). The name is common in the Hebrew epigraphic material and it is recorded 22 times in its full spelling and seven times in its shortened form (Davies 1991:333–4). The name also occurs on the next bulla, no. 42.

*r*ʾ*yhw* — Raʾayahu is a Hebrew theophoric personal name meaning "Yahweh saw". Only the shortened form of the name: *r*ʾ*yh* is found in the Bible (I Chr. 4:2, 5:5; Ezra 2:47). The name is rare in the Hebrew epigraphic material and is found only on two identical bullae: *lr*ʾ*yhw ḥlṣyhw* "Belonging to Raʾayahu (son of) Ḥalaṣyahu" (Avigad 1986, 157a-b; WSS 624a-b).

42. Hoshaʿayahu son of Shemaʿyahu

A complete bulla made of brownish-grey clay, measuring 14.5x10.9 mm. The back of the bulla is convex and covered with fingerprints. This points towards a different use of the bulla, probably as a receipt rather than to seal a document. This type of bullae were called "Fiscal bullae" by Avigad (1990:262). The inscription is divided between two registers by two parallel lines and surrounded by a framing circular line which survives only on the lower part. The left edge of the bulla is not entirely impressed but the inscription is clear.

The Hebrew inscription reads:

להושעיה[ו] / בן שמעיהו
*lhwš*ʿ*yh[w] / bn šm*ʿ*yhw*
"Belonging to Hoshaʿayahu son of Shemaʿyahu"

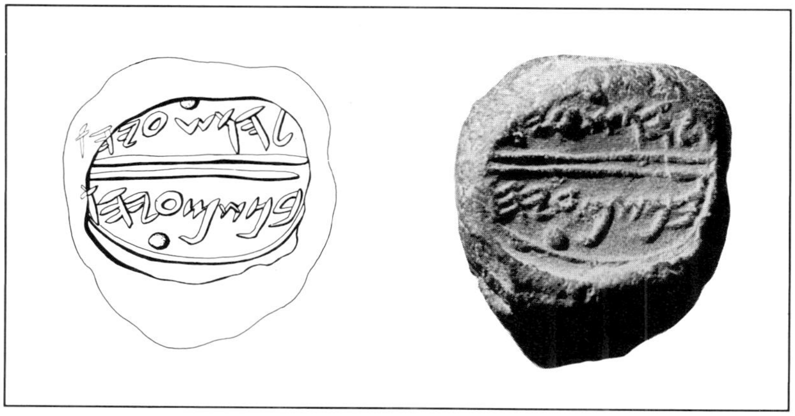

*hwš*ʿ*yhw* — Hoshaʿayahu is a Hebrew theophoric personal name meaning "Yahweh has saved". In the Bible it appears in its shortened form *hwš*ʿ which is also the name of the last king of Israel: Hoshea son of Elah (II Kgs. 15:30). The nickname of Joshuah son of Nun was also Hoshea (Num. 13:8). The name is common in the Hebrew epigraphic material and it is recorded 22 times in its full spelling and seven times in its shortened form (Davies 1991:333–4). The name also occurs on the previous bulla, no. 41.

*šm*ʿ*yhw* — Shemaʿyahu is a Hebrew theophoric personal name meaning "Yahweh has listened". The name is very common in the Bible and appears also in its shortened forms: *šm*ʿ, *šm*ʿ*y* and *šm*ʿ*yh* (Kimchi 1991:834, 836–842). In the Hebrew epigraphic material the name is recorded 20 times in its full spelling and 10 times in its shortened forms (Davies 1991:500–2; Deutsch and Heltzer 1994, 38; 1995, 64). The name also occurs on bulla no. 90 below.

43. Hiṣṣil son of Shaḥar

A complete bulla of elliptic shape made of dark brown clay, measuring 19.0x14.5 mm. The impression is 12.5x9.8 mm. in size. Around the seal impression a thick groove is present. This indicates that the seal was set in a metal bezel, probably of a signet ring or a pendant, while it served to impress the bulla. The edges are covered with fingerprints. On the back of the bulla the imprint of the texture of the papyrus to which the bulla was affixed is visible, along with a groove where the cord which tied the papyrus ran. The inscription is divided between two registers by a double line and is surrounded by a framing circular line. An Egyptian *s3* symbol appears on the left side of the upper register. This sign also occurs on nine identical Aramaic bullae from Nineveh: *l*ʿ*tr*ʿ*zr* (Layard, 1853, 155; WSS 837). The first letter bet in the lower register is missing as a result of a hole in the clay.

The Hebrew inscription reads:

להצל / [ב]ן שחר

lhṣl / [b]n šḥr

"Belonging to Hiṣṣil son of Shaḥar"

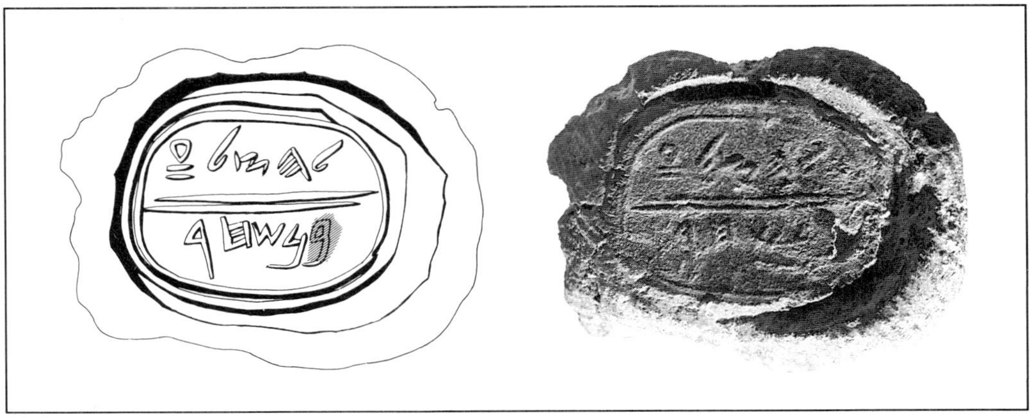

hṣl — Hiṣṣil is the hypocoristicon of the Hebrew theophoric personal name *hṣlyhw* "Hiṣṣilyahu" meaning "Yahweh rescued". The name is not found in the Bible but is common in the Hebrew epigraphic material in its full spelling. It is found on three ostraca, one from Lachish: *gmryhw bn hṣlyhw* "Gemaryahu son of Hiṣṣilyahu" (Lachish III:331, 1:1), the second from Ḥorvat ʿUza: *mky bn hṣlyhw mmqdh* "Mikay son of Hiṣṣilyahu from Maqedah" (Beit-Arieh 1986–7) and the third from Judah: *hṣlyhw bn bnyhw* "Hiṣṣilyahu son of Benayahu" (Deutsch and Heltzer 1995, 79:18). The name appears on several handles from Gibeon: *lnḥm hṣlyhw* "Belonging to Naḥum son of Hiṣṣilyahu" (Pritchard 1959:27), is common on seals and bullae (Davies, 1991:336) and it occurs again on bulla no. 77 below.

šḥr — Shaḥar is a hypocoristicon of the Hebrew personal name *šḥryhw* "Shaḥariyahw" meaning "To search for Yahweh". The name appears only once in the Bible and belonged to Shaḥariya son of Jeroham who was a man of Benjamin (I Chr. 8:26). In the Hebrew epigraphic material the name is common and was recorded 14 times by Davies (1991:492) and once again on an ostracon from Judah: *bn šḥr lʾḥqm* "Son of Shaḥar, belonging to ʾAḥiqam" (Deutsch and Heltzer 1995, 79:8).

44. Zakkur son of Ṭobiyahu

A complete bulla of elliptic shape made of brown clay, measuring 14.5x14.0 mm. On the back of the bulla the imprint of the texture of the papyrus to which the bulla was affixed is visible, along with a groove where the cord which tied the papyrus ran. On the left side of the surface is a hole made by the cord while the bulla was wet. The inscription is divided between two registers by a double line and is surrounded by a circular border line.

The Hebrew inscription reads:

לזכר̇ בן / טביהו̇

lzkr̊ bn / ṭbyhẘ

"Belonging to Zakkur son of Ṭobiyahu"

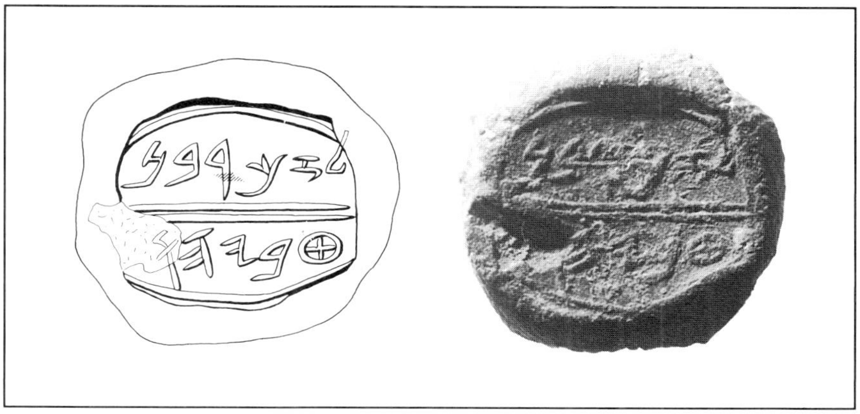

zkr — Zakkur is a hypocoristicon of the Hebrew personal name *zkryhw* meaning "Yahweh has remembered". The name in its shortened form occurs only once in the Bible (I Chr. 8:31), but is very common in its other spellings such as: *zkry*, *zkryh* and *zkryhw*. 42 different individuals are recorded in the Bible bearing these names (Kimchi 1991:266–273). The name is also common in the Hebrew epigraphic material and was recorded 20 times by Davies (1991:342–3).

ṭbyhw — Ṭobiyahu is a Hebrew theophoric personal name meaning "Yahweh is my good". In the Bible it appears in a different spelling: *ṭwbyhw* (II Chr. 17:8; Neh. 2:10; Ezra 2:60; Zech. 6:10). The name occurs on an ostracon from Lachish: *ṭbyhw ʿbd hmlk* "Ṭobiyahu, servant of the king" (Lachish III:333, 3:19) and on two Hebrew bullae: *lʾḥqm bn ṭbyhw* "Belonging to ʾAḥiqam son of Ṭobiyahu" and *lṭbyhw ʿbdʾ* "Belonging to Ṭobiyahu (son of) ʿAbdaʾ" (Avigad 1986, 14, 65). In addition, the name appears on bullae no. 46a-b below.

45. Ḥagab son of ʾAmaryahu

A complete bulla made of light-brown clay, measuring 18.0x16.0 mm. On the back of the bulla the imprint of the texture of the papyrus to which the bulla was affixed is visible, along with a groove where the cord which tied the papyrus ran. The inscription is divided between two registers by a double line and is surrounded by a circular border line.

The Hebrew inscription reads:

לחגב בן / אמריהו

lḥgb bn / *ʾmryhw*

"Belonging to Ḥagab son of ʾAmaryahu"

ḥgb — Ḥagab is a Hebrew personal name meaning "locust, grasshopper", given after this insect. Names derived from animals such as this are common and are known both from the

Bible and from the Hebrew epigraphic material. Such names are: "ʿAkhbor" (mouse), (II Kgs. 22:12), "ʿOreb" (crow), (WSS 693) etc. This name is rare and occurs only once in the Bible (Ezra 2:46). In the Hebrew epigraphic material the name is found on two ostraca: one from Lachish *ḥgb bn yʾznyhw* "Belonging to Ḥagab son of Yaʾazanyahu" (Lachish III:331, 1:3) and one from Ḥorvat ʿUza: *bn ḥgb* "son of Ḥagab" (Beit-Arieh 1988–9), as well as on four bullae (Avigad 1986, 53a-b, 54a-b). The name Ḥagab appears also on bulla no. 92 below.

ʾmryhw — ʾAmaryahu is a Hebrew theophoric personal name meaning "Yahweh established". This name and its shortened forms *ʾmry* and *ʾmryh* are common in the Bible (I Chr. 5:33; Ezra 10:42; Neh. 10:4). An official by the name ʾAmaryahu, in the time of Hezekiah was appointed by the king over the "freewill offerings of God" (II Chr. 31:14,15). The Hebrew epigraphic material provides us with a seal: *lyšʿyhw ʾmryhw* "Belonging to Yeshaʿyahu (son of) ʾAmaryahu (Avigad 1963:324; WSS 212), with two identical bullae: *lʾmryhw bn yhwʾb* "Belonging to ʾAmaryahu son of Yehoʾab" (Avigad 1986, 31a-b; WSS 449a-b), with two graffiti from Beer-Sheba: *lnryhw lʾmryhw and lʾm[ryhw]* "Belonging to Neriyahu, Belonging to ʾAmaryahu" and "Belonging to ʾAmaryahu" (Beer-Sheba I:73, 74) and several jar handles from Gibeon: *gbʿn gdr ʾmryhw* "Gibeon, Gdor, ʾAmaryahu" (Pritchard 1959, 3). The name occurs also on bullae nos. 35 above and 62 below.

46. Ṭobiyahu son of Ḥanni

Two fragmentary bullae impressed with the same seal, made of brown clay, and measuring: a. 15.0x9.3 mm., b. 13.0x6.1 mm. On the back of both bullae a weak imprint of the texture of the papyrus is visible, along with grooves where the cord which tied the papyrus ran. The field is divided into two registers by a double line and is surrounded by a circular border line. In the upper and larger register, of which only the lower part has survived, a sphinx facing an *ankh* is depicted. The inscription in the lower register is divided into two lines without a divider. The inscription is complete in the first bulla and fragmentary in the second.

The Hebrew inscription reads:

a. **לטביהו / חני**
lṭbyhw / ḥny

b. **[לט]ביהו / [ח]ני**
[lṭ]byhw / [ḥ]ny
"Belonging to Ṭobiyahu son of Ḥanni"

ṭbyhw — Ṭobiyahu is a Hebrew theophoric personal name meaning "Yahweh is my good". In the Bible it appears in a different spelling: *ṭwbyhw* (II Chr. 17:8; Neh. 2:10; Ezra 2:60; Zech. 6:10). The name occurs on an ostracon from Lachish: *ṭbyhw ʿbd hmlk* "Ṭobiyahu, servant of the king" (Lachish III:333, 3:19) and on two Hebrew bullae: *lʾḥqm bn ṭbyhw* "Belonging to ʾAḥiqam son of Ṭobiyahu" and *lṭbyhw ʿbdʾ* "Belonging to Ṭobiyahu (son of) ʿAbdaʾ" (Avigad 1986, 14, 65). In addition, the name appears on bulla no. 44 above.

ḥny — Ḥanni is a hypocoristicon of the Hebrew personal name *ḥnyhw* — "Ḥanniyahu" meaning "Yahweh is gracious". The name is not found in the Bible but there is a similar one in a full spelling with the theophoric element El: *ḥnyʾl* (Num. 34:23). The name is very rare in the Hebrew epigraphic material and it occurs only once restored on an ostracon from Tell en-Naṣbeh, the biblical Mizpah: *ṣdq ḥn[y]*(Naṣbeh I:169). The name in its full spelling is found on a seal which belonged to two persons, probably two generations: *lšʿryhw bn ḥnyhw* // *lhwdyhw šʿryhw* "Belonging to Sheʿaryahu son of Ḥanniyahu // Belonging to Hodiyahu (son of) Sheʿaryahu" (Bordreuil and Lemaire 1976:46f; WSS 380).

47. Yaʾazanyahu

A complete bulla made of dark-grey clay, measuring 12.1x9.7 mm. On the back of the bulla the imprint of the texture of the papyrus to which the bulla was affixed is visible, along with a groove where the cord which tied the papyrus ran. The inscription is divided between four groups of two letters by a four petaled lotus-bud motifs and is surrounded by two circular border lines.

The Hebrew inscription reads:

לי/אז/ני/הו

ly/ʾz/ny/hw

"Belonging to Yaʾazanyahu"

yʾznyhw — Yaʾazanyahu is a common Hebrew theophoric personal name meaning "Yahweh has listened, heard" (*yʾzn* is an archaic past form). Four individuals are named Yaʾazanyahu in the Bible: 1) Yaʾazanyahu son of Maʿakhati, captain of the army in the time of Gedalayah (II Kgs. 25:23), 2) Yaʾazanyahu son of Shapan, one of the seventy elders of the house of Israel in the time of Ezekiel the prophet (Ezek. 8:11), 3) Yaʾazanyahu son of ʿAzzur, a minister of the people in the time of Ezekiel the prophet (Ezek. 11:1), 4) Yaʾazanyahu son of Jeremiah son of Havazzinya, from the house of the rekhavim, in the time of Jeremiah the prophet (Jer. 35:3). The name is also common in the Hebrew epigraphic material and it occurs on an agate seal found at Tell en-Naṣbeh: *lyʾznyhw ʿbd hmlk* "Belonging to Yaʾazanyahu, servant of the king" (Naṣbeh I:163; WSS 8), twice on an ostracon from Lachish: *yʾznyhw bn ṭbšlm* "Yaʾazanyahu son of Ṭobshalem" and *ḥgb bn yʾznyhw* "Ḥagab son of Yaʾazanyahu" (Lachish III:331, 1:2–3), on an ostracon from Arad: *yʾznyhw bn bnyhw* "Yaʾazanyahu son of Benayahu" (Aharoni 1981, 39:9), on an ostracon from Judah: *yʾznyhw bn ʿzr* "Yaʾazanyahu son of ʿEzer" (Deutsch and Heltzer 1994, 77:3), on two bullae from Jerusalem: *lšmʿyhw bn yʾznyhw* "Belonging to Shemaʿyahu son of Yaʾazanyahu" and *lyʾznyhw bn mʿśyhw* "Belonging to Yaʾazanyahu son of Maʿaśeyahu" (Shoham 1994:58, nos. 15, 41; WSS 511, 636) and on other items (Davies 1991:361). The patronym on this bulla is absent, therefore the owner of the seal could be one of the above-mentioned persons.

48. Yedaʿyahu

The upper part of a light brown clay bulla measuring 14.3x11.4 mm. On the back of the bulla the imprint of the texture of the papyrus to which the bulla was affixed is visible. The partly-preserved inscription appears above a two-winged *uraeus* and is surrounded by a circular border line.

The Hebrew inscription reads:

ידע/י[הו]

ydʿ/y[hw]

"(Belonging to) Yedaʿyahu"

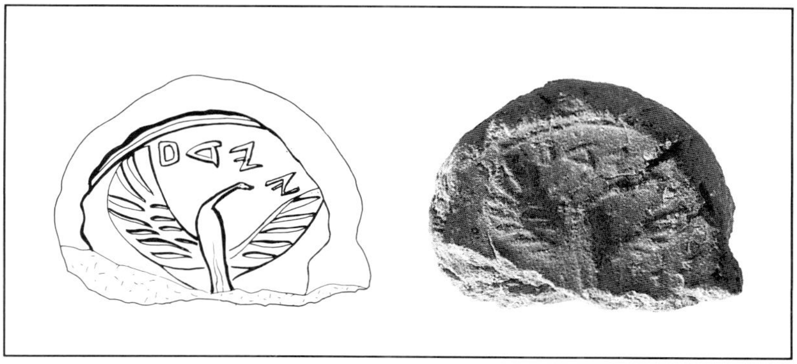

ydʿyhw — Yedaʿyahu is a Hebrew theophoric personal name meaning "Yahweh knows, has favored". The name is common in the Bible in its shortened forms *ydʿ* and *ydʿyh* (I Chr. 2:28, 24:7; Ezra 2:36 etc.). In the Hebrew epigraphic material it was recorded 13 times by Davies (1991:361–2). Additionally, the name appears on the bulla: *lʿbdʾ bn ydʿyhw* "Belonging to ʿAbdaʾ son of Yedaʿyahu", and on three seal impressions on two jar handles: *ydʿyh(w) ʾlʿzr* "(Belonging to) Yedaʿyahu (son of) ʾElʿazar" (Deutsch and Heltzer 1994, 17; 1995, 53a-c) and on bulla no. 91 below.

49. Yehoʾab son of Shapaṭ

A complete bulla made of brown clay, measuring 15.8x15.1 mm. On the back of the bulla the imprint of the texture of the papyrus to which the bulla was affixed is visible, along with a groove where the cord which tied the papyrus ran. The inscription is divided between two registers by a lotus-bud motif and surrounded by a single circular border line which is visible on the right side. The first letter in the lower register is missing but it should be the letter *bet* of the word *bn* "son".

The Hebrew inscription reads:

ליהואב / [ב]ן שפט
lyhwʾb / [b]n špṭ
"Belonging to Yehoʾab son of Shapaṭ"

yhwʾb — Yehoʾab is a Hebrew theophoric personal name meaning "Yahweh is father". The name is missing in the Bible but is known from the Hebrew epigraphic material. It occurs on three ostraca from Arad: 1) *yhwʾb bn ḥldy* "Yehoʾab son of Ḥeldai", 2) *yhwʾb* "Yehoʾab", 3) *yhwʾb bn ...* "Yehoʾab son of ..." (Aharoni 1981, 39:10, 49:9, 59:1), as well as on the seal: *lʾḥmlk yhwʾb* "Belonging to ʾAḥimelek (son of) Yehoʾab" (Avigad 1989, 8; WSS 58), on four bullae, two from Jerusalem: 1) *lʾlšmʿ bn yhwʾb* "Belonging to ʾElishamaʿ son of Yehoʾab", 2) *lʾḥyʾb bn yhwʾb* "Belonging to ʾAḥiʾab son of Yehoʾab" (Shoham 1994:58, 18, 37; WSS 427, 447) and on two identical bullae (from the Tell Beit Mirsim area?): *[l]ʾmryhw bn yhwʾb* "[Belonging to]

ʾAmaryahu son of Yehoʾab" (Avigad 1986, 31a-b; WSS 449a-b) and once again on bulla no. 65 below.

špṭ — Shapaṭ is a hypocoristicon of the Hebrew personal name *špṭyhw* or *yhwšpṭ* meaning "Yahweh has judged". Five persons in the Bible bear this name (Kimchi 1991:848–849). In the Hebrew epigraphical material it occurs on two seals: 1) *lšpṭ* — "Belonging to Shapaṭ" (Hestrin and Dayagi-Mendels 1978, 37; WSS 381), 2) *lmlkyhw nʿr špṭ* — "Belonging to Malkiyahu steward of Shapaṭ" (Avigad 1976:295–296; WSS 25) and on a bulla (from the Tell Beit Mirsim area?): *lšpṭ bn ʾḥyhw* — "Belonging to Shapaṭ son of ʾAḥiyahu" (Avigad 1986, 166; WSS 641). In our group the name appears on bulla no. 91 and in its full spelling: *špṭyhw* on bulla no. 69 below.

50a-b. Yehoʿaz son of ʾElʿaśa

Two bullae impressed with two different seals belonging probably to the same person:

a. A complete bulla made of brown clay, measuring 13.4x13.3 mm. On the back of the bulla the imprint of the texture of the papyrus to which the bulla was affixed is visible, along with a groove where the cord which tied the papyrus ran. The inscription is divided between two registers by two parallel lines and surrounded by two circular border lines.

The Hebrew inscription reads:

ליהועז / בן אלעשה

lyhwʿz / bn ʾlʿśh

"Belonging to Yehoʿaz son of ʾElʿaśa"

b. A slightly damaged bulla made of light brown clay, measuring 19.1x22.0 mm. On the back of the bulla the imprint of the texture of a fabric, probably a sack or a pouch to which the bulla was affixed is visible. On the edges fingerprints are also visible. The inscription is divided between two registers by two parallel lines and surrounded by three circular border lines.

The Hebrew inscription reads:

ליהועז ב/[ן] אׄלעשה

lyhwʿz b/[n] ʾlʿśh

"Belonging to Yehoʿaz son of ʾElʿaśa"

yhwʿz — Yehoʿaz is a Hebrew theophoric personal name meaning "Yahweh is my strength". The name is found in the Bible only in its reversed version: *ʿzyhw* (I Chr. 27:25) or in its shortened reversed version *ʿzyh* which was the name of the king of Judah: ʾUzziah son of Amaziah (II Kgs. 15:1, 2, 13, 32) and of other three persons (I Chr. 6:9; Ezra 10:21; Neh. 11:4). The element *ʿz* which means "strength, courage" appears also in Ammonite and Phoenician names such as *mlkmʿz* and *ʿštrʿz* (Bordreuil 1986, nos. 17, 84) and in Moabite *kmšʿz* (Avigad 1992). The name is known from the Hebrew epigraphic material and it appears twice on ostraca from Arad (Aharoni 1981, 31:3, 49:7), on a glass seal from Tell eṣ-Ṣafi: *yhwʿz ʾḥʾb* "Belonging to

a

b

Yehoʿaz (son of) ʾAḥʾab" (Reifenberg 1942:109, no. 2; WSS 178) and on two identical bullae (from the Tell Beit Mirsim area?): *yhwʿz bn mtn* "Belonging to Yehoʿaz son of Mattan" (Avigad 1986, 74a-b; WSS 525a-b). Yeho[ʿaz] is apparently the name which is to be restored on bulla 74 below.

ʾlʿśh — ʾElʿaśa is a Hebrew theophoric personal name meaning "The God (Yahweh) has made, created". Four persons in the Bible bear this name: 1) The son of Heleṣ (I Chr. 2:39), 2) The son of Raphah (I Chr. 8:37), 3) The son of Shaphan and brother of ʾAḥiqam and Gemaryahu (Jer. 29:3), 4) The son of Pashḥur (Ezra 10:22). The name is very rare in the Hebrew epigraphic material and occurs only once before on the bulla: *lšknyhw ʾlʿśh* "Belonging to Shekanyahu (son of) ʾElʿaśa" (Deutsch and Heltzer 1994, 16), and again in our group, on an identical bulla, no. 86 below.

51. Yehoqam (son of) Ḥaggi

A partly-impressed bulla made of black clay, measuring 14.6x12.2 mm. On the back of the bulla the imprint of the texture of the papyrus to which the bulla was affixed is visible, along with a groove where the cord which tied the papyrus ran. The field is divided into three registers by two double lines. In the upper register a quadruped is depicted, probably a grazing doe. The inscription is divided between the two lower registers. Around the impression a framing groove is visible. This indicates that the seal was set in a metal bezel, probably of a signet ring or a pendant, while it served to impress the bulla.

The Hebrew inscription reads:

[ל]יהוק/[ם] חגי

[l]yhwq/[m] ḥgy

"Belonging to Yehoqam (son of) Ḥaggi"

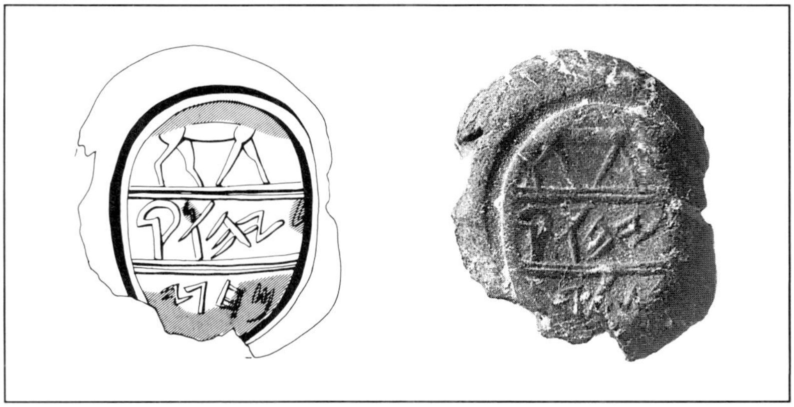

yhwqm — Yehoqam is a Hebrew theophoric personal name meaning "Yahweh raises, establishes". The name occurs in the Bible only in its reversed version: *yqmyh* "Yeqamyah" (I Chr. 2:41, 3:18). The name is found on two Hebrew seals: 1) *yhwqm* "Yehoqam", 2) *yhwqm yhwndb* "Yehoqam (son of) Yehonadab" (Avigad 1975:69, 12, 13; WSS 182, 183) and on two Hebrew bullae (from the Tell Beit Mirsim area?): 1) *lpdyhw yhwqm* "Belonging to Pedayahu (son of) Yehoqam" 2) ... *yhwqm* "(Belonging to ... son of) Yehoqam" (Avigad 1986, 12, 171; WSS 608, 650). The reversed name *yqmyhw* appears on bulla no. 53 below.

ḥgy — Ḥaggi is a shortened form of the Hebrew personal name *ḥgyh* "Ḥaggiya" literally meaning "Feast of Yahweh", yet if the suffix is not a theophoric element, one can argue that the name means: "Born on a feast day" (Willett 1992:23). Ḥaggi is the name of the tenth book in the Masoretic ordering of the Book of the Twelve. Ḥaggi the prophet began to prophesy in Jerusalem on the second year of the Persian king Darius I, i.e., 520 B.C.E. (Hag. 1:1). Another person in the Bible bears this name: Ḥaggi son of Gad, who accompanied Jacob to Egypt (Gen. 46:16; Num. 26:15). The name is common in the Hebrew epigraphic material and was recorded eleven times: nine times by Davies (1991:347), including a seal: *lbnyh/w nʿr ḥgy* "Belonging to Benayahu, steward of Ḥaggi" (Avigad 1976:296f, Pl.12:3; WSS 24), once on an ostracon from Judah" *ḥgy bn yšmʿʾl* "Ḥaggi son of Yshmaʿʾel" (Deutsch and Heltzer 1995:83, 77:2) and on another bulla: *lḥgy bn hwšʿyhw* "Belonging to Ḥaggi (sic) son of Hoshaʿyahu" (DHL:8, no. 33).

52. Yoʿalyahu son of Shebnʾa

A partly-impressed bulla made of black clay, measuring 15.5x11.8 mm. On the back of the bulla the imprint of the texture of the papyrus to which the bulla was affixed is visible, along with a groove where the cord which tied the papyrus ran. The field is divided into two registers by a double line which terminates in palmette motifs and is surrounded by a double framing border line.

The Hebrew inscription reads:

ליועליהו / בן שבנא

l̇ywʿlyhw / ḃn šbnʾ

"Belonging to Yoʿalyahu son of Shebnʾa"

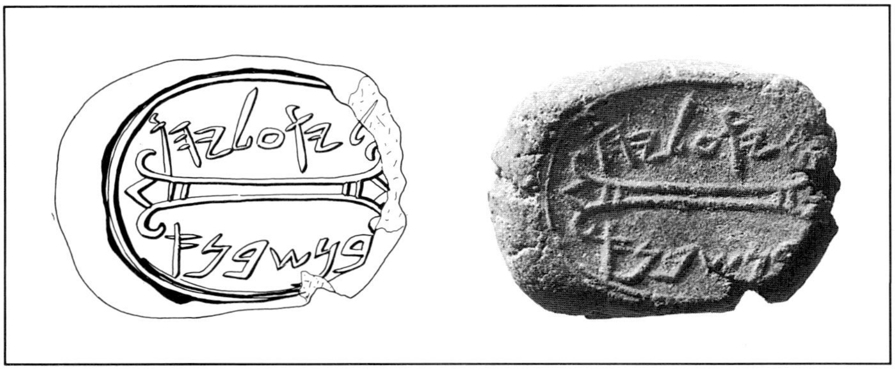

ywʿlyhw — Yoʿalyahu is a Hebrew theophoric personal name literally meaning "Yahweh will be useful" and according to Lemaire (1985:29): "Yahweh is efficient". The name is missing from the Bible but is recorded five times in the Hebrew epigraphic material: on the seal: *lywʿlyhw yšmʿʾl* "Belonging to Yoʿalyahu son of Yshmaʿʾel" (Lemaire 1985:29, no. 1; WSS 191), on the bulla: *lmlkyhw bn ywʿlyhw* "Belonging to Malkiyahu son of Yoʿalyahu" (Deutsch and Heltzer 1994:47 no. 20) and three times on two ostraca from Judah (Deutsch and Heltzer 1995, 78:1, 79:9, 16). The name appears on another bulla in our group, no. 59 below.

šbnʾ — Shebnʾa is a hypocoristicon of the Hebrew theophoric personal name *šbnyhw* meaning "Pray, God (Yahweh) return". The name is known from the Bible (Isa. 22:15) and from the Hebrew epigraphic material. It appears on several jar handles from the end of the eight century B.C.E.: *lšwky šbnʾ* "Belonging to *šwky* (son of) Shebnʾa" (Vaughn 1996:275; WSS 704a-b), *šbnʾ šḥr* "Belonging to Shebnʾa (son of) Shaḥar", *lnrʾ šbnʾ* "Belonging to Nerʾa (son of)

Shebn'a" (WSS 686, 687, 701), as well as on two seals, one from Lachish: *lšbn' 'ḥ'b* "Belonging to Shebna' (son of) ʾAḥ'ab" (Lachish, III:348, 171; WSS 350) and one without provenance: *šbn'* "(Belonging to) Shebna'" (Avigad 1954:147, 1; WSS 349). The name appears on another bulla in this group, no. 78 below.

53. Yeqamyahu son of ʾAsap

A worn bulla which was partially impressed, made of brown clay, measuring 11.9x12.2 mm. On the back of the bulla the imprint of the texture of the papyrus to which the bulla was affixed is visible, along with a groove where the cord which tied the papyrus ran. The field is divided into two registers by a double line and surrounded by a single circular border line. Despite the poor condition of the bulla the script is clear and readable.

The Hebrew inscription reads:

ליקמי/הו בן אסף
l̇yqmẏ/ḣw ḃn 'sṗ
"Belonging to Yeqamyahu son of ʾAsap"

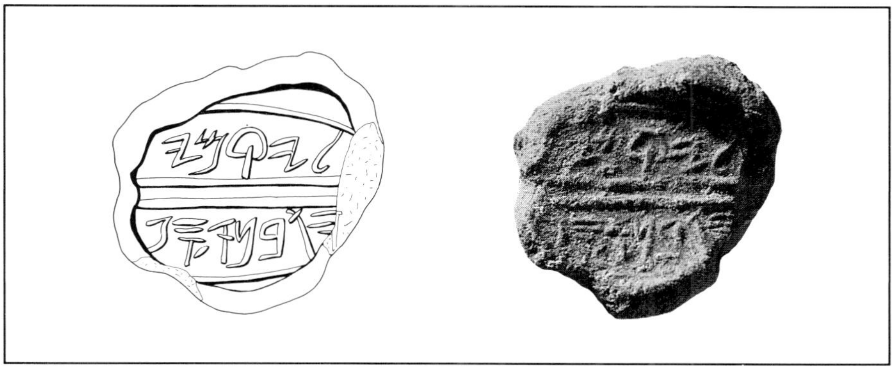

yqmyhw — Yeqamyahu is a Hebrew theophoric personal name meaning "Yahweh raises, establishes". Two persons in the Bible bear the shortened form of this name *yqmyh*: the son of Jehoiachin king of Judah (I Chr. 3:18) and the son of Shallum (I Chr. 2:41). The name is common in the Hebrew epigraphic material and it is recorded 15 times, 12 times by Davies (1991:377), on a seal of a woman: *lʿmd bt yqmyhw* "Belonging to ʿAmad daughter of Yeqamyahu" (Deutsch and Heltzer 1994, 26), on an ostracon from Judah (Deutsch and Heltzer 1995, 79:3) and on a bulla: *l'lntn yqmyhw* "Belonging to ʾElnatan (son of) Yeqamyahu" (DHL no. 42). The reversed version of the name: *yhwqm* appears on bulla no. 51 above.

'sp — ʾAsap is a hypocoristicon of the Hebrew personal name ʾAsapyahu meaning "Yahweh gathered (me)". Four individuals bear this name in the Bible (I Chr. 6:24, 26:1; II Kgs. 18:18; Neh. 2:8). The epigraphic material provides us with two seals, one found at Megiddo: *l'sp* " Belonging to ʾAsap" (Guthe, Erman and Kautzsch 1906; WSS 85) and another without

provenance: *lmšlm ʾsp* "Belonging to Meshullam (son of) ʾAsap" (Bordreuil and Lemaire 1982, no. 14; WSS 253). The name appears on another bulla in our group, no. 35 above.

54. Yoram (son of) Neriyahu

A worn and damaged bulla made of brown clay, measuring 12.9x12.9 mm. On the back of the bulla are grooves made by the cord which tied the sealed object. The field is divided into two registers by a cross-hatched rectangular column terminating in volute palmettes and surrounded by a single border line visible only on the upper edge. Despite the poor condition of the bulla the reading is certain.

The Hebrew inscription reads:

ירם / נ̇רי[הו]

yrm / ṅry[yhw]

"(Belonging to) Yirmi (son of) Neriyahu"

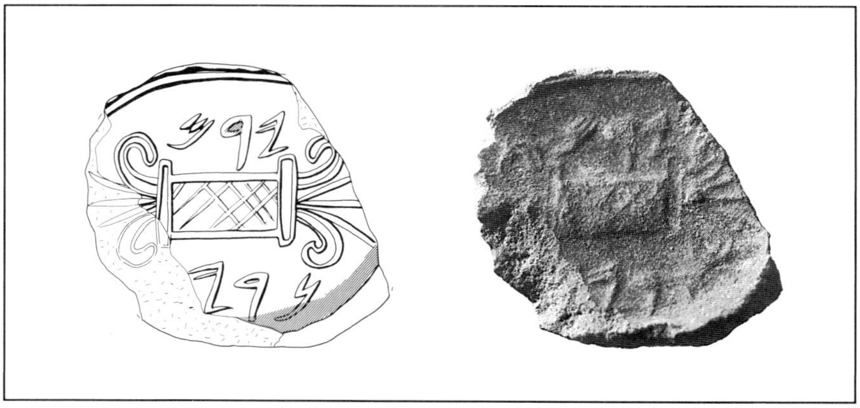

yrm — Yirmi is probably a shortened form of the Hebrew theophoric personal name Yirmiyahu meaning "Yahweh is exalted" or "My Yahweh raise up". This shortened form of the name is not found in the Bible, yet two other spellings: *yrmyh* and *yrmyhw* are common and ten individuals bear this name including Jeremiah the prophet and the book named after him (I Chr. 12:5, 11, 14, 5:24 etc.). The name in its shortened form is rare in the Hebrew epigraphy and appears on a seal: *lyrm zmryhw* "Belonging to Yirmi (son of) Zimriyahu" (Millard 1988; WSS 203) and is inscribed on a jar: *lyrm* "Belonging to Yirmi" (Avi-Yonah, and Stern 1978). The fully-spelled name *yrmyhw* appears on two bullae in our group nos. 30 and 55.

nryhw — Neriyahu is a Hebrew theophoric personal name meaning "My light is Yahweh". The name occurs only once in the Bible (Berekyahu son of Neriyahu the scribe, Jer. 32:12, 36:14 etc.). Two bullae of "Berekyahu son of Neriyahu the scribe" were published (Avigad 1986, 9; Deutsch and Heltzer 1994, 11; WSS 417). The name is very common in the Hebrew epigraphy where it is recorded 26 times (Davies 1991:444, Deutsch and Heltzer 1994:54, 23) and again on bulla no. 39 above.

55. Yirmiyahu son of *ʾyʿm*

A complete bulla made of brown clay, in a good state of preservation, measuring 19.1x17.5 mm. On the reverse of the bulla, the imprint of the texture of a fabric, a sack?, to which the bulla was affixed is visible, along with grooves where the cord ran. Around the edges fingerprints are preserved. The script is divided into two registers by a ladder-motif and surrounded by a single circular border line which is visible only on the lower part. The letters are thick and eminent.

The Hebrew inscription reads:

לירמיהו / בן איעם̇

lyrmyhw / bn ʾyʿṁ

"Belonging to Yirmiyahu son of *ʾyʿm*"

yrmyhw — Yirmiyahu is a Hebrew theophoric personal name meaning "May Yahweh raise up". Ten individuals bear this name in the Bible. Among them are the prophet Jeremiah son of Hilkiah (Jer. 1:1) and the father of Hamutal, mother of Jehoahaz and Zedekiah, kings of Judah (II Kgs. 23:31; Jer. 52:1). The name is very common in the Hebrew epigraphic material and it is recorded 12 times by Davies (1991:379). The name occurs on another bulla in our group, no. 32 above, and it's hypocoristicon *yrm* on bulla no. 54 above.

ʾyʿm — A new, hitherto unrecorded, Hebrew personal name. It contains the possible theophoric element *ʾy* similar to the biblical name: *ʾyʿzr* (Num. 26:30, called *ʾbyʿzr* in the book of Joshua 17:2) and the names *ʾyndb* found on an ostracon from Nimrud (Segal 1957) and *ʾyʿdh* found on a Hebrew seal (Hestrin and Dayagi-Mendel 1978, 52; WSS 62). A possible meaning of the element *ʾy* as lit. "where", together with the theophoric component *ʿm* is less likely but is also to be considered.

56. Yishma

A complete bulla made of black clay, in a very good state of preservation, measuring 13.4x13.1 mm. On the reverse of the bulla, the imprint of the texture of the papyrus is visible, along with grooves where the cord ran. The script is divided into two registers by a double line. The letters are of high calligraphic quality.

The Hebrew inscription reads:

ליׁשמעא[ל] / בן שפן

lyšmʿʾ[l] / bn špn

"Belonging to Yishmaʿʾel son of Shapan"

yšmʿʾl — Yishmaʿʾel is a theophoric personal name meaning "The God (Yahweh) will listen", similar to names such as "ʾElishamaʿ and Yishmaʿ. Six persons in the Bible bear this name (Gen. 16:15; I Chr. 8:38; II Chr. 19:11; II Kgs. 25:25 etc.). This is also a common name in the Hebrew epigraphic material and was recorded 20 times by Davies (1991:380) and once on an ostracon from Judah (Deutsch and Heltzer 1995, 77:2). The name occurs on two additional bullae in this group, nos. 82 and 100 below.

špn — Shapan, lit. "rabbit", is a Hebrew personal name. Names derived from animals such as this are common and are known from the Bible and from the Hebrew epigraphic material. Such names are: "Shuʿal" (fox), "ʿAkhbor" (mouse), (II Kgs. 22:12), "ʿOreb" (crow), (WSS 693) etc. The name "Shapan" is rare and it appears only once in the Bible. He is the son of ʾAṣalyahu the scribe (II Kgs. 22:3) and the father of ʾAḥiqam. ʾAṣalyahu was the man sent by Josiah the King to Ḥilqiyahu the high priest with the command to repair the "House of the Lord" (II Kgs. 22:3–6). Shapan the high priest received the Book, the Torah, found in the Temple by Ḥilqiyahu and brought it to the king (II Kgs. 22:8–9). The name Shapan is rare also in the Hebrew epigraphy and appears on a bulla from the City of David: *lgmryhw / bn špn* "Belonging to Gemaryahu son of Shapan" (Shoham 1994:57, no. 2; WSS 470), on the seal: *lšpn / pdyhw* "Belonging to Shapan (son of) Pedayahu" (Avigad 1989:12, no. 9; WSS 388) and on a burial inscription from Jerusalem (Prignaud 1978:136). Despite the rarity of the name, it appears on another four bullae in this group, nos. 25, 92–94.

57. Mi᾿amen (son of) Meshullam

A fragmentary bulla, with a small chip missing on the left side, made of white-grey clay and measuring 11.3x10.6 mm. The back of the bulla is convex. This fact points towards a different use of the bulla, probably as a receipt rather than to seal a document. This type of bullae were called "Fiscal bullae" by Avigad (1990:262). The inscription is divided between two registers by a double line and surrounded by a single circular border line.

The Hebrew inscription reads:

למיאמן / משל[ם]

lmy᾿mṅ / mšl[m]

"Belonging to Mi᾿amen (son of) Meshullam"

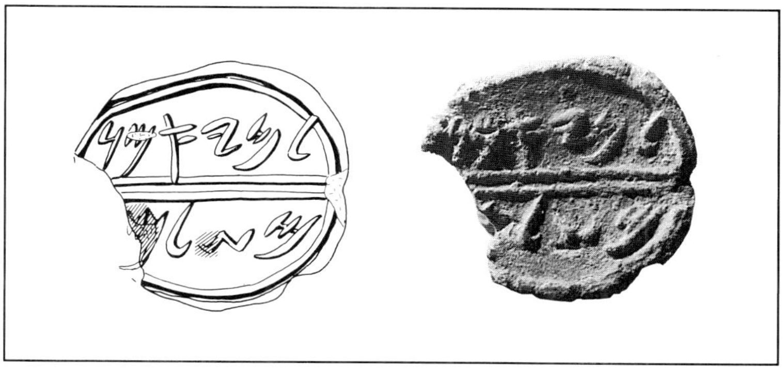

my᾿mn — Mi᾿amen is a Hebrew personal name, an interrogative deriving from the root "faith", "Who is faithful (to god Yahweh)", such as the names Micaiah or Michael (Avigad 1986:68), or simply "Faithful". Variants of the name are mentioned both in the Bible: *mymn* (Neh. 10:8) and in the Hebrew epigraphy, on the seal: *my᾿mn ..ʿdd* "Belonging to Mi᾿amen (son of) ..ʿ*dd*" (Hestrin and Dayagi-Mendels 1978, 94; WSS 228) and on four bullae: 1) *[lmʿ]śyhw my᾿mn* "Belonging to Maʿaśeyahu (son of) Mi᾿amen", 2) *[lm]y᾿mn [bn] ʿpy* "Belonging to Mi᾿amen son of ʿEpai" (Avigad 1986, 87, 88; WSS 647, 539), 3) *lyhw᾿l my᾿mn* "Belonging to Yeho᾿el (son of) Mi᾿amen" found at Lachish (Lachish V:21, 4; WSS 523), 4) *lmy᾿mn bnyhw* "Belonging to Mi᾿amen (son of) Benayahu" (Deutsch and Heltzer 1995, 60). The name appears on bulla no. 84 below and in its shortened form: *m᾿mn* on bulla no. 21 above.

mšlm — Meshullam is a Hebrew personal name of the verbal root *šlm* and probably means "One recompensed (by Yahweh)". The name is common in the Bible (Kimchi 1991:611–613) as well as in the Hebrew epigraphic material, and it is recorded 15 times by Davies (1991:435). The feminine form of the name is *mšlmt* "Meshullemet" and appears in the Bible (II Kgs. 21:19), on a

Hebrew seal (Avigad 1987:206; WSS 255) and on an ostracon from Judah (Deutsch and Heltzer 1995, 77:6). The name Meshullam occurs on another bulla in this group, no. 67 below.

58. Malyahu (son of) Neḥemyahu

A complete bulla made of dark brown clay, measuring 28.5x30.4 mm. The size of the impression is 13.5x11.1 mm. On the reverse of the bulla, the imprint of the texture of a fabric is visible. The script is divided into two registers by a double line and surrounded by a single circular border line. The letters are slightly worn but the reading is certain.

The Hebrew inscription reads:

לׄמליהו / נחמׄיׄהו

l̇mlyhw / nḥṁẏhw

"Belonging to Malyahu (son of) Neḥemyahu"

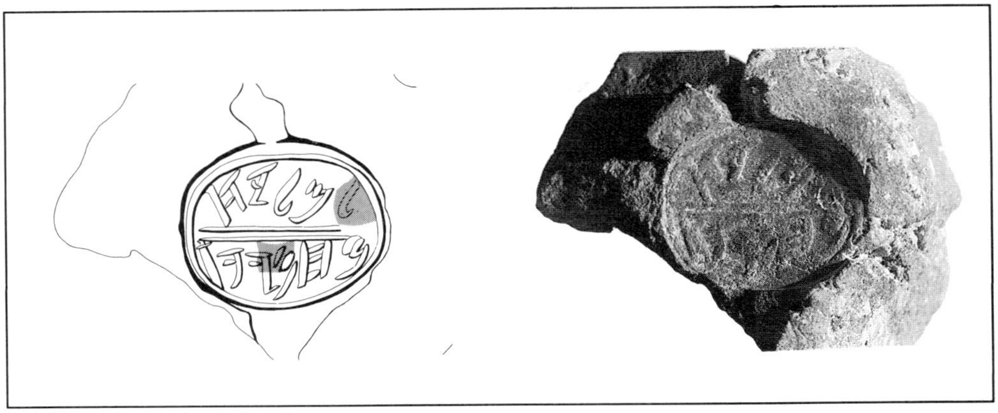

mlyhw — Malyahu is a Hebrew personal name apparently meaning "Yahweh circumcise". According to Avigad (1989:10), the element *ml* seems to represent the *qal* pf. 3m sq. of the root *mwl* "circumcise", which is used in the Bible also in the figurative sense. Thus Moses says to the people of Israel: "ומל יהוה אלהיך את לבבך ואת לבב זרעך לאהבה את יהוה ...". "And the Lord thy God will circumcise thy heart, and the heart of thy seed to love the Lord ..." (Deut. 30:6). Malyahu is a very rare name not found in the Bible and occurs on a single Hebrew seal from the Hecht Museum collection: *lmlyhw yhwšᶜ* "Belonging to Malyahu (son of) Yehoshuaᶜ" (Avigad 1989:9–10, no. 4; WSS 233).

nḥmyhw — Neḥemyahu is a Hebrew theophoric personal name meaning "My comfort is Yahweh". In the Bible it occurs in its shortened form *nḥmyh* (Neh. 1:1, 3:16; Ezra. 2:2). The name appears in the Hebrew epigraphic material on ostraca from Arad (Aharoni 1981, 25:5, 31:3, 36:1, 40:1, 59:3), on the seal: *lnḥmyhw bn mykyhw* "Belonging to Neḥemyahu son of Mikayahu" (Wright 1882:54, no. 1; WSS 265), on two bullae: 1) *lḥnnyhw nḥmyhw* "Belonging to Ḥananyahu (son of) Neḥemyahu" (Avigad, 1986, 61; WSS 506), 2) *lnḥmyhw* ... "Belonging to

Neḥemyahu ..." (no. 202 in the Borowsky collection, to by published by A. Lemaire, no. 19 in *Eretz Israel* 26, *F.M. Cross* Vol.[14]) and on another two bullae in our group, nos. 36 above and 65 below. The shortened form of the name, "Naḥum", appears on bulla no. 64 below.

59. Malkiyahu son of Yoᶜalyahu

A complete bulla made of brown-grey clay and measuring 16.1x16.0 mm. The back of the bulla is convex. This fact points towards a different use of the bulla, probably as a receipt rather than to seal a document. This type of bullae were called "Fiscal bullae" by Avigad (1990:262). The inscription is divided between two registers by a double lotus-bud motif and surrounded by a circular ladder-pattern frame.

The Hebrew inscription reads:

למלכיהו ב/ן יועליהו

lmlkyhw b/n ywᶜlyhw

"Belonging to Malkiyahu son of Yoᶜalyahu"

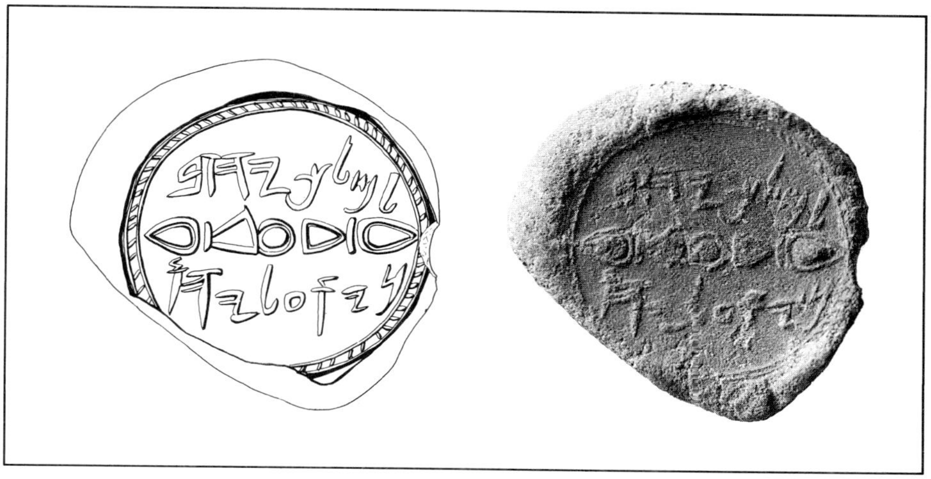

mlkyhw — Malkiyahu is a very common Hebrew theophoric personal name meaning "Yahweh is my King". 12 individuals bear this name in the Bible (Kimchi 1991:575–576) and it is recorded 18 times in the Hebrew epigraphic material (Davies 1991:426; Deutsch and Heltzer 1994, 20; 1977, 85, 86). The name appears in three other bullae in our group, nos. 33 above and 66a-b below.

ywᶜlyhw — Yoᶜalyahu is a Hebrew theophoric personal name literally meaning "Yahweh will be useful" and according to Lemaire (1985:29): "Yahweh is efficient". The name is missing from the Bible but is recorded five times in the Hebrew epigraphic material: on the seal: *lywᶜlyhw*

14. Lemaire suggest that this bulla and bulla no. 65 below are identical, and were sealed with the same seal.

yšmʿʾl "Belonging to Yoʿalyahu son of Yshmaʿʾel" (Lemaire 1985:29, no. 1; WSS 191), on the bulla: *lmlkyhw bn ywʿlyhw* "Belonging to Malkiyahu son of Yoʿalyahu" (Deutsch and Heltzer 1994:47 no. 20) and three times on two ostraca from Judah (Deutsch and Heltzer 1995, 78:1, 79:9, 16). The name appears on another bulla in our group, no. 52 above.

60. Maʿaśeyahu son of *ḥṣp...*

A damaged bulla made of light-brown clay, measuring 13.0x11.0 mm. The back of the bulla is pyramidal and covered with fingerprints. This fact points towards a different use of the bulla, probably as a receipt rather than to seal a document. The inscription is divided between two registers by a double line and surrounded by a single circular border line.

The Hebrew inscription reads:

למעשיהו / בן חצפ..

lmʿśyhw / bn ḥṣp...

"Belonging to Maʿaśeyahu son of *ḥṣp...*"

mʿśyhw — Maʿaśeyahu is a Hebrew theophoric personal name meaning "Creation of Yahweh". Several high officials in the Bible bear this name: The governor of the city (of Jerusalem), in the time of Josiah the king (II Chr. 34:8), an officer in the time of Uzziah the king (II Chr. 26:11), a military commander in the time of Athaliah the Queen (II Chr.23:1) and other officials (Kimchi 1991:588–9). The name is also common in the Hebrew epigraphic material and was recorded seven times in its full spelling and three times in two shortened forms: *mʿśyh* and *mʿśy* (Davies 1991:432). The name appears on another recently-published bulla: *lʾlšmʿ bn mʿśyhw* "Belonging to ʾElshamaʿ son of Maʿaśeyahu (Deutsch and Heltzer 1994, 19).

The patronym begins with three clearly visible letters: *ḥṣp...* but the restoration of the name is difficult. The name חֲצְפִית *ḥṣpyt* is known from the Second Temple period. This was the name of the "translator" to the ten Rabbinic martyrs of the Roman persecution (Kiddushin 39).

61a-b. **Miṣri (son of) Shebanyahu**

Two fragmentary bullae impressed by the same seal.

a. Made of light-brown clay, measuring 23.2x29.5 mm. On the back of the bulla, the imprint of a fabric is visible along with grooves where the cord ran. The upper part was damaged when it was still wet. The field is divided by a double horizontal line terminating in a short vertical line and dot.

b. Made of black clay, measuring 16.0x12.2 mm. On the back of the bulla, the imprint of papyrus is visible. On the upper edge fingerprints are preserved. Despite the fragmentary condition of the two bullae they enable us to reconstruct the entire inscription.

The Hebrew inscription reads:

a. **למׄצריׄ / שבניהו**
lṁṣrẏ / šbnyhw

b. **למצריׄ / [שבניהו]**
lmṣrẏ / [šbnyhw]
"Belonging to Miṣri (son of) Shebanyahu"

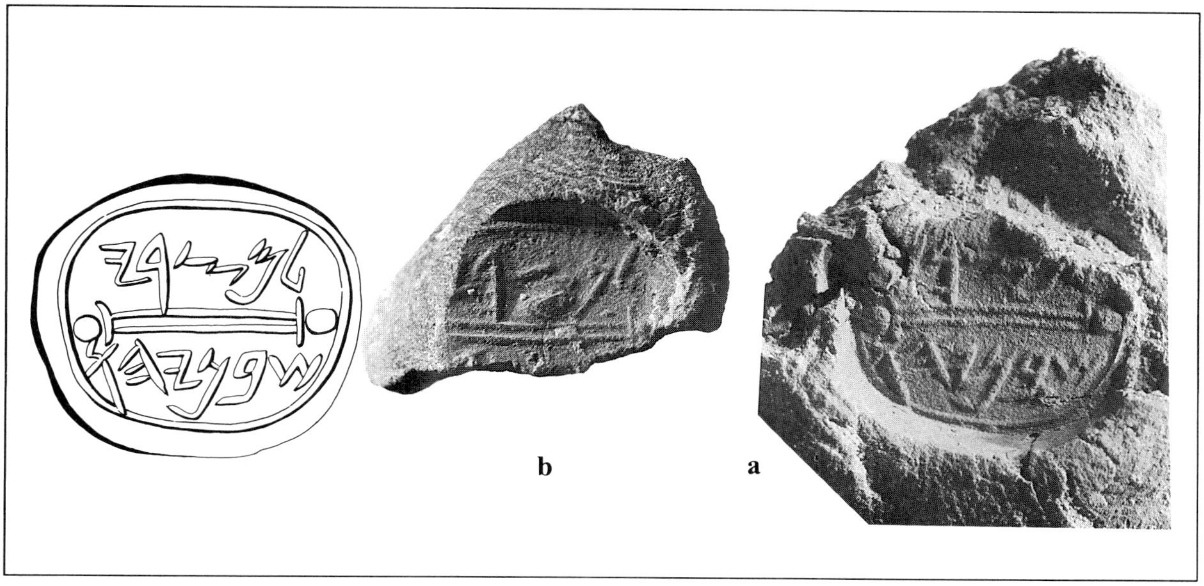

b a

mṣry — Miṣri is a rare personal name, literally meaning "My boundary". It is not found in the Bible. The name occurs in the unpublished epigraphic material from Kuntillet ʿAjrud (Zadok 1988:279, 72127:13) and on a Hebrew ostracon from Judah: *mṣry bn šknyhw* "Belonging to Miṣri son of Shekanyahu" (Deutsch and Heltzer 1995:92, 79:10). A shortened form of the name: *mṣr*, appears on the bulla: *mṣr bn šlm* "Belonging to Miṣr(i) son of Shallum" (Avigad 1986, 108; WSS 556 *mṣr[i] mšlm*?).

šbnyhw — Shebanyahu is a Hebrew theophoric personal name meaning "God Yahweh, return" (Avigad 1986:48, no. 49). The name appears in the Bible (I Chr. 15:24) and in the Hebrew epigraphy, where it is recorded 18 times by Davies (1991:490). This is also the name of ʿImmadiyahu's father which appears on her personal seal: "ʿImmadiyahu daughter of Shebanyahu" (Clermont-Ganneau 1902:264; WSS 41). The name also occurs on bullae no. 16 above and no. 85 below.

62. Mattanyahu (son of) ʾAmaryahu

A damaged bulla made of brown clay, with the lower left corner missing and measuring 18.5x21.5 mm. On the back of the bulla wooden fibres are visible. The field is divided into two registers by a double line and surrounded by a dotted double border line. The letters are of high calligraphic quality.

The inscription reads:

למתניהו / אמרי[הו]

lmtnyhẇ / ʾmry[hw]

"Belonging to Mattanyahu (son of) ʾAmaryahu"

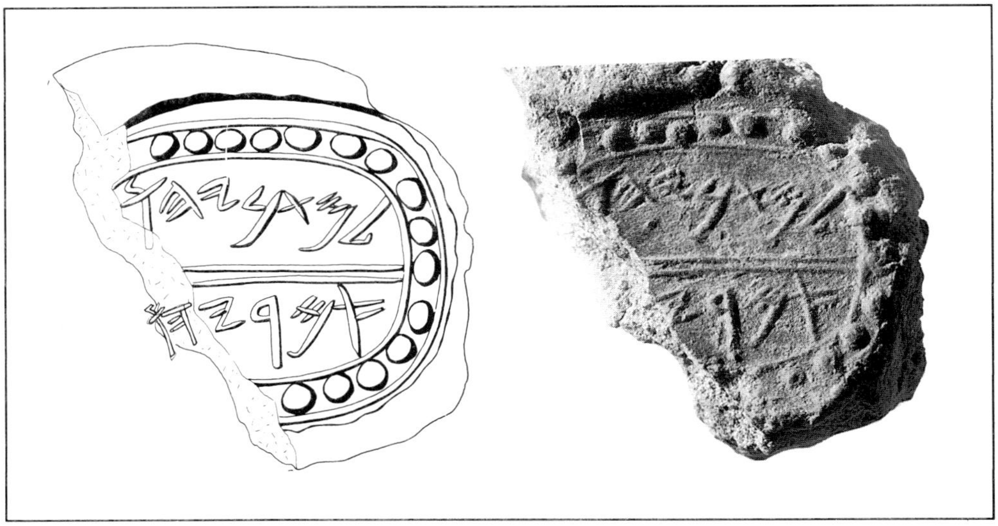

mtnyhw — Mattanyahu is a theophoric personal name meaning "Gift of the God Yahweh". It is a biblical name (I Chr. 25:4; II Chr. 29:13), which is also common in the Hebrew epigraphy. It is listed 11 times by Davies (1991:436–437) and appears on two other bullae in this chapter, nos. 22 and 63. The shortened form of the name: "Mattan", has been presented above (bullae nos. 15a-b).

ʾmryhw — ʾAmaryahu is a Hebrew theophoric personal name meaning "Yahweh established". This name and its shortened forms *ʾmry* and *ʾmryh* are common in the Bible (I Chr. 5:33; Ezra 10:42; Neh. 10:4). An official by the name ʾAmaryahu, in the time of Hezekiah was appointed by the king over the "freewill offerings of God" (II Chr. 31:14, 15). The Hebrew epigraphic material provide us with a seal: *lyšʿyhw ʾmryhw* "Belonging to Yeshaʿyahu (son of) ʾAmaryahu (Avigad 1963:324; WSS 212), with two identical bullae: *lʾmryhw bn yhwʾb* "Belonging to ʾAmaryahu son of Yehoʾab" (Avigad 1986, 31a-b; WSS 449a-b), with two graffiti from Beer-Sheba: *lnryhw lʾmryhw and lʾm[ryhw]* "Belonging to Neriyahu, Belonging to ʾAmaryahu" and "Belonging to ʾAmaryahu" (Beer-Sheba I:73, 74) and on several jar handles from Gibeon: *gbʿn gdr ʾmryhw* "Gibeon, Gdor, ʾAmaryahu" (Pritchard 1959, 3). The name occurs also on bullae nos. 35 and 45 above.

63. Mattanyahu son of ʾUriyahu

A complete bulla made of black clay, in a very good state of preservation, measuring 17.0x14.0 mm. On the back of the bulla the imprint of the texture of the papyrus to which the bulla was affixed is visible, along with a groove where the cord which tied the papyrus ran. Around the edges fingerprint are visible. The field is divided into two registers by a double line and surrounded by a groove which indicates that the seal was set in a metal bezel of a ring or a pendant. The letters are of high calligraphic quality.

The inscription reads:

למתניהו / בן אריהו
lmtnyhw / bn ʾryhw
"Belonging to Mattanyahu son of ʾUriyahu"

mtnyhw — Mattanyahu is a theophoric personal name meaning "Gift of the God Yahweh". For the name see bullae nos. 20 and 62 above. For the shortened form of the name: "Mattan" see bullae nos. 15a-b.

ʾryhw — ʾUriyahu is a Hebrew theophoric personal name meaning "My light is Yahweh". In the Bible it occurs in its full spelling *ʾwryhw* (Jer. 26:20) and in its shortened form *ʾwryh* (II Sam. 11:3; II Kgs. 16:10 etc.). The name, which is common in the Hebrew epigraphic material, was recorded nine times by Davies (1991:290) and appears on two other bullae in this chapter, nos. 23 and 37 above.

64. Naḥum son of *Mqmyhw*

A broken and glued bulla made of brown clay, measuring 21.0x22.8 mm. On the back of the bulla the imprint of the texture of the papyrus to which the bulla was affixed is visible, along with a groove where the cord which tied the papyrus ran. The upper edge was damaged while the bulla was wet. The field is divided into two registers by a dotted ladder-pattern and surrounded by a single lentoid border line which is visible only in the lower part. The letters are large and carelessly executed.

The inscription reads:

לנחם בן / מקמיהו
lnḥm bn / mqmyhw
"Belonging to Naḥum son of *mqmyhw*"

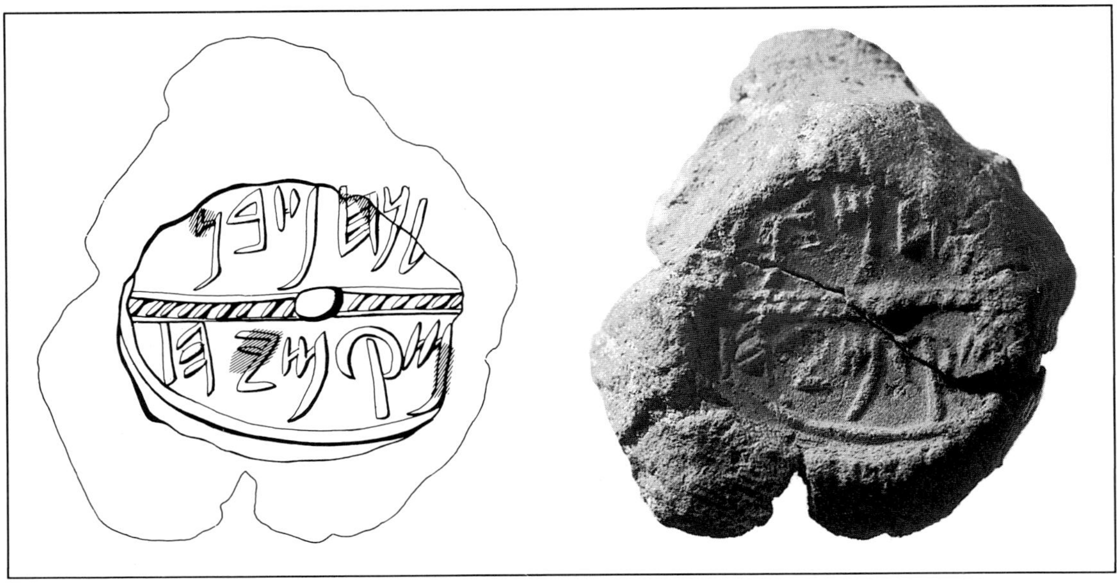

nḥm — Naḥum is a shortened form of the Hebrew personal name *nḥmyhw* "Neḥemyahu" meaning "Yahweh has comforted". The name Naḥum occurs only once in the Bible and is borne by the father of Keʿila the Garmite of the tribe of Judah (I Chr. 4:19). However, the name in its fuller spelling appears another three times: 1) Nehemiah the son of Hacaliah, governor of Judah (*hpḥh*) (Neh. 1:1, 5:14), who is the central figure in the book of Nehemiah in the Bible, 2) Neḥemyah the son of Azbuk, ruler of half the district of Beth-Zur (Neh. 3:16), 3) Neḥemyah, a leader of the Jewish community who returned with Zerubbabel from the Babylonian exile (Ezra 2:2). The name Naḥum is very common in the Hebrew epigraphic material and it is recorded 23 times, as well as seven times in its full spelling "Neḥemyahu" (Davies 1991:439–40). On three other bullae in this group we find the full spelling, nos. 36, 58 and 65.

mqmyhw — A Hebrew theophoric personal name hitherto unrecorded, meaning "Yahweh raises up". Similar reversed names are Jehoiakim and Eliakim.

65. Neḥemyahu (son of) Yeho'ab

A complete bulla made of grey clay, measuring 20.5x22.0 mm. The back of the bulla is conoid and it probably served as a stopper. The field is divided into three registers by two double lines and surrounded by a single circular border line. In the upper register a fish is depicted.[15] The inscription is divided between the two lower registers. The surface of the bullae was damaged while it was wet but the script is clearly visible.

The inscription reads:

לנחמיהו / יׄהואב

lnḥmyhw / ẏhw'b

"Belonging to Neḥemyahu (son of) Yeho'ab"[16]

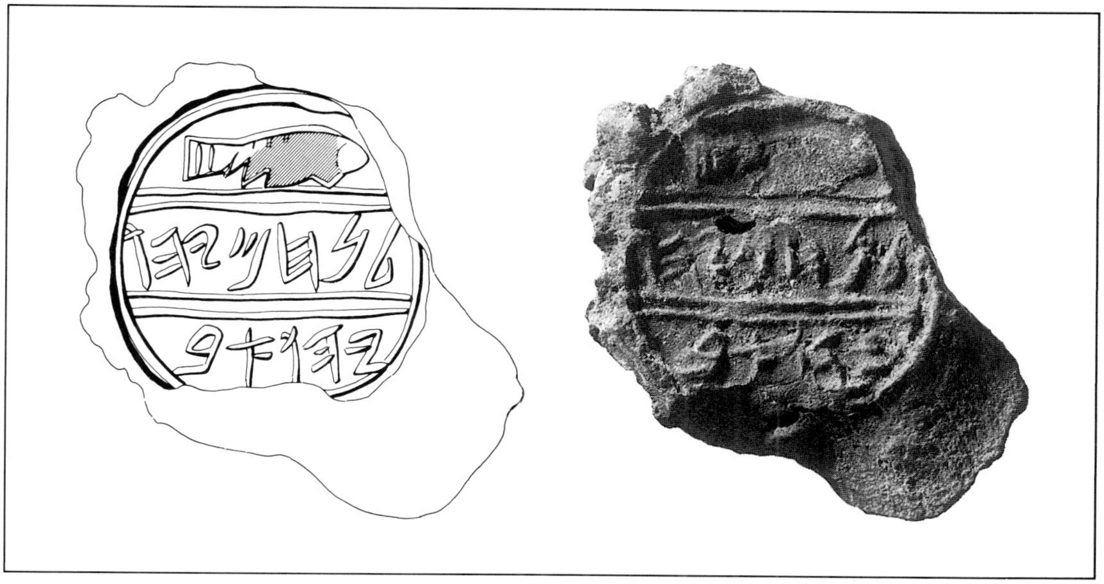

nḥmyhw — Neḥemyahu is a Hebrew theophoric personal name meaning "My comfort is Yahweh". In the Bible it occurs in its shortened form *nḥmyh* (Neh. 1:1, 3:16; Ezra 2:2). The name appears in the Hebrew epigraphic material on ostraca from Arad (Aharoni 1981, 25:5,

15. For similar iconography on Hebrew seals and bullae see: WSS 25, 35, 52, 215, 386, 553, 589.
16. Another bulla sealed with the same seal was acquired in 1995 on the Jerusalem antiquities market by a private collector from Tel Aviv. The bulla is damaged and the lower part is lost.

31:3, 36:1, 40:1, 59:3), on the seal: *lnḥmyhw bn mykyhw* "Belonging to Neḥemyahu son of Mikayahu" (Wright 1882:54, no. 1; WSS 265), on two bullae: 1) *lḥnnyhw nḥmyhw* "Belonging to Ḥananyahu (son of) Neḥemyahu" (Avigad 1986, 61; WSS 506), 2) *lnḥmyhw* ... "Belonging to Neḥemyahu ..." (no. 202 in the Borowsky collection, to by published by A. Lemaire, no. 19 in *Eretz Israel* 26, *F. M. Cross* Vol.)[17] and on other two bullae in our group, nos. 36 and 58 above. The shortened form of the name "Naḥum" appears on bulla no. 64 above.

yhw'b — Yeho'ab is a Hebrew theophoric personal name meaning "Yahweh is father". The name is missing in the Bible but is known from the Hebrew epigraphic material. It occurs on three ostraca from Arad: 1) *yhw'b bn ḥldy* "Yeho'ab son of Ḥeldai", 2) *yhw'b* "Yeho'ab", 3) *yhw'b bn* ... "Yeho'ab son of ..." (Aharoni 1981, 39:10, 49:9, 59:1), on the seal: *l'ḥmlk yhw'b* "Belonging to 'Ahimelek (son of) Yeho'ab" (Avigad 1989, 8; WSS 58), on four bullae, two from Jerusalem: 1) *l'lšmʿ bn yhw'b* "Belonging to 'Elishamaʿ son of Yeho'ab", 2) *l'ḥy'b bn yhw'b* "Belonging to 'Aḥi'ab son of Yeho'ab" (Shoham 1994:58, 18, 37; WSS 427, 447) and on two identical bullae (from the Tell Beit Mirsim area?): *[l]'mryhw bn yhw'b* "[Belonging to] 'Amaryahu son of Yeho'ab" (Avigad 1986, 31a-b; WSS 449a-b) and once again on bulla no. 49 above.

66a-b. Nera' (son of) Malkiyahu

Two identical bullae impressed by the same seal.

a. The first one is made of light-brown clay and measures 13.0.x13.5 mm. On the back the imprint of the texture of the papyrus to which the bulla was affixed is visible.

b. The second bulla is made of black clay and measures 15.4x12.8 mm. The reverse of this bulla is conoid and was probably used as a stopper. The Hebrew script is divided into two lines within an oval double line cartouche, surrounded by a chain of pomegranates, all enclosed by a framing border line. The surfaces of both bullae are slightly worn but the fusion of both scripts enables us to decipher the entire inscription.

b a

17. Lemaire suggest that this bulla and bulla no. 65 above are identical, and were sealed with the same seal.

The Hebrew inscription reads:

a) לנֿרא / מלכיהו
*lṅr*ʾ / *mlkyhw*

b) לנֿרא֗ / מלכֿיֿהוֿ
*lṅr*ʾ / *mlk̇ẏhẇ*
"Belonging to Neraʾ (son of) Malkiyahu"[18]

*nr*ʾ — Neraʾ is a shortened form of the Hebrew personal name Neriyahu meaning "Yahweh is my light". The name is rare and is not found in the Bible. It appears in the Hebrew epigraphic material impressed on several jar handles: *lnr*ʾ *šbn*ʾ "Belonging to Neraʾ (son of) Shebnaʾ" (WSS 686, 687), and engraved on 16 jar handles from Gibeon: *lḥnnyhw nr*ʾ "Belonging to Ḥananyahu (son of) Neraʾ" (Pritchard 1959:3–6). The name occurs also on the next bulla, no. 67.

mlkyhw — Malkiyahu is a very common Hebrew theophoric personal name meaning "Yahweh is my King". 12 individuals bear this name in the Bible (Kimchi 1991:575–576) and it is recorded 18 times in the Hebrew epigraphic material (Davies 1991:426; Deutsch and Heltzer 1994, 20; 1977, 85, 86). The name appears on two other bullae in our group, nos. 33 and 59 above.

Bulla no. 66a has been recently published erroneously in WSS (no. 583) as: "Belonging to Neriyahu, son of Malkiyahu".

67. Neraʾ son of Meshullam

A complete bulla made of black clay, measuring 14.5x16.5 mm. On the back of the bulla a groove is visible along with the imprint of the texture of the papyrus to which the bulla was affixed. The edges are covered with fingerprints. The field is divided into three registers by two double lines and surrounded by a single circular border line. In the upper register a schematic two-winged sun is depicted. The inscription is divided between the two lower registers. The lower part of the bulla was damaged while it was wet but the letters are clear.

The Hebrew inscription reads:

לנרא בנֿ / משלם
*lnr*ʾ *bṅ* / *mšlm*
"Belonging to Neraʾ son of Meshullam"

18. An additional two identical bullae are known to the author, one unpublished kept in a private collection in Tel-Aviv and the second in the private collection of Mr. L. Wolfe of Jerusalem (Deutsch and Heltzer 1997, 86).

*nr*ʾ — Neraʾ is a shortened form of the Hebrew personal name Neriyahu meaning "Yahweh is my light". The name is rare and is not found in the Bible. For parallels see the previous bullae, nos. 66a-b.

mšlm — Meshullam is a Hebrew personal name of the verbal root *šlm* and probably means "One recompensed (by Yahweh)". The name is common in the Bible (Kimchi 1991:611–613) as well as in the Hebrew epigraphic material, where it is recorded 15 times by Davies (1991:435). The feminine form of the name is *mšlmt* "Meshullemet" and appears in the Bible (II Kgs. 21:19), on a Hebrew seal (Avigad 1987:206; WSS 255) and on an ostracon from Judah (Deutsch and Heltzer 1995, 77:6). The name Meshullam occurs on another bulla in this group, no. 57 above.

68. Samakh (son of) Rapaʾ

A worn but complete bulla made of brown clay, measuring 13.5x16.2 mm. The back of the bulla is also worn and it possibly served to seal an artifact made of fabric. The inscription is divided between two registers by a single line and surrounded by a circular border line. The letters were damaged while the clay was still wet, yet they are easily decipherable.

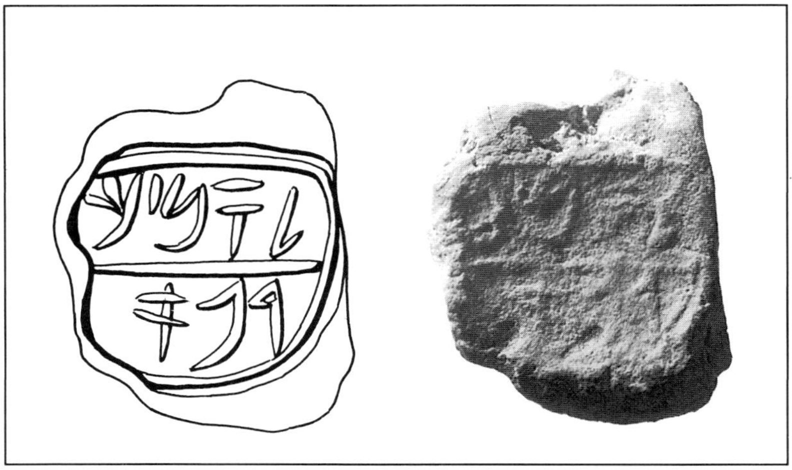

The Hebrew inscription reads:

לסמך / רפא

*lsmk / rp*ʾ

"Belonging to Samakh (son of) Rapaʾ"

smk — Samakh is a hypocoristicon of the Hebrew personal name Semakhyahu meaning "Yahweh has supported". The name occurs only once in the Bible in its full spelling, Semakhyahu son of Shemaʿyahu, who was an official listed among the gatekeepers at the temple in Jerusalem (I Chr. 26:7). The name is common in the Hebrew epigraphic material and was recorded eight times in its shortened form and 13 times in its fuller spellings: *smky*, *smkyh*, *smkyhw* and *smkyw* (Davies 1991:448-9). The name appears on the next bulla, no. 69 and as *smky* on bulla 96 below.

*rp*ʾ — Rapaʾ is a hypocoristicon of the Hebrew personal name Rapaʾyahu or Rephaeʾl meaning "God (Yahweh) has healed". In the Bible this is the name of the fifth son of Benjamin (I Chr. 8:2). The name is common in the Hebrew epigraphic material and was recorded seven times in its shortened form and three times in its full spelling: *rp*ʾ*yhw* (Davies 1991:487). The name occurs also in Aramaic on a 5th century B.C.E. bronze cymbal from Eliachin: *zy yhb rp*ʾ *lḥyy npšh l*ʿ*štrm* "This which Rapaʾ offered for the life of his soul to the ʿAshtars" (Deutsch and Heltzer 1994:73). The full spelled name: *rp*ʾ*yhw* occurs on bulla no. 94 below.

69. Samakh son of Shepaṭyahu

A complete bulla made of brown clay, measuring 12.5x10.6 mm. On the reverse of the bulla the imprint of the texture of the papyrus to which the bulla was affixed is visible, along with grooves where the cord which tied the papyrus ran. On the edges fingerprints are visible. The inscription is divided between two registers by three parallel lines and surrounded by a double circular border line. The left side of the surface of the bulla was slightly damaged while it was wet, yet all the letters are complete.

The Hebrew inscription reads:

לסמך בן / שפטיהו

lsmk bn / špṭyhw

"Belonging to Samakh son of Shepaṭyahu"

smk — Samakh is a hypocoristicon of the Hebrew personal name Semakhyahu meaning "Yahweh has supported". The name occurs only once in the Bible in its full spelling, Semakhyahu son of Shemaʿyahu, who was an official listed among the gatekeepers at the temple in Jerusalem (I Chr. 26:7). For parallels see the previous bulla, no. 68.

špṭyhw — Shepaṭyahu is a Hebrew theophoric personal name meaning "Yahweh has judged". 15 individuals bear this name in the Bible (Kimchi 1991:848–849, including shortened forms of the name), and it is recorded eleven times in the Hebrew epigraphic material (Davies 1991:504; Deutsch and Heltzer 1997, 102). The name in its shortened form: *špṭ* appears on two bullae in our group, nos. 49 and 91.

70. Saʿadyahu

A complete bulla made of light-brown clay, measuring 15.0x16.0 mm. The back of the bulla is of conoid shape. This indicates a use which is different than to seal a document and it probably served as a document itself, similar to a receipt. The field is divided into three registers by two double lines. In the upper and larger register a four-winged beetle is depicted. The inscription appears in the two lower registers. Around the seal impression, a deep groove is present indicating that the seal was set in a metal bezel, while it served to impress the bulla. Several letters were hidden under the bezel, therefore the beginning and the end of the owner's name, along with the patronym, are missing. However, the owner's name is easily restored based on the four letters.

The Hebrew inscription reads:

... / [ל[סֹעדי]הו]

[l]šʿdy[hw] / ...

"[Belonging to] Saʿadyahu ..."

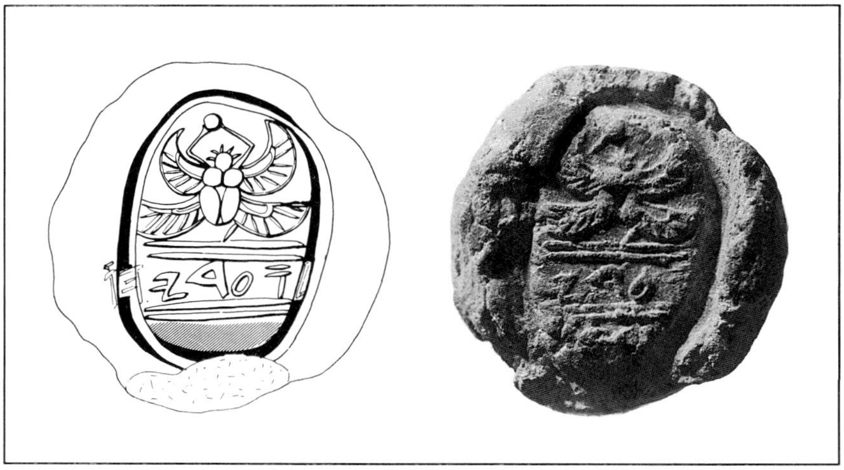

sᶜdyhw — Saᶜadyahu is a Hebrew theophoric personal name meaning "The support is Yahweh", probably based on the biblical verse: "When I said, 'My foot is slipping', your love, O Lord, supported me" (Ps. 94:18). The name is rare and is not found in the Bible. It appears on an ostracon from Arad (Aharoni 1981, 31:4)[19] and on two identical fragmentary bullae (probably from the Tell Beit Mirsim area): *lsᶜdyh[w b]n z...* "Belonging to Saᶜadyahu son of Z..." (Avigad 1986, 133; WSS 591a-b). The shortened forms of the name: *sᶜdyh and sᶜdh* occurs on two Hebrew seals: *sᶜdyh ʾlsmk* "Belonging to Saᶜadyah (son of) ʾElsamak" (Lemaire, 1985:30, no. 3; WSS 285) and *lsᶜdh* "Belonging to Saᶜadah" (Avigad 1989, 2; WSS 284).

71. ᶜObadyah (son of) Menaḥemo

A complete bulla made of light-brown clay, measuring 11.2x14.0 mm. The back of the bulla is convex. This points towards a different use of the bulla, probably as a receipt rather than to seal a document. This type of bullae was called "Fiscal bullae" by Avigad (1990:262). Another similar fiscal bulla belonged to: *ᶜzryhw šᶜr hmsgr* — "ᶜAzaryahu the gate-keeper of the prison" (Deutsch and Heltzer 1994:41, 14). The field is divided into two registers by a single line and surrounded by a circular border line. The letters are large and carelessly executed. The letter *dalet* is placed high in the center and a small redundant horizontal line appears in the middle.

The Hebrew inscription reads:

עבדיה / מנחמו

ᶜbdyh / mnḥmw

"(Belonging to) ᶜObadyah (son of) Menaḥemo"

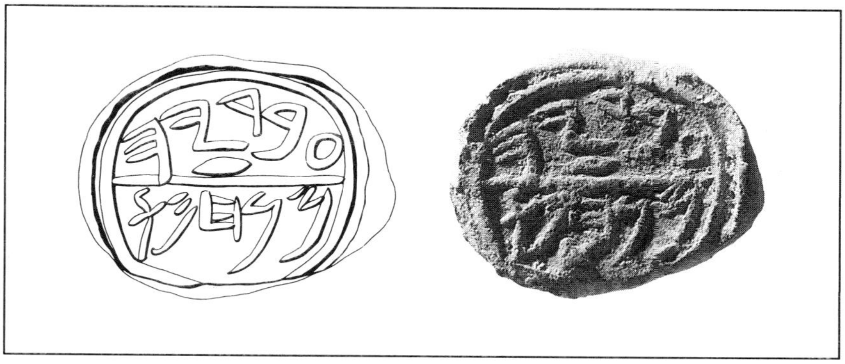

ᶜbdyh — ᶜObadyah is a shortened form of the Hebrew theophoric personal name "ᶜObadyahu" meaning "Servant of Yahweh". This was the name of one of the twelve minor prophets (The Book of ᶜObadiah). Another eleven individuals bear this name in the Bible (Kennedy 1992:1–2),

---

19. The original reading was *sᶜryhw* and the correct reading by F.M. Cross to *sᶜdyhw* was not accepted by Aharoni (1981:58, Cross misspelled as Kraus). The letter in question is clearly a *dalet* based on the upper horizontal line which protruding at the right side. Moreover, the letter *dalet* with such a cursive curving leg is similar to the letter *dalet* which appears on another ostracon from Judah (Deutsch and Heltzer 1995:82, 76:3).

including an official "who is over the house" in the time of Ahab the king of Israel (I Chr. 18:3). The name is common in the Hebrew epigraphic material and was recorded 12 times by Davies (1991:454), and in its full spelling on an ostracon from Judah (Deutsch and Heltzer 1995:92, 79:9). In the group presented here it appears again on the next bulla, no. 72 below.

mnḥmw — Menaḥemo is a Hebrew personal name, hitherto unrecorded in this form in the Hebrew epigraphic material. Similar names are: Menaḥem, Menaḥemet, Neḥemiah and Tanḥumet, with the general meaning "To comfort".

A second yet less probable reading, based on a possible scribal error where the letter *waw* at the end of the lower register belongs in fact to the end of the upper register, will be: *ʿbdyh/w mnḥm* "(Belonging to) ʿObadyahu (son of) Menaḥem", names which basically have the same meaning.

72. ʿObadyahu son of ʾAḥʾab

A fragmentary bulla made of clay.[20] The field is divided into two registers by a double line and surrounded by a single circular border line. The letters are large and carelessly executed.

The Hebrew inscription reads:

לעבד̇[יהו] / בן אחא̇[ב]
lʿbḋ[yhw] / bn ʾḥʾ̇[b]
"Belonging to ʿObadyahu son of ʾAḥʾab"

20. The bulla was lost and the author examined only the specified picture. The color of the clay, the size and the features of the back of the bulla are unknown.

ʿbdyhw — ʿObadyahu is a Hebrew theophoric personal name meaning "Servant of Yahweh". This was the name of one of the twelve minor prophets (The Book of Obadiah). For a shortened form of the name and parallels see the previous bulla, no. 71.

ʾḥʾb — ʾAḥʾab is a Hebrew theophoric personal name meaning "The Brother (which is a divine epithet of the God), is the father". ʾAḥʾab is the name of the seventh king of Israel, the son and successor of ʿOmri in the 9th century B.C.E. (I Kgs. 16:28). Another biblical figure bearing this name is ʾAḥʾab son of Kolaiah, who was condemned by Jeremiah for prophesying false things in the Babylonian exilic period (Jer. 29:21–23). The name is very common in the Hebrew epigraphy. It appears on seven bullae (Avigad 1986, 16–19, 60), on a seal found in Lachish: *lšbnʾ (bn) ʾḥʾb* "Belonging to Shebnʾa (son of) ʾAḥʾab" (Lachish III:348, no. 171; WSS 350), on another seal found at Tell eṣ-Ṣafi: *lyhwʿz ʾḥʾb* "Belonging to Yehoʿaz (son of) ʾAḥʾab" (WSS 178), and on a seal in the Hecht Museum: *lmtn (bn) ʾḥʾb* "Belonging to Mattan (son of) ʾAḥʾab" (Avigad 1989:10, no. 5; WSS 257). In addition, the name is incised on a handle found at Tell el-Ḥamme (Gophna and Porat 1972:214). The name ʾAḥʾab occurs on three other bullae in this chapter, nos. 18a-b and 19 above.

73. ʿEzer (son of) ʾAḥʾa

A broken and glued bulla made of light-brown clay and measuring 18.8x16.2 mm. On the back of the bulla the impressions of fabric fibres are visible. The surface is worn and was damaged, probably while the bulla was wet. The field is divided into two registers by a ladder-type divider and surrounded by a double circular border line.

The Hebrew inscription reads:

לעזר׳ / אחא׳

lʿzr̊ / ʾḥʾ

"Belonging to ʿEzer (son of) ʾAḥʾa"

ʿzr — ʿEzer is a hypocoristicon (shortened form), of the Hebrew personal name ʿAzriʾel or ʿAzaryahu meaning "Yahweh is my help". This name and its shortened forms are very common in the Bible (Kimchi 1991:687–8, 692–5) and in the Hebrew epigraphic material. It was recorded 19 times by Davies (1991:458), three times by Deutsch and Heltzer (1994, 24, 77:3; 1995, 56), and it appears on bulla no. 34 above. The name in its full spelling occurs also on bullae nos. 3, 10 above and 74 below.

ʾḥʾ — ʾAḥʾa is a shortened form of the Hebrew theophoric personal name ʾAḥiyahu or Yehoʾaḥ, both meaning "Yahweh is my brother". The name is not found in the Bible but is common in the Hebrew epigraphic material. It appears on six identical seal impressions on jar handles: *lšlm / ʾḥʾ* "(Belonging to) Shallum (son of) ʾAḥʾa" (WSS 705a-f), on two bullae from Jerusalem: *lḥnnyhw bn ʾḥʾ* "Belonging to Ḥananyahu son of ʾAḥʾa" and *lʿzryhw bn ʾḥʾ* "Belonging to ʿAzaryahu son of ʾAḥʾa", which is similar to our bulla (Shoham 1994:58, nos. 34, 42; WSS 503, 595 *lʿzryh[w] / bn ʾ*...) and on three ostraca from Arad (Aharoni 1981, 49:16, 67:4, 74:2). The name is also found on two recently-published Phoenician bronze arrowheads from the 11th century B.C.E. (Deutsch and Heltzer 1995:21–23).

74. ʿAzaryahu (son of) ...ʿaz

A worn but intact bulla made of grey clay and measuring 15.0x13.2 mm. The inscription is divided between two registers by a double line and surrounded by a single circular border line which is only partly visible. From the patronym only the last two letters have survived.

The Hebrew inscription reads:

לעזריהו / ...עז

lʿzryhẘ / ...ʿż

"Belonging to ʿAzaryahu (son of) ...ʿaz"

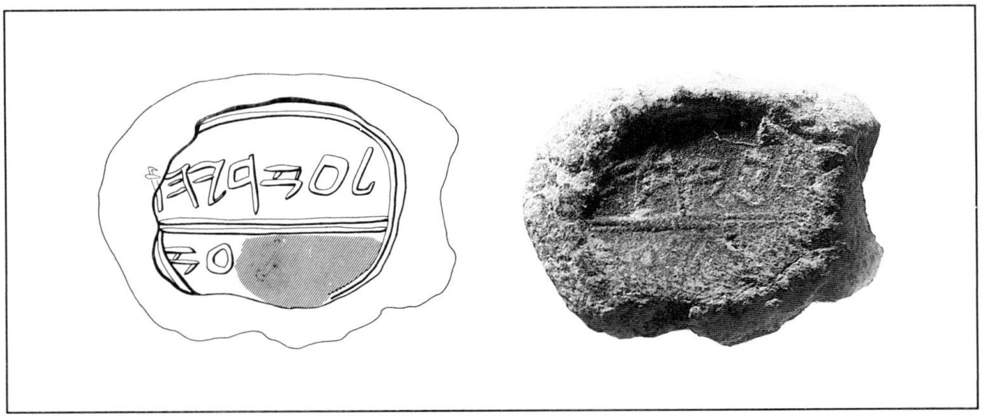

ʿzryhw — ʿAzaryahu is a Hebrew theophoric personal name meaning "Yahweh has helped". This is the name of one of the Judean kings: "ʿAzaryah the son of ʾAmazyah and Yekholyahu the Jerusalemite" (II Kgs. 15:1). "ʿAzaryah" and "ʿAzaryahu" are the names of other biblical high officials: "ʿAzaryah son of Yeroham, captain of hundreds" (II Chr. 23:1), "ʿAzaryah the son of Yohanan, priest in the House built by Solomon in Jerusalem" (I Chr. 5:36), "ʿAzaryah the son of Ḥilqiyyah, the ruler of the house of God" (I Chr. 9:11), "ʿAzaryah the son of Zadok the priest, high official in the time of Solomon (I Kgs. 4:2), "ʿAzaryahu the son of Natan, who was over the officers" (I Kgs. 4:5), "ʿAzaryahu the son of ʿOded, the prophet" (II Chr. 15:1), "ʿAzaryahu the son of ʿOved, captain of hundreds" (II Chr. 23:1), "ʿAzaryahu the high priest" (II Chr. 26:17), "ʿAzaryahu the chief priest" (II Chr. 31:10), as well as two sons of kings: "ʿAzaryah the son of king Yehoshafat" (II Chr. 21:2) and "ʿAzaryah the son of king Yoram" (II Chr. 22:6). ʿAzaryahu is also the name of the "gate keeper of the prison", as it is known from his bulla (Deutsch and Heltzer 1994, 41). The name is one of the most frequent names in the Hebrew epigraphy and has been recorded thirty times by Davies (1991:459). It appears also on bullae nos. 3 and 10 (above).

The damaged patronym is to be restored as: *(yhw)ʿz* "Yehoʿaz", but other names such as *(ʾl)ʿz* "ʾEliʿaz" or *(ʾly)ʿz* ʾElyʿaz" are also to be considered. All three versions have the same meaning: "My God (Yahweh) is my strength". The name Yehoʿaz is found in the Bible only in its reversed version: *ʿzyhw* (I Chr. 27:25) or in its shortened reversed version *ʿzyh* which was the name of the king of Judah: ʾUzziah son of Amaziah (II Kgs. 15:1, 2, 13, 32) and of other three persons (I Chr. 6:9; Ezra 10:21; Neh. 11:4). Also the names ʾEliʿaz and ʾElyʿaz are found in the Bible only in their reversed versions (Exod. 6:18; I Chr. 4:42, 7:7, 25:4; II Chr. 29:14; Neh. 3:8). The element *ʿz* which means "strength, courage" appears also in Ammonite and Phoenician names such as *mlkmʿz* and *ʿštrʿz* (Bordreuil 1986, nos. 17, 84) and in Moabite *kmšʿz* (Avigad 1992). The name Yehoʿaz is known from the Hebrew epigraphic material and it appears twice on ostraca from Arad (Aharoni 1981, 31:3, 49:7), on a glass seal from Tell eṣ-Ṣafi: *yhwʿz ʾḥʾb* "Belonging to Yehoʿaz (son of) ʾAḥʾab" (Reifenberg 1942:109, no. 2; WSS 178) and on two identical bullae (from the Tell Beit Mirsim area?): *yhwʿz bn mtn* "Belonging to Yehoʿaz son of Mattan" (Avigad 1986, 74a-b; WSS 525a-b). The name Yehoʿaz appears on bullae nos. 50a-b above.

75. ʿAzryqam son of Mikay

A complete bulla made of brown clay, measuring 13.2x10.9 mm. On the back of the bulla the imprint of the texture of the papyrus to which the bulla was affixed is visible, along with a groove where the cord which tied the papyrus document ran. The field is divided into two registers by a double line and surrounded by a single circular border line which is visible only on the left edge. The right edge is damaged but the reading is certain.

The Hebrew inscription reads:

[ל]עזריקם / בן מכי

[l]ʿzryqm / bn mky

"Belonging to ʿAzryqam son of Mikay"

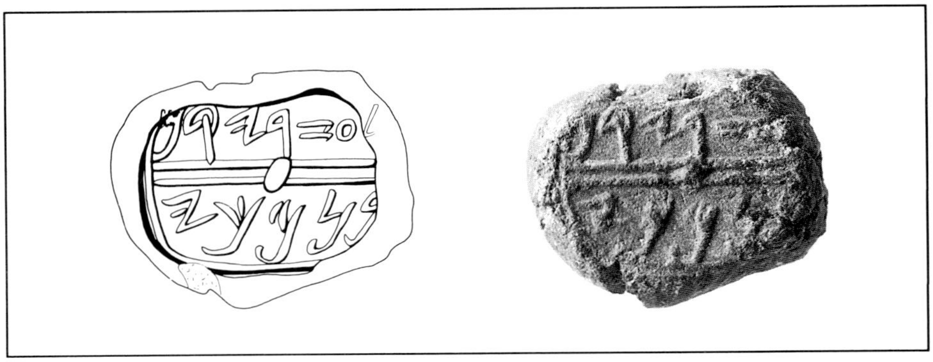

ʿzryqm — ʿAzryqam is a Hebrew personal name meaning "My (Divine) help has arisen". Four individuals bear this name in the Bible (I Chr. 3:23, 8:38, 9:14), among them a state official, "steward of the royal palace" of Ahaz king of Judah, in the second half of the 8th century B.C.E. (II Chr. 28:7), mentioned without his father's name. In the Hebrew epigraphic material the name (in its defective spelling *ʿzrqm*) is found on three bullae, one from the city of David in Jerusalem: *lʿzrqm mkyhw* "Belonging to ʿAzriqam (son of) Mikayahu" (Shoham 1994, 32; WSS 599), which is similar to our bulla, and two with no provenance: 1) *lʿzrqm bn prpr* "Belonging to ʿAzriqam son of Parpar", 2) *lʿzrqm [bn] ṣdqʾ* "Belonging to ʿAzriqam son of Ṣidqʾa" (Avigad 1986, 138, 139; WSS 600, 601). The name occurs also on bulla no. 83 and in the defective spelling: *ʿzrqm* on bulla no. 93 below.

mky — Mikay is a shortened form of the Hebrew theophoric personal name *mkyhw* meaning "Who is like God Yahweh". The name is attested only once in the Bible as the father of Geuel, the representative of the tribe of Gad, who was one of the twelve individuals sent to spy out the land of Canaan (Num. 13:15). In the Hebrew epigraphic material the name appears on two seals: *lšʿl bn mky* "Belonging to Shuʿal son of Mikay" (Deutsch and Heltzer 1994, 25), and *mky yqmyh* "Belonging to Mikay (son of) Yeqamyah" (Hestrin and Dayagi-Mendels 1978, 84; WSS 229), on two ostraca, one from Ḥorvat ʿUza: *mky bn hṣlyhw mmqdh* "Mikay son of Hiṣṣilyahu from Maqedah" (Beit-Arieh 1986–7:32) and one from Arad: *mky nʿr gdlyh* "Mikay steward of Gedalyah" (Rainey 1981, 110:2). The name is also known from Elephantine in the Persian period (Kornfeld 1978, 58).

76a-c. ʿAkbor son of Palṭi"

Three identical bullae made of brown clay, measuring: a) 15.5x28.6, b) 21.3x19.0, c) 25.0x20.5 mm. On the back of all three bullae imprints of wooden fibres are visible and apparently they were used to seal a box-like object. On the edges of the bullae fingerprints are visible. The field is divided into two registers by a dotted double line and surrounded by a single framing border line. The letters are large and carelessly executed.

The Hebrew inscription reads:

a. **לעכבר ב/ן פלטי**

lʿkbr b/n plṭy

b. לעכבר [ב]/ן פלטי
lᶜkbr [b]/n plṭẏ

c. לעכ̇בר ב/ן̇ פל̇[טי]
lᶜk̇br b/ṅ pl̇[ṭy]
"Belonging to ᶜAkbor son of Palṭi"

ᶜkbr — ᶜAkbor, lit. "mouse" is a Hebrew personal name given after this rodent. Names such as this derived from animals are common and are known from the Bible and from the Hebrew epigraphic material. Such names are: "Shapan" (rabbit), "Shuʿal" (fox), "Ḥagab" (grasshopper) etc.[21] The name occurs only once in the Bible in its full spelling *ʿkbwr*. "Achbor son of Micaiah" is mentioned as a courtier of King Josiah who, after the book of the law was found, was sent as part of a royal delegation to inquire of Huldah the prophetess concerning the words of this book (II Kgs. 22:11–20). His son Elnathan was a high official in the administration of King Jehoiakim (Jer. 36:12). The name is more common in the Hebrew epigraphic material and it appears on two identical bullae: *lʿkbr bn ṣpnyhw* "Belonging to ʿAkbor son of Ṣefanyahu (Avigad 1986, 140; Deutsch and Heltzer 1995:50, no. 55),[22] on two seals: 1) *lḥnnyhw bn ʿkbr* "Belonging to Ḥananyahu son of ʿAkbor" (Diringer 1934:185, no. 25; WSS 166), 2) *ʿkbr ʾḥqm* "(Belonging to) ʿAkbor (son of) Aḥiqam" (Avigad 1963:322, Pl.34:C; WSS 312) and on an ostracon from Judah: *lnḥmyhw bn ʿkbr* "Belonging to Neḥemyahu son of ʿAkbor" (Deutsch and Heltzer 1995:92, 79:11).

plṭy — Palṭi is a shortened form of the Hebrew personal name *plṭyhw* "Pelaṭyahu", meaning "Yahweh has rescued". The name is common in the Bible and is found in its full spelling as well as in its shortened versions: *plṭ*, *plṭy*, *plṭyh* and *plṭyhw* (I Chr. 2:47, 3:21; I Sam. 25:44 etc.). The name is also very common in the Hebrew epigraphic material and was recorded 20 times in its full spelling and three times in its shortened form *plṭh* (Davies 1991:471–472; Deutsch and Heltzer 1995, 57; DHL, 8, no. A34[23]). For the fully-spelled name see also bullae nos. 79–81 below. The thermoluminescence analysis report for bulla 76c is shown on plate XIV.

77. ʿAliyahu son of Hiṣṣilyahu

A complete bulla made of brown clay, measuring 16.3x12.3 mm. On the reverse of the bulla, the imprint of the texture of the papyrus to which the bulla was affixed is visible, along with grooves where the cord which tied the papyrus ran. On the upper edge finger prints are visible. The field is divided into two registers by a double line and is surrounded by a border line which survives only on the lower edge.

The Hebrew inscription read:

לעליהו בן / הצליהו

lʿlyhw bn / hṣlyhw

"Belonging to ʿAliyahu son of Hiṣṣilyahu"

---

21. See also bullae nos. 25, 34, 38, 45, 56, 92, 93, 94.

22. The bulla published by Avigad (1986, no. 140), is fragmentary and only four letter survived: *lʿkb*, yet, the inscription is to be completed based on the second intact bulla published by Deutsch and Heltzer (1995, 55), due to the fact that both bullae were impressed by the same seal.

23. See the bulla *lʿmdy.. bt pltyh* in the Samel collection (DHL A34). There the reading of the word *bt* (daughter) instead of the word *bn* (son), is based on the upper part of the damaged letter *nun* as *taw*. Therefore, the correct reading should be *lʿmdy[hw] bn pltyh[w]*.

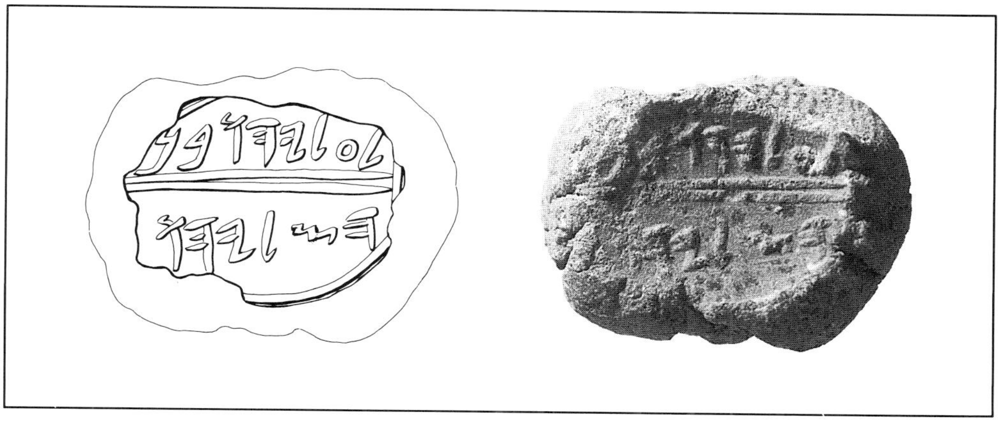

ʿlyhw — ʿAliyahu is a Hebrew theophoric personal name meaning "Yahweh is exalted". The name is found in the Bible only in its shortened form *ʿly*. ʿEli was a priest of the Lord at Shiloh (I Sam. 1:3). The name is also rare in the Hebrew epigraphic material and is known on only three bullae published by Avigad: 1) *lbnyhw ʿlyhw* "Belonging to Benayahu (son of) ʿAliyahu", 2) *lʿlyhw rpʾ* "Belonging to ʿAliyahu (son of) Raphʾa", 3) *lʿlyhw hlṣ* "Belonging to ʿAliyahu (son of) Heleṣ" (Avigad 1986, 35, 141, 142; WSS 460, 603, 604). The Israelite form of the name with the *yw* theophoric suffix is found on the seal: *lʿlyw* "Belonging to ʿAlayau" (Avigad 1987, note 18; WSS 313).

hṣlyhw — Hiṣṣilyahu is a Hebrew theophoric personal name meaning "Yahweh rescued". The name is not found in the Bible but is common in the Hebrew epigraphic material. It occurs on three ostraca, one from Lachish: *gmryhw bn hṣlyhw* "Gamaryahu son of Hiṣṣilyahu" (Lachish III, 1:1), the second from Ḥorvat ʿUza: *mky bn hṣlyhw mmqdh* "Mikay son of Hiṣṣilyahu from Maqedah" (Beit-Arieh 1986–7), and the third from Judah: *hṣlyhw bn bnyhw* "Hiṣṣilyahu son of Benayahu" (Deutsch and Heltzer 1995, 79:18). The name appears on several handles from Gibeon: *lnḥm hṣlyhw* "Belonging to Naḥum son of Hiṣṣilyahu" (Pritchard 1959:27), it is common on seals and bullae (Davies, 1991:336) and it occurs in its shortened form on bulla no. 43 above.

78. ʿAśayahu (son of) Shebnʾa

A fragmentary bulla made of light-brown clay, measuring 15.1x12.3 mm. On the back of the bulla the impression of wooden fibres is visible. The field is divided into two registers by a double line and is surrounded by dots. Despite the missing parts the entire inscription has been preserved except for the upper half of the letter *waw*.

The Hebrew inscription reads:

לעשיהו / שבנא

lʿśyhẇ / šbnʾ

"Belonging to ʿAśayahu (son of) Shebnʾa"

ʿśyhw — ʿAśayahu is a Hebrew theophoric personal name meaning "Yahweh created". The name is found in the Bible in its shortened form *ʿśyh* "ʿAśayah" (I Chr. 4:36, 6:15, 9:5; II Kgs. 22:12). The name is very common in the Hebrew epigraphic material and was recorded eight times by Davies (1991:466), and three times by Deutsch and Heltzer: on a seal of a high official: *lʿśyhw ʿbd hmlk* "Belonging to ʿAśayahu, servant of the king" (1994:50, no. 21), and on two ostraca from Judah: 1) *ʿśyhw bn ʾlnr* "ʿAśayahu son of ʾElinur", 2) *ʿśyhw hgzh* "ʿAśayahu the shearer" (1995:83, 77:1).

šbnʾ — Shebnʾa is a hypocoristicon of the Hebrew theophoric personal name *šbnyhw* meaning "Pray, God (Yahweh) return". The name is known from the Bible (Isa. 22:15) and from the Hebrew epigraphic material. It appears on several jar handles from the end of the eight century B.C.E.: *lšwky šbnʾ* "Belonging to *šwky* (son of) Shebnʾa" (Vaughn 1996:275; WSS 704a-b), *šbnʾ šḥr* "Belonging to Shebnʾa (son of) Shaḥar", *lnrʾ šbnʾ* "Belonging to Nerʾa (son of) Shebnʾa" (WSS 686, 687, 701) and on two seals, one from Lachish: *lšbnʾ ʾḥʾb* "Belonging to Shebnaʾ (son of) ʾAḥʾab" (Lachish, III:348, 171; WSS 350) and one without provenance: *šbnʾ* "(Belonging to) Shebnaʾ" (Avigad 1954:147, 1; WSS 349). The name appears on another bulla in this group, no. 52 above.

79. Pelaṭyahu (son of) Shekanyahu

A worn and damaged bulla made of grey clay, measuring 24.5x17.8 mm. On the back of the bulla an imprint of fabric fibres is visible. The inscription is divided between two registers by a double line and surrounded by a single framing border line visible on the upper part. Despite the poor condition of the bulla the reading is certain.

The Hebrew inscription reads:

לפלטיה[ו] / שכ[ניהו]

lplṭyh[w] / šk[nyhw]

"Belonging to Pelaṭyahu (son of) Shekanyahu"

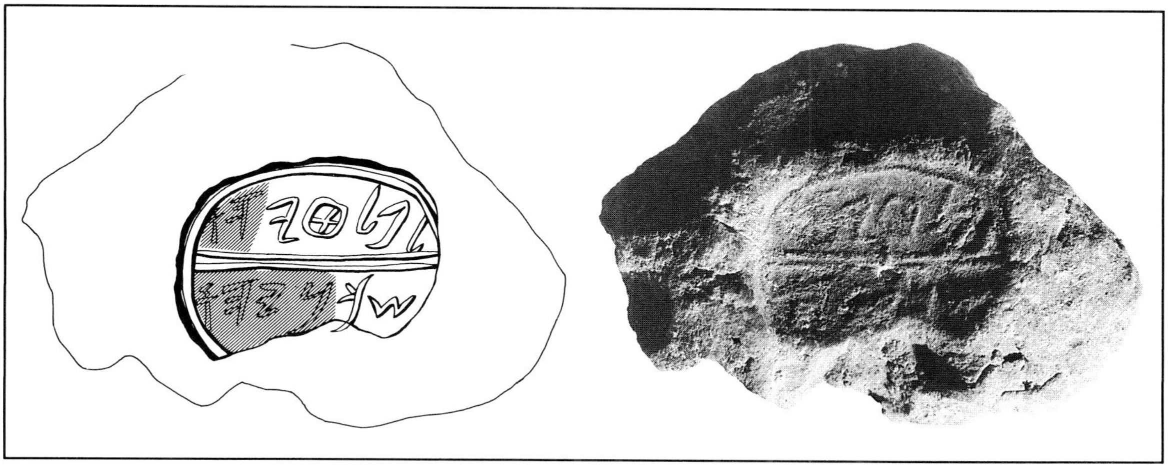

plṭyhw — Pelaṭyahu is a Hebrew personal name meaning "Yahweh has rescued". The name is common in the Bible and is found in its full spelling as well as in its shortened versions: *plṭ*, *plṭy*, *plṭyh* and *plṭyhw* (I Chr. 2:47, 3:21; I Sam. 25:44, etc.). The name is also very common in the Hebrew epigraphic material and was recorded 20 times in its full spelling and three times in its shortened form *plṭh* (Davies 1991:471–472; Deutsch and Heltzer 1995, 57; DHL, 8, no. A34, and see note no. 20 with bulla no. 76 above). The name also appears on the next two bullae, nos. 80–81 below and in its shortened form *plṭy* on bullae nos. 76a-c above.

šknyhw — Shekanyahu is a Hebrew theophoric personal name meaning "Yahweh dwells (with us)". Seven individuals bear this name in the Bible (Fuller 1992:1173–1174), including an high official in charge of apportioning the freewill offerings during the reign of Hezekiah, king of Judah (II Chr. 31:15). The name is rare in the Hebrew epigraphic material and it is recorded in the above mentioned identical bulla (Deutsch and Heltzer 1994, 16), on another bulla from the Hecht Museum collection: *lšknyhw bn gmr* — "Belonging to Shekanyahu son of Gomer" (AHL, 39), on a seal: *lšknyhw ḥylʾ* — "Belonging to Shekanyahu (son of) Ḥilʾa" (Avigad 1975:67, no. 4), and on an ostracon from Judah: *mṣry bn šknyhw* — "Miṣry son of Shekanyahu" (Deutsch and Heltzer 1995:92, 79:10). The name occurs also on bulla no. 86 below.

80. Pelaṭyahu (son of) ..l..yahu

A complete bulla made of black clay and measuring 18.0x13.6 mm. On the back of the bulla an imprint of papyrus fibres is visible. On the left edge fingerprints are preserved. The inscription is divided between two registers by a double line and surrounded by a single framing border line visible mainly on the upper part. The lower register is damaged.

The Hebrew inscription reads:

לפלטיהו / ..ל..יהו

lplṭyhw / ..l..yhw

"Belonging to Pelaṭyahu (son of) .. l..yahu"

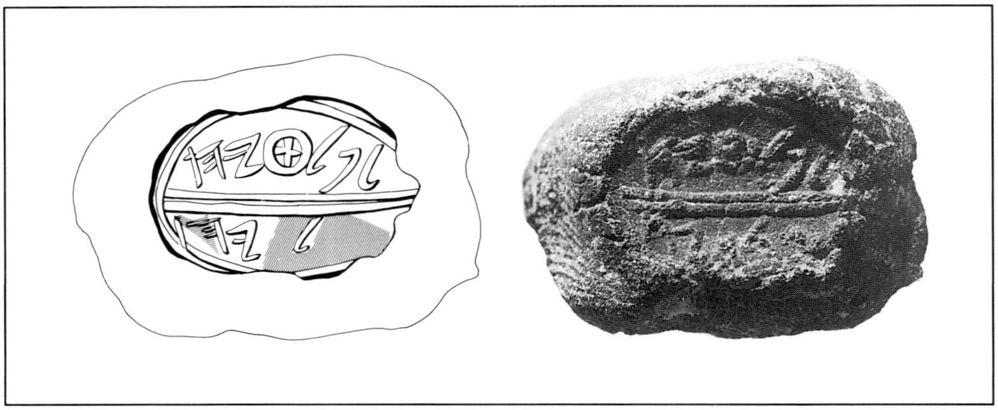

plṭyhw — Pelaṭyahu is a Hebrew personal name meaning "Yahweh has rescued". The name is common in the Bible and is found in its full spelling as well as in its shortened versions: *plṭ*, *plṭy*, *plṭyh* and *plṭyhw* (I Chr. 2:47, 3:21; I Sam. 25:44, etc.). For parallels see the previous bulla, no. 79. The name also appears on the next bulla, no. 81 below and in its shortened form *plṭy* on bullae nos. 76a-c above.

In the lower register only the four letters: *..l..yhw* are certain, therefore there are several possibilities for reconstructing the patronym, such as: *ḥlqyhw*, *šlmyhw*, *mlkyhw*, *ḥlṣyhw* or *plṭyhw*.

81. Pelaṭyahu (son of) ...

A damaged bulla made of brown clay, measuring 16.3x12.6 mm. On the back of the bulla an imprint of papyrus fibres is visible. The inscription is divided between two registers by a double line and surrounded by a single framing border line visible only on the upper part.

The Hebrew inscription reads:

לפלטיה̇[ו] / ...

lplṭyḣ[w] / ....

"Belonging to Pelaṭyahu (son of) ...."

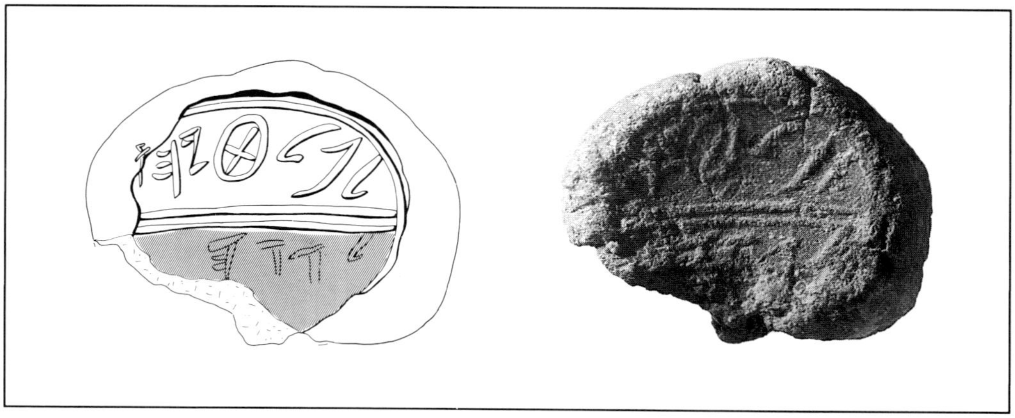

plṭyhw — Pelaṭyahu is a Hebrew personal name meaning "Yahweh has rescued". For parallels see bulla no. 79 above. The name also appears on the previous bulla, no. 80 and in its shortened form *plṭy* on bullae nos. 76a-c above.

Only remnants of letters are visible in the lower register and the patronym is undecipherable.

82. Pashḥur son of Yishmaʿʾel

A fragmentary bulla made of light-brown clay and measuring 11.3x12.3 mm. On the back of the bulla cord grooves are visible. The inscription is divided between two registers by a double line and remnants of a single circular border line are visible on the upper edge. A peculiar rectangular-framed zigzag pattern is depicted at the bottom.

The Hebrew inscription reads:

לפשחר בׄ[ן] / יׄשמעא[ל]

lpšḥr ḃ[n] / ẏšmʿʾ[l]

"Belonging to Pashḥur son of Yishmaʿʾel"

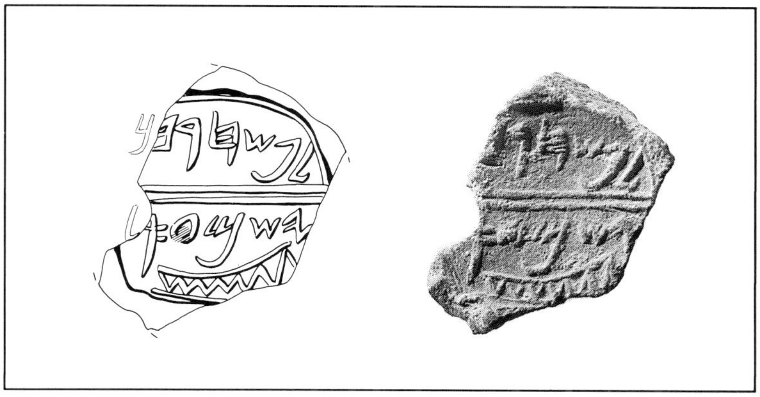

pšḥr — Pashḥur is an Egyptian personal name which contains the theophoric element *ḥor* with a possible meaning: "Son of Horus" or "Portion of Horus" (Bracke 1992; WSS, p. 544). The name was adopted by the Hebrews and is common in the post-exilic period. Five individuals bear this name in the Bible in its full spelling *pšḥwr*: 1) "Pashḥur son of Immer the priest", opponent of the prophet Jeremiah (Jer. 20:1–6), 2) "Pashḥur son of Malchiah", a high official in the time of Zedekiah the last king of Judah (Jer. 20:1–6), 3) "Pashḥur, father of Gedaliah", another high official in the time Zedekiah king of Judah (Jer. 38:1), 4) One of the ancestors of the priests who returned from the exile (Ezra 2:38; Neh. 7:41), 5) An individual who participate in the sealing of the covenant with Nehemiah (Neh. 10:3). The name is also common in the Hebrew epigraphic material and is found on three bullae: 1) *lpšḥr bn ʾḥʾmh* "Belonging to Pashḥur son of ʾAḥiʾimmo", 2) *lpšḥr bn mnḥm* "Belonging to Pashḥur son of Menaḥem", 3) ...*yhw [pš]ḥr* "(Belonging to) ...yahu (son of) Pashḥur" (Avigad 1986, 151, 152, 183; WSS 618,

619),[24] on three seals: 1) *lʾdtʾ ʾšt pšḥr* "Belonging to *ʾdtʾ* wife of Pashḥur" (Reifenberg 1938:115, no. 7; WSS 33), 2) *lpšḥr* "Belonging to Pashḥur" (Avigad 1989a:94, no. 14; WSS 335), 3) *lpšḥr bn ʿdyhw* "Belonging to Pashḥur son of ʿAdayahu" (Moscati 1951, no. 28; WSS 336), and on two ostraca, one from Arad (Aharoni 1981:86, no. 54) and one from Aroer (Lemaire 1980:20).

yšmʿʾl — Yishmaʿʾel is a theophoric personal name meaning "The God (Yahweh) will listen", similar to names such as "ʾElishamaʿ and Yishmaʿ. Six persons in the Bible bear this name (Gen. 16:15; I Chr. 8:38; II Chr. 19:11; II Kgs. 25:25 etc.). This is also a common name in the Hebrew epigraphic material and was recorded twenty times by Davies (1991:380), and once on an ostracon from Judah (Deutsch and Heltzer 1995, 77:2). The name occurs on two additional bullae in this group, nos. 56 above and 100 below.

83. Ṣapan son of ʿAzryqam

A fragmentary and worn bulla made of brown clay, measuring 16.8x13.3 mm. On the back of the bulla the impression of wooden fibres are visible. The field is divided into two registers by a dotted double line and is surrounded by a single border line. Despite the missing corner and the poor state of preservation, the letters are easily legible.

The Hebrew inscription reads:

לצפן בן / עזריקם

l̇ṣpn bn / ʿzryqm

"Belonging to Ṣapan son of ʿAzryqam"

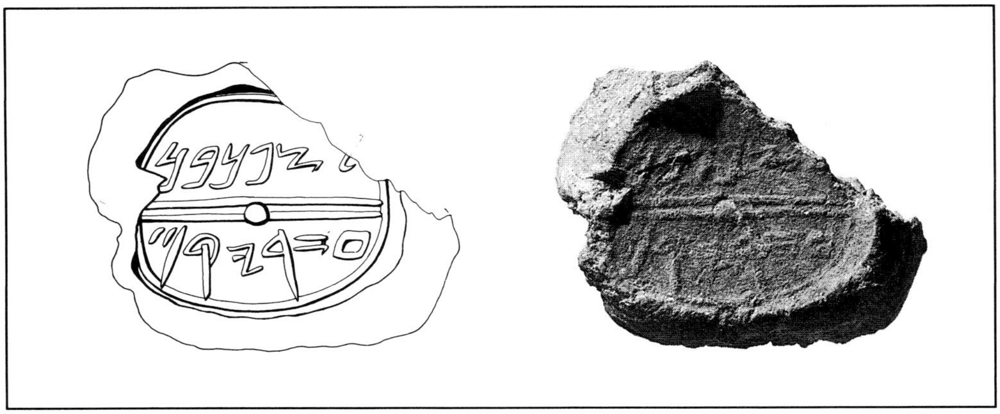

ṣpn — Ṣapan is a hypocoristicon of the Hebrew theophoric personal name *ṣpnyhw* meaning "Yahweh has hidden, treasured". For biblical and other epigraphic parallels see two other bullae in our group which bear the fully spelled name, nos. 84 and 90 below.

ʿzryqm — ʿAzryqam is a Hebrew personal name meaning "My (Divine) help has arisen".

24. Avigad 1986, no. 183 is not listed in WSS.

Four individuals bear this name in the Bible (I Chr. 3:23, 8:38, 9:14), among them a state official, "steward of the royal palace" of Ahaz king of Judah, in the second half of the 8th century B.C.E. (II Chr. 28:7), who is mentioned without his father's name. In the Hebrew epigraphic material the name, (in its defective spelling *ʿzrqm*) is found on three bullae, one from the city of David in Jerusalem: *lʿzrqm mkyhw* "Belonging to ʿAzriqam (son of) Mikayahu" (Shoham 1994, 32; WSS 599) and on two bullae with no provenance: 1) *lʿzrqm bn prpr* "Belonging to ʿAzriqam son of Parpar", 2) *lʿzrqm [bn] ṣdqʾ* "Belonging to ʿAzriqam son of Ṣidqʾa" (Avigad 1986, 138, 139; WSS 600, 601). The name occurs also on bulla no. 75 above and in the defective spelling: *ʿzrqm* on bulla no. 93 below.

84. Ṣapanyah (son of) Miʾamen

A fragmentary and worn bulla made of reddish-brown clay, measuring 14.1x10.2 mm. On the back of the bulla the impression of papyrus fibres is visible. The field is divided into two registers by a double line and is surrounded by a single framing border line which is fragmentary. Despite the poor condition of the bulla the letters are easily legible.

The Hebrew inscription reads:

לצפניה / מיאמן

lṣpnẏḣ / ṁyʾmṅ

"Belonging to Ṣapanyah (son of) Miʾamen"

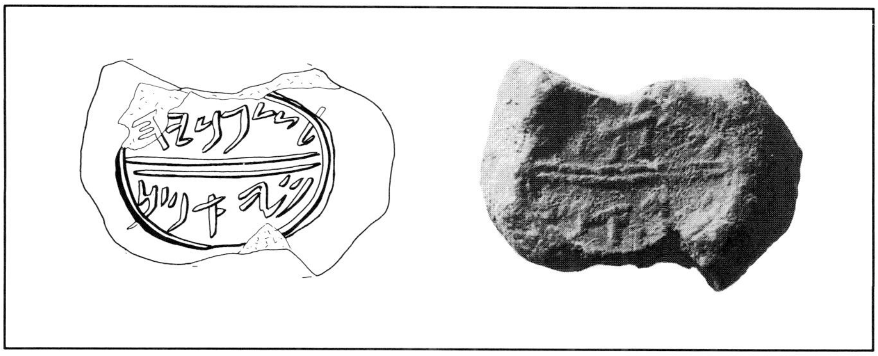

ṣpnyh — Ṣapanyah is a shortened form of the Hebrew theophoric personal name *ṣpnyhw* "Ṣapanyahu", meaning "Yahweh has hidden, treasured". In the Bible this is the name of the ninth book of the twelve minor prophets, containing the oracles of the prophet Zephaniah son of Kushi, and of three other individuals (I Chr. 6:21; Jer. 52:24–27; Zech. 6:10). The name is very common in the Hebrew epigraphic material and was recorded 23 times in its full and shortened spellings (Davies 1991:477–478). The name Ṣapan appears on bulla no. 83 above and Ṣapanyahu on bulla no. 90 below.

myʾmn — Miʾamen is a Hebrew personal name, an interrogative deriving from the root "faith", "Who is faithful (in god Yahweh)", such as the names Micaiah or Michael (Avigad

1986:68), or simply "Faithful". Variants of the name are mentioned both in the Bible: *mymn* (Neh. 10:8) and in the Hebrew epigraphy, on the seal: *my'mn ..ʿdd* "Belonging to Miʾamen (son of) ..ʿ*dd*" (Hestrin and Dayagi-Mendels 1978, 94; WSS 228) and on four bullae: 1) *[lmʿ]śyhw myʾmn* "Belonging to Maʿaśeyahu (son of) Miʾamen", 2) *[lm]yʾmn [bn] ʿpy* "Belonging to Miʾamen son of ʿEpai" (Avigad 1986, 87, 88; WSS 647, 539), 3) *lyhwʾl myʾmn* "Belonging to Yehoʾel (son of) Miʾamen" found at Lachish (Lachish V:21, 4; WSS 523), 4) *lmyʾmn bnyhw* "Belonging to Miʾamen (son of) Benayahu" (Deutsch and Heltzer 1995, 60). The name appears on bulla no. 57 and in its shortened form: *mʾmn* on bulla no. 21 above.

85. Shebanyahu (son of) Maḥseyahu

A bulla made of brown clay, measuring 22.0x24.5 mm. On the back of the bulla an impression of wooden fibres is visible. The seal impression is triangular with a rounded top. The field is divided into three registers and surrounded by a framing border line. The upper register is decorated with a net pattern, while the two lower registers contain the inscription. The surface of the bulla is worn but the script is easily decipherable.

The Hebrew inscription reads:

לשבנׄיׄהׄוׄ / מחסׄיׄהׄוׄ

lšbṅẏḣẇ / mḥṡẏḣẇ

"Belonging to Shebanyahu (son of) Maḥseyahu"

šbnyhw — Shebanyahu is a Hebrew theophoric personal name meaning "God Yahweh, return" (Avigad 1986:48, no. 49). The name appears in the Bible (I Chr. 15:24), as well as in the

Hebrew epigraphy, recorded eighteen times by Davies (1991:490). This is also the name of ʿImmadiyahu's father which appears on her personal seal: "ʿImmadiyahu daughter of Shebanyahu" (Clermont-Ganneau 1902:264; WSS 41). The name also occurs on bullae nos. 16 and 61a-b above.

mḥsyhw — Maḥseyahu is a Hebrew theophoric personal name meaning "God Yahweh is shelter, refuge". The name appears in the Bible in a shortened form: *mḥsyh* "Maḥseyah", who was the grandfather of Baruch the scribe and Seraiah the quartermaster (Jer. 32:12, 51:59). The name is recorded eight times in the Hebrew epigraphic material, six times by Davies (1991:420–21) and twice by Deutsch and Heltzer (1995, 59 and 79:3). See also the thermoluminescence analysis report for this bulla (Plate XV).

86. Shekanyahu (son of) ʾElʿaśa

A worn bulla made of grey clay, measuring 10.2x12.8 mm. On the back of the bulla cord grooves are visible. The field is divided into three registers by two double lines and surrounded by a framing border line visible only on the upper edge. In the middle, largest register a four-winged *uraeus* is depicted. The script is of high calligraphic quality. The inscription is divided between the upper and lower registers with two letters, *he* and *waw* in the middle decorated register. The inscription has been restored based on a previously-published identical bulla (Deutsch and Heltzer 1994:43, no. 16).

The Hebrew inscription reads:

לשכּנּיּ/[ה/ו] / [א]לעש[ה]

lšk̇ṅẏ/[h/w] / [ʾ]lʿś[h]

"Belonging to Shekanyahu (son of) ʾElʿaśa"

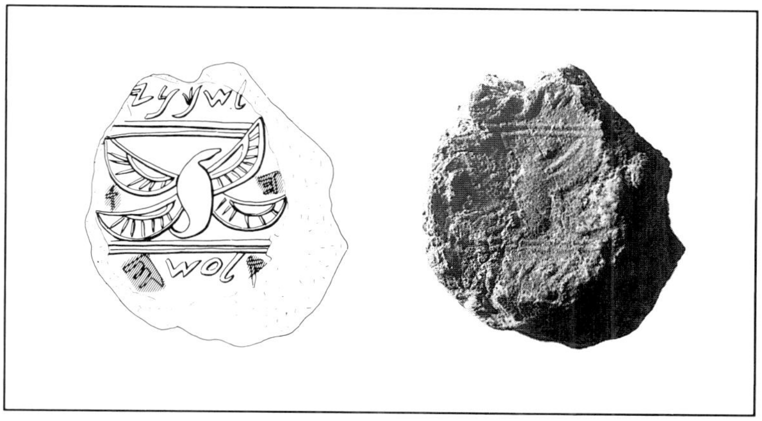

šknyhw — Shekanyahu is a Hebrew theophoric personal name meaning "Yahweh dwells (with us)". Seven individuals bear this name in the Bible (Fuller 1992:1173–1174), including an high official in charge of apportioning the freewill offerings during the reign of Hezekiah, king of Judah (II Chr. 31:15). The name is rare in the Hebrew epigraphic material and it is recorded in the above-mentioned identical bulla (Deutsch and Heltzer 1994, 16), on another bulla from the Hecht Museum collection: *lšknyhw bn gmr* "Belonging to Shekanyahu son of Gomer" (AHL, 39), on a seal: *lšknyhw ḥylʾ* "Belonging to Shekanyahu (son of) Ḥilʾa" (Avigad 1975:67, no. 4), and on an ostracon from Judah: *mṣry bn šknyhw* "Miṣry son of Shekanyahu" (Deutsch and Heltzer 1995:92, 79:10). The name occurs also on bulla no. 79 above.

ʾlʿśh — ʾElʿaśa is a Hebrew theophoric personal name meaning "The God (Yahweh) has made, created". Four persons in the Bible bear this name: 1) The son of Heleṣ (I Chr. 2:39), 2) The son of Raphah (I Chr. 8:37), 3) The son of Shaphan and brother of ʾAḥiqam and Gemaryahu (Jer. 29:3), 4) The son of Pashḥur (Ezra 10:22). The name is very rare in the Hebrew epigraphic material and occurs only once before on an identical bulla: *lšknyhw ʾlʿśh* "Belonging to Shekanyahu (son of) ʾElʿaśa" (Deutsch and Heltzer 1994, 16) and again in our group, nos. 50a-b above.

87. Shallum son of ʾElyaqim

A fragmentary bulla made of light-brown clay, measuring 20.6x19.0 mm. On the back of the bulla cord grooves are visible along with wooden fibre impressions. The field is divided into two registers by a double line and surrounded by a single framing border line. The lower part of the bulla is missing but the inscription is complete except for the lower half of the letter *yod.*

The Hebrew inscription reads:

לשלם ב/ן אליקם

lšlm b/n ʾlẙqm

"Belonging to Shallum son of ʾElyaqim"

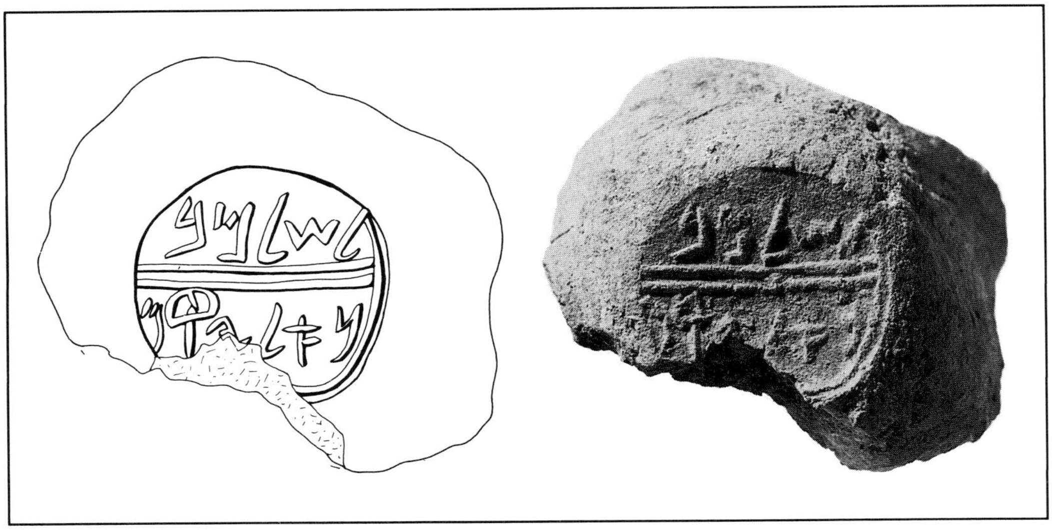

šlm — Shallum is a Hebrew biblical theophoric personal name (Gen. 46:24; I Chr. 4:25), a shortened version of "Shelemyahu" meaning "Yahweh has recompensed". This is a very common name in the Hebrew epigraphy and was recorded nineteen times by Davies (1991:495), twice by Deutsch and Heltzer (1995, nos. 57, 65), once in DHL (no. 36), once in WSS 366 (*editio princeps*) and once on the bulla *lʾḥyʾm / bn šlm* "Belonging to ʾAḥyʾem son of Shallum", which is no. 22 above.

ʾlyqm — ʾElyaqim is a Hebrew theophoric personal name meaning "The god will raise, establish". Similar names are Yehoyaqim and Yeqamyahu. Two other biblical figures bearing the name ʾElyaqim are recorded: ʾElyaqim son of Josiah who was made king by Pharaoh Neco and changed his name to Yehoyaqim (II Kgs. 23:34) and a priest in the time of Nehemiah known as participating in the dedication ceremony of the restored temple (Neh. 12:41). The name is common in the Hebrew epigraphical material and appears on four identical seal impressions on jar handles: *lʾlyqm nʿr ywkn* "Belonging to ʾElyaqim steward of Yokin", found at Ramat Rahel, Beth Shemesh and Tell Beth Mirsim (Hestrin and Dayagi-Mendels 1978, 8–9; WSS 663), on three bullae, two identical from Jerusalem: *lʾlyqm bn ʾwhl* "Belonging to ʾElyaqim son of ʾOhel" (Shoham 1994:58, nos. 29–30; WSS 437) and *lʾlyqm bn mʿśyh* "Belonging to ʾElyaqim son of Maʿaśeyah" (Avigad 1969:4, no. 8; WSS 438). Two seals are also recorded: *lʾlyqm ʿzʾ* "Belonging to ʾElyaqim (son of) ʿUzzaʾ" (Hestrin and Dayagi-Mendels 1978, 91; WSS 69) and *lʾlyqm ʿbd hmlk* "Belonging to ʾElyaqim son of the king" (Bordreuil 1992, pl. 1016). The name appears also on the bulla *lʾlyqm / ḥlqyhw* "Belonging to ʾElyaqim (son of) Ḥilqiyahu", no. 30 above (possibly his father).

88. *Šlmh* son/daughter of Yeshaʿyahu

A fragmentary bulla made of brown clay, measuring 17.0x20.5 mm. On the back of the bulla cord grooves are visible along with wooden fibre impressions. The field is divided into two registers by a ladder-pattern and surrounded by a single framing border line visible on the left side. Despite the missing edges the inscription is almost complete.

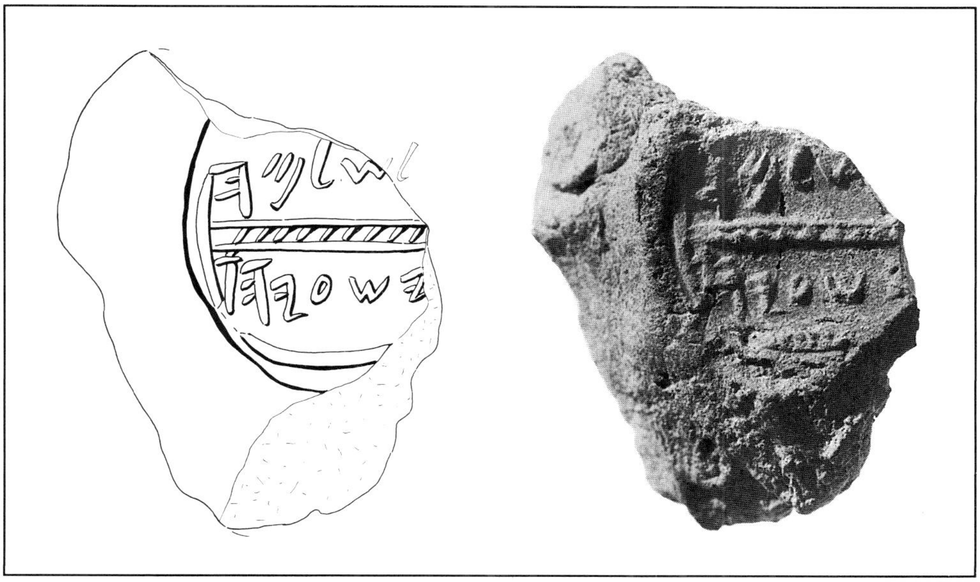

The Hebrew inscription reads:

[ל]שׁלמה / ישעיהו

[l]šlmh / yšʿyhw

"Belonging to *Šlmh* son/daughter of Yeshaʿyahu"

šlmh — Shalomeh/Shlomo, the name means "The God has completed", or "The God is entire". A third possibility is the adjectives "entire, complete, perfect", similar to names like Yaffa "beautiful", Neʾehebet "loved" and Maʿadanah "delight". The name does not appear as the name of a woman in the Hebrew Bible, but is the name of the third king of the United Kingdom, the son of David with Bath-Sheba (II Sam. 5:14). Likewise, the name is absent from the First Temple period Hebrew epigraphy, but it appears on another bulla in this chapter as a feminine name: *lšlmh bt šbnyhw* (no. 16 above). In our bulla, the filiation is not mentioned and therefore it could have belonged to a woman or a man. Nevertheless, names such as: *šlm*, *šlmy*, *šlmyh* and *šlmyhw*, are very common in the Hebrew epigraphy and are recorded 32 times by Davies (1991:495–497).

yšʿyhw — Yeshaʿyahu is a Hebrew theophoric personal name meaning "Yahweh has saved". Seven individuals in the Bible bear this name and its shortened form *yšʿyh*, including the son of Amoz the prophet, and the book named after him (I Chr. 3:21, 25:3, 26:25; Ezra 8:7, 19; Neh. 11:7). The name is common in the Hebrew epigraphic material and was recorded twelve times (Davies 1991:495–497; Deutsch and Heltzer 1997, 87, 89).

89. Shelemyahu son of ʾEliykon

A complete bulla made of brown clay, measuring 15.7x13.0 mm. On the back of the bulla the imprint of the texture of the papyrus to which the bulla was affixed is visible, along with grooves where the cord which tied the papyrus ran. The inscription is divided between two registers by a double line and surrounded by a single circular border line. The bulla is in a very good state of preservation.

The Hebrew inscription reads:

לשלמיהו / בן אליכן

lšlmyhw / bn ʾlykn

"Belonging to Shelemyahu son of ʾEliykon"

šlmyhw — Shelemyahu is a Hebrew theophoric personal name meaning: "Yahweh has recompensed" or "Yahweh has completed". The name *šlmyhw* and its shortened forms: *šlm*, *šlmy* and *šlmyh* are common in the Bible (Kimchi 1991:815, 823, 824), and was recorded 33 times in the Hebrew epigraphic material (Davies 1991:495–497).

ʾlykn — ʾEliykon is a very rare Hebrew personal name which is not attested in the Bible. Similar names are *yhwykn*, *ywkn*, *knyhw* and *knyw*, all having the same meaning: "The God (Yahweh) will establish". In the Hebrew epigraphic material the name was recorded three times in *scriptio defective*: *ʾlkn*, on two ostraca from Judah (Deutsch and Heltzer 1995, 77:6, 78:3).

90. Shemaʿyahu (son of) Ṣapanyahu

A fragmentary bulla made of light-brown clay and measuring 12.9x10.3 mm. On the back of the bulla the imprint of the texture of the papyrus to which the bulla was affixed is visible, along with grooves where the cord which tied the papyrus ran. The inscription is divided between two registers by a double line and surrounded by a single circular border line visible on the left edge. The right edge is missing but the restoration of the letter *ṣade* is certain.

The Hebrew inscription reads:

[ל]שמעיהו / צפניהו

[l]šmʿyhw / ṣpnyhw

"Belonging to Shemaʿyahu (son of) Ṣapanyahu"

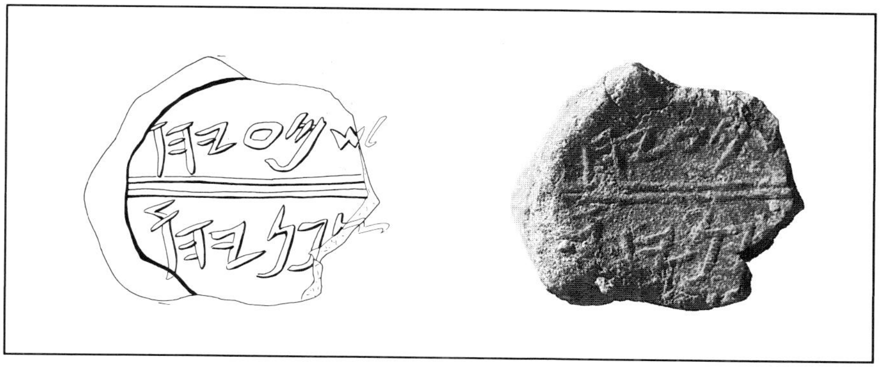

šmʿyhw — Shemaʿyahu is a Hebrew theophoric personal name meaning "Yahweh has listened". The name is very common in the Bible and appears also in its shortened forms: *šmʿ*,

šm^cy and *šm^cyh* (Kimchi 1991:834, 836–842). In the Hebrew epigraphic material the name is recorded 20 times in its full spelling and 10 times in its shortened forms (Davies 1991:500–2; Deutsch and Heltzer 1994, 38; 1995, 64). The name occurs also on bulla no. 42 above.

ṣpnyhw — Ṣapanyahu is a Hebrew theophoric personal name meaning "Yahweh has hidden, treasured". In the Bible this is the name of the ninth book of the twelve minor prophets, containing the oracles of the prophet Zephaniah son of Kushi, and of three other individuals (I Chr. 6:21; Jer. 52:24–27; Zech. 6:10). The name is very common in the Hebrew epigraphic material and was recorded 25 times in its full and shortened spellings (Davies 1991:477–478; Deutsch and Heltzer 1995, 52, 55). The shortened forms of the name *ṣpnyhw*: *ṣpn* and *ṣpnyh* appear on bullae nos. 83 and 84 above.

91. Shapaṭ son of Yeda^cyahu

A complete bulla in a good state of preservation, made of brown clay and measuring 14.8x15.1 mm. On the back of the bulla the imprint of the texture of a wooden artifact to which the bulla was affixed is visible, along with grooves where the cord which tied the artifact ran. The inscription is divided between three registers by two double lines and surrounded by a double circular border line. In the upper register a four-winged beetle is depicted.

The Hebrew inscription reads:

לשפט בן / ידעיהו

lšpṭ bn / yd^cyhw

"Belonging to Shapaṭ son of Yeda^cyahu"

špṭ — Shapaṭ is a hypocoristicon of the Hebrew personal name *špṭyhw* or *yhwšpṭ* meaning "Yahweh has judged". Five persons in the Bible bear this name (Kimchi 1991:848–849). In the Hebrew epigraphical material it occurs on two seals: 1) *lšpṭ* — "Belonging to Shapaṭ" (Hestrin and Dayagi-Mendels 1978, 37; WSS 381), 2) *lmlkyhw n^cr špṭ* — "Belonging to Malkiyahu steward of Shapaṭ" (Avigad 1976:295–296; WSS 25) and on a bulla (from the Tell Beit Mirsim area?): *lšpṭ bn ʾḥyhw* — "Belonging to Shapaṭ son of ʾAḥiyahu" (Avigad 1986, 166; WSS 641). In our group the name appears on bulla no. 49 and in its full spelling: *špṭyhw* on bulla no. 69 above.

ydʿyhw — Yedaʿyahu is a Hebrew theophoric personal name meaning "Yahweh knows, has favored". The name is common in the Bible in its shortened forms *ydʿ* and *ydʿyh* (I Chr. 2:28, 24:7; Ezra 2:36, etc.). In the Hebrew epigraphic material it was recorded 13 times by Davies (1991:361–2). Additionally, the name appears on the bulla: *lʿbdʾ bn ydʿyhw* "Belonging to ʿAbdaʾ son of Yedaʿyahu" and on three seal impressions on two jar handles: *ydʿyh(w) ʾlʿzr* "(Belonging to) Yedaʿyahu (son of) ʾElʿazar" (Deutsch and Heltzer 1994, 17; 1995, 53a-c) and on bulla no. 48 above.

92. Shapan son of Ḥagab

A damaged bulla made of brown clay, measuring 14.5x12.8 mm. On the back of the bulla the imprint of the texture of the papyrus to which the bulla was affixed is visible, along with grooves where the cord which tied the papyrus ran. The inscription is divided between two registers by a double line and surrounded by a single circular border line visible on the lower edge. On the left side of the lower register a palm branch motif is depicted serving as a space filler.

The Hebrew inscription reads:

לשפן ב/ן חגב
lšpn b/n ḥgb
"Belonging to Shapan son of Ḥagab"

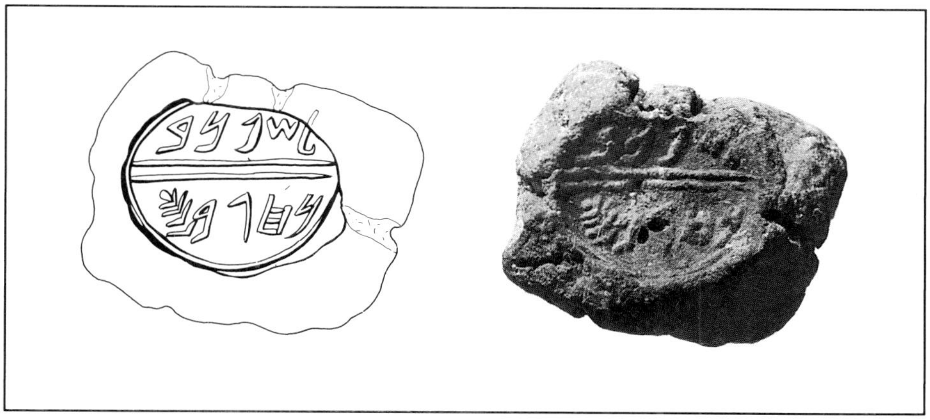

špn — Shapan, lit. "rabbit", is a Hebrew personal name. Names such as this derived from animals are common and are known from the Bible and from the Hebrew epigraphic material. Such names are: "Shuʿal" (fox), "ʿAkhbor" (mouse), (II Kgs. 22:12), "ʿOreb" (crow), (WSS 693) etc. The name "Shapan" is rare and it appears only once in the Bible. He is the son of ʾAṣalyahu the scribe (II Kgs. 22:3) and the father of ʾAḥiqam. ʾAṣalyahu was the man sent by Josiah the King to Ḥilqiyahu the high priest with the command to repair the "House of the Lord" (II Kgs. 22:3–6). Shapan the high priest received the Book, the Torah, found in the Temple by Ḥilqiyahu and brought it to the king (II Kgs. 22:8–9). The name Shapan is rare also in the Hebrew epigraphy and appears on a bulla from the City of David: *lgmryhw / bn špn* "Belonging to Gemaryahu son of Shapan" (Shoham 1994:57, no. 2; WSS 470), on the seal: *lšpn / pdyhw* "Belonging to Shapan (son of) Pedayahu" (Avigad 1989:12, no. 9; WSS 388) and on a burial inscription from Jerusalem (Prignaud 1978:136). Despite the rarity of the name, it appears on another four bullae in this group, nos. 25, 56, 93 and 94.

ḥgb — Ḥagab is a Hebrew personal name meaning "locust, grasshopper", given after this insect. The name occurs only once in the Bible (Ezra 2:46). In the Hebrew epigraphic material the name is found on two ostraca: one from Lachish *ḥgb bn yʾznyhw* "Belonging to Ḥagab son of Yaʾazanyahu" (Lachish III:331, 1:3) and one from Ḥorvat ʿUza *bn ḥgb* "son of Ḥagab" (Beit-Arieh 1988-9), as well as on four bullae (Avigad 1986, 53a-b, 54a-b). The name Ḥagab appears also on bulla no. 45 above.

93. Shapan son of ʿAzriqam

A complete bulla made of grey clay, measuring 15.8x12.0 mm. On the back of the bulla the imprint of the texture of the papyrus to which the bulla was affixed is visible, along with grooves where the cord which tied the papyrus ran. The inscription is divided between two registers by a lotus-bud motif and is surrounded by a single circular border line. The seal impression is weak but the letters are visible.

The Hebrew inscription reads:

לשפן ב/ן עזרקם̇

lšpn b/n ʿzrqṁ

"Belonging to Shapan son of ʿAzriqam"

špn — Shapan, lit. "rabbit", is a Hebrew personal name. The name is rare and it appears only once in the Bible (II Kgs. 22:3). For the name and the parallel epigraphic material see the previous bulla, no. 92. Despite the rarity of the name, it appears on another four bullae in our group, nos. 25, 56, 92 and 94.

ʿzrqm — ʿAzriqam is a Hebrew personal name meaning "My (Divine) help has arisen". In the Bible four individuals bear this name in its full spelling: *ʿzryqm* (I Chr. 3:23, 8:38, 9:14), among them a state official, "steward of the royal palace" of Ahaz king of Judah, in the second half of the 8th century B.C.E. (II Chr. 28:7), mentioned without his father's name. In the Hebrew epigraphic material the name is found on three bullae, one from the city of David in Jerusalem: *lʿzrqm mkyhw* "Belonging to ʿAzriqam (son of) Mikayahu" (Shoham 1994, 32; WSS 599), and two with no provenance: 1) *lʿzrqm bn prpr* "Belonging to ʿAzriqam son of Parpar", 2) *lʿzrqm [bn] ṣdqʾ* "Belonging to ʿAzriqam son of Ṣidqʾa" (Avigad 1986, 138, 139; WSS 600, 601). The name in its full spelling occurs on bullae nos. 75 and 83 above.

94. Shapan (son of) Rapaʾyahu

A bulla made of light-brown clay, measuring 16.5x17.0 mm. On the back of the bulla an imprint of wooden fibres is visible. The upper edge is large and covered with fingerprints. The inscription is divided between two registers by a dotted double line and is surrounded by a single circular border line. The seal impression is weak but the letters are visible and certain, except for the second letter in the upper register which is a *shin* or a *ṣade*. It seems to be the upper part of the letter *shin*.

The Hebrew inscription reads:

לשׁפן / רפאיהו

lšpn / rpʾyhw

"Belonging to Shapan (son of) Rapaʾyahu"

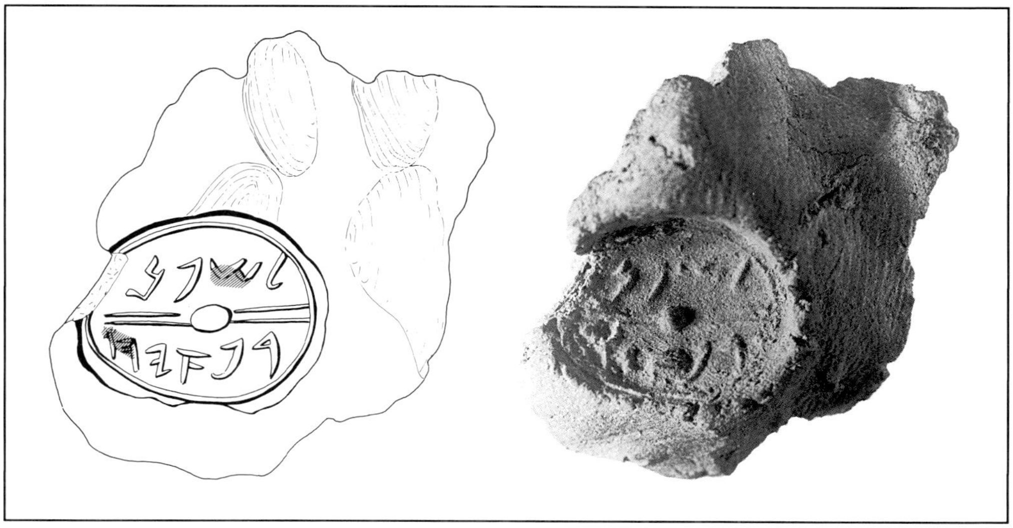

špn — Shapan, lit. "rabbit", is a Hebrew personal name. The name is rare and it appears only once in the Bible (II Kgs. 22:3). For the name and the parallel epigraphic material see bulla no. 92 above. Despite the rarity of the name, it appears on another four bullae in our group, nos. 25, 56, 92 and 93.

rpʾyhw — Rapaʾyahu is a Hebrew theophoric personal name meaning "Yahweh has healed". The name occurs only once in the Bible in its shortened form: Rapaʾ and is the name of the fifth son of Benjamin (I Chr. 8:2). The name is also found in the Hebrew epigraphic material and was recorded three times by Davies (1991:487) and once by Deutsch and Heltzer (1995:53, no. 58). The shortened form of the name: *rpʾ* was recorded seven times (Davies 1991:487) and occurs in our group on bulla no. 68 above.

95. ... Son of Baʿadiyahu

A fragmentary bulla made of black clay and measuring 12.0x10.3 mm. On the back of the bulla grooves are visible. The field is divided into two registers by a double line and is surrounded by a single line visible on the lower part. The upper part of the bulla is missing, therefore the seal owner's name is lost and only the patronym is preserved.

The Hebrew inscription reads:

... / [ב]ן בעדיהו

... / *[b]n bʿdyhw*

"... son of Baʿadiyahu"

bʿdyhw — Baʿadiyahu is a Hebrew theophoric personal name meaning "Yahweh protects me", in accordance with Psalms 3:4: *wʾth yhwh mgn bʿdy kbwdy wmrym rʾšy* "And now Yahweh protects me, my glory, and lifts my head". The name is rare and is not found in the Bible. It occurs only on two bullae: *lbʿdyhw šryhw* "Belonging to Baʿadiyahu (son of) Śerayahu", and *lbʿdyhw* ... "Belonging to Baʿadiyahu ..." (Avigad 1986, 36, 37). The shortened form of the name: *bʿdyh* "Baʿadiyah" is found in the 5th century B.C.E. documents from Elephantine (Cowley 1923, 19:2 25:18).

96. **..ʾ.. (son of) Semakhy**

A fragmentary bulla made of light-brown clay, measuring 11.2x14.2 mm. On the back of the bulla the imprint of the texture of the papyrus to which the bulla was affixed is visible, along with grooves where the cord which tied the papyrus ran. On the left side a two-winged *uraeus* (cobra snake), is depicted. On the upper right side of the field, a section of a double lined cartouche is visible. All is surrounded by a double circular border line. Only the letter *alef* has survived from the owner's name and it is impossible to determine its position within the name, nevertheless the patronym is complete.

The Hebrew inscription reads:

..א.. / סמכי

..ʾ.. / *smky*

"..ʾ.. (son of) Semakhy"

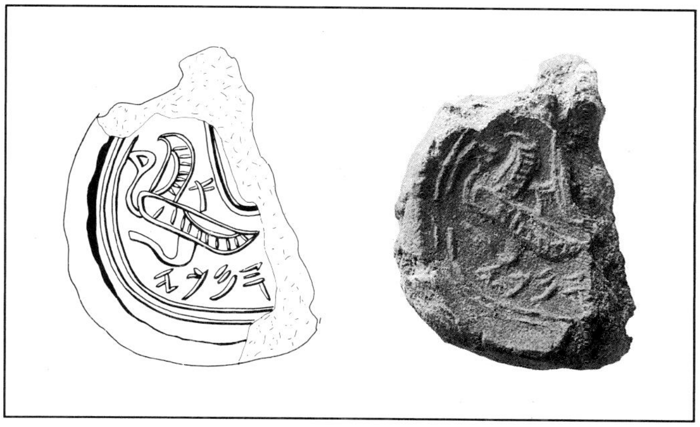

smky — Semakhy is a shortened form of the Hebrew theophoric personal name *smkyhw* "Semakhyahu" meaning "Yahweh has supported". The name occurs only once in the Bible and is the name of a gatekeeper at the temple in Jerusalem (I Chr. 26:7). Yet, it is very common in the Hebrew epigraphic material and was recorded 21 times in different spellings: *smk*, *smky*, *smkyh*, *smkyhw* and *smkyw* (Davies 1991:448–449). It appears in its shortened form: *smk* on two other bullae in our group, nos. 68, 69 above.

Fiscal Bullae

The next five bullae are not of individuals and are called "fiscal", a term used by Avigad with the publication of the bulla: *b 26 / šnh / ʾltld / lmlk* "In the 26th year, (from the city of) Eltolad, to the king" (Avigad 1990:262–266).[25] In this group, contrary to the personal seals, the prefix *lamed* means: "To, for", instead of "Belonging to", similar to the formula found on the Samaria ostraca (Rainey 1967).

97a-b. In the 14th year, the first (crop, from the city of) Lachish, to the king

Two identical bullae:

a. The first is in a very good state of preservation, made of brown clay and measures 22.5x21.3 mm. It has a conoid shape covered with fingerprints and measures 16.5 mm. in height.

b. The second is in a very poor state of preservation, made of brown clay and measures 17.5x19.5 mm. It also has a conoid shape covered with fingerprints and measures 15.5 mm. in height.

Both bullae did not seal documents and probably served as receipts.

The field is divided into five registers by four lines and surrounded by a circular border line. The letters are angular and it seems that the seal used to impress these bullae was made of wood. The variable thickness of the lines and the style of the letters indicate that the material itself dictated to the seal-maker the shapes of the letters. Several tiny lines which are clearly visible between the letters are the unavoidable result of the workmanship on the wooden seal.

The Hebrew inscription reads:

a. ב 14 / שנה / ראשנה / לכש ל/מלך
b 14 / šnh / rʾšnh / lkš l/mlk

b. ב̇ 1[4] / ש̇נ̇ה̇ / ר̇א[שנ]ה̇ / ל̇כ̇ש̇ ל/מל̇ך̇
ḃ 1[4] / šṅḣ / ṙʾ[šn]ḣ / l̇k̇š l/ml̇k̇

25. This bulla together with the bulla of "Taḥat son of Besai", [ʾḥʾb ʾbsy (sic.)], were published by Avigad (1990:262–266; WSS 421, 424). Yet, they belong to our group and therefore are listed as nos. 101 and 102, without discussion.

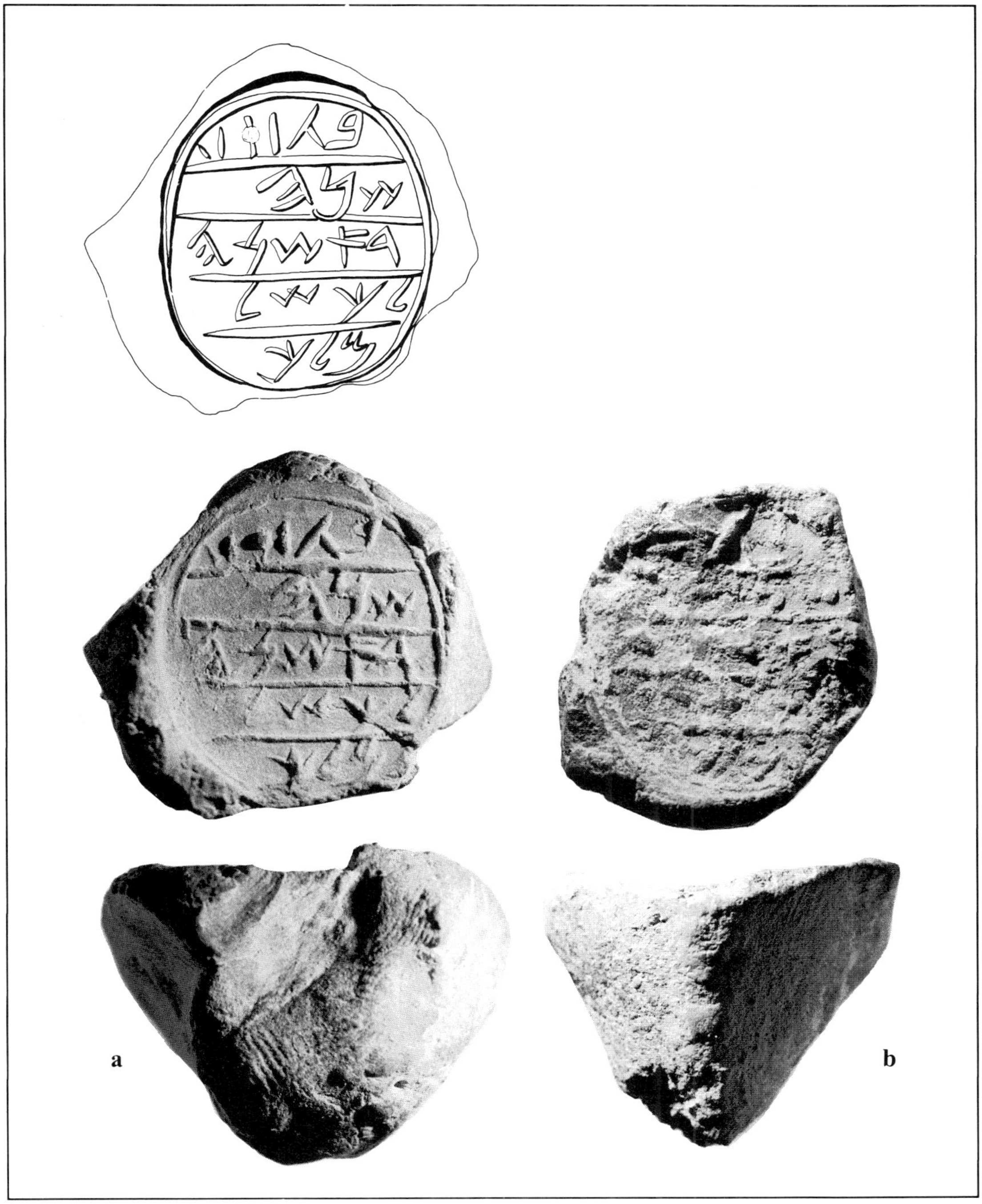

"In the 14th year (of the king PN), the first (crop, from the city of) Lachish, to the king"

The formula on this bulla is very similar to that on two other bullae in our group:

1) *b 26 / šnh / ʾltld / lmlk* "In the 26th year, (from the city of) Eltolad, to the king" (Avigad 1990:262–266).

2) *b 20 šnh / nṣb / lmlk* "In the 20th year, (from the city of) Naṣib, to the king" (no. 98).

Line 1.

b 14 — "In the 14th". The inscription begins with the preposition *b* "in", followed by the hieratic numeral 10 and four vertical strokes, equal to the number 14. The use of Egyptian hieratic numerals in the First Temple Period is known from Hebrew ostraca and Judean weights (Noth 1927; Aharoni 1966), and now is also found on Hebrew bullae. The Egyptian hieratic numerals are used in Judah due to the fact that an individual Hebrew numerical system had not yet developed in the First Temple Period.

Line 2.

šnh — "year". The first two lines marks the date: "In the 14th year", which is the regnal year of a king. The name of the king is omitted since his identity was well known to the public. This kind of formulae is known from the Bible: "In the 18th year of the king Josiah" (II Kgs. 22:3).

Line 3.

r'šnh — "The first". The term probably indicates the agricultural product from the first harvest. In the Bible the term *r'šyt*, indicates the first harvest: *wlqḥt mr'šyt kl pry h'dmh* ... "That thou shalt take of the first of all the fruit of the earth ..." (Deut. 26:2), *r'šyt dgnk tyršk wyṣhrk* "The firstfruit also of thy corn, of thy wine, and of thy oil ..." (Deut. 18:4; II Chr. 31:5), *kbd 't-yhwh mhwnk wmr'šyt kl-tbw'tk* "Honor the Lord with thy substance, and with the firstfruit of all thy increase" (Prov. 3:9), *r'šyt qṣyrkm 'l-hkhn* "the firstfruits of your harvest to the priest" (Lev. 23:10), *mr'šyt ʿrstykm ttnw lyhwh trwmh ldrtykm* "Of the first of your dough you shall give to the Lord an offering throughout your generations" (Num. 15:21). A second possible, yet less probable interpretation of the term *r'šnh* as a type or a quality of flour, is to be found on two ostraca from Arad: *hqmḥ hr'šn* "The first flour", according to Aharoni: a *terminus technicus* for a certain type of flour (1981, 1:5–6, 5:3–4).

Line 4.

lkš — "Lachish", (Tell ed-Duweir), is the name of a biblical city in the Shephelah (Ussishkin 1992). Lachish was probably the most important city after Jerusalem in the 8th century B.C.E. Sennacherib conquered Lachish in 701 B.C.E. and this victory was commemorated by decorating the walls of one of the rooms in his palace at Nineveh with scenes of the siege of the city. The name of Lachish is also mentioned on an ostracon found there (Lachish I:79, 4:10).

Line 5.

l/mlk — "For the King". The prefix *lamed* (at the end of line 4), stands for the word: "For, to", similar to the formula found on the Samaria ostraca (Rainey 1967).

98. In the 20th year, (from the city of) Naṣib, to the king

A complete bulla made of brown clay and in a very good state of preservation. It measures 14.2x12.5 mm. and the size of the impression is 9.6x9.6 mm. On the back of the bulla the imprint of the texture of the papyrus to which the bulla was affixed is visible, along with grooves where the cord which tied the papyrus ran. On the edges fingerprints are visible. The inscription is divided between three registers by two double lines and is surrounded by a double circular border line. The upper left corner was damaged while the bulla was still wet, yet all the letters are preserved. At the end of the central register are two strokes which served as space fillers. This is a fiscal bulla which was used to seal a papyrus document in contrast to the two previously-presented fiscal bullae which served as receipts.

The Hebrew inscription reads:

ב 20 שנה / נצב .. / למלך

b 20 šnh / nṣb .. / lmlk

"In the 20th year (of king PN, from the city of) Naṣib, to the king"

Line 1.

b 20 šnh — "In the 20th year". The inscription begins with the preposition *b* "in", followed by the hieratic numeral 20, similar to the numeral 20 which appears on an ostracon from Arad (Aharoni 1981, 17:8), and with some resemblance to the numeral 20 which occurs on the "Eltolad" fiscal bulla, no. 101 below. After the numeral and above the letter *šhin* two strokes are visible. These are probably the result of defects in the seal itself, due to the fact that they are thicker and misplaced. Nevertheless, an intended later addition of these two strokes to the seal is also possible. The seal which was made and used in the 20th year, may have been used two additional consecutive years by adding a stroke after the numeral 20 to obtain the 21st year and another stroke to creature the 22nd year. Therefore, the first line indicates the 20th (22nd) regnal year of a king whose name was omitted. This formula is known from the Bible: *bšmnh ʿšrh šnh lmlk yʾšyhw* "In the 18th regnal year of king Josiah" (II Kgs. 22:3), or: *bʿšrym wšbʿ šnh* "In the 27th year" (Ezek. 29:17).

Line 2.

nṣb — The name of the biblical city of "Naṣib" (Kalai 1968), followed by two strokes serving as space fillers. The name of the city appears in *scriptio defective* just as in the biblical version: *wypth wʾšnh wnṣb* "And Yiftaḥ and ʾAshnah, and Naṣib" (Josh. 15:43). The only reference to this settlement occurs in the list of towns within the tribal allotment of Judah and belongs to the third district of the Judean Shephelah. The city has preserved its name in Arabic and it was identified at the site of Khirbet Beit Neṣib (UTM 1105–1510). The ancient city is located at the bottom of the Hebron hills, the lowlands of Judah, some three km. south south-east of Keilah (Ḥorvat Qe'ila). According to Eusebius (On. 136:21), Naṣib was located at the ninth mile on the way from Beth-Guvrin to Hebron, while according to Hieronymus (On. 136:24), the distance was only seven miles. The famous US orientalist and surveyor Edward Robinson visited the place in 1838. He identified the site and knew of the biblical verse mentioning Naṣib, as well as the ancient source of Eusebius mentioning its location. (Robinson 1841, II:344, 404, III:12–13). In the 1931 survey made on the site, an abundance of Iron Age II pottery was observed (Saarisalo 1931:101).

Line 3.

lmlk — "For the King". The prefix *lamed* stands for the word: "For, to", similar to the formula found on the Samaria ostraca (Rainey 1967).

On both bullae presented here (nos. 97 and 98), and on the bulla published by Avigad (1990:262–266), we find the same formula:

b 14 šnh, r'šnh, lkš, lmlk

b 20 šnh, nṣb, lmlk

b 26 šnh, 'ltld, lmlk

The three bullae belong to the same group, therefore we can assume that the dates are related to the same king. The three paleographical variations could be the result of three different scribal handwritings and not of a chronological factor.

99. In the Third (Year), for the Customs/Tribute

A complete bulla made of reddish-grey clay and in a very good state of preservation. It measures 16.0x16.0 mm. and the size of the impression is 12.0x10.5 mm. On the edges fingerprints are visible. On the back of the bulla the imprint of the texture of the papyrus to which the bulla was affixed is visible, along with grooves where the cord which tied the papyrus ran. This bulla, like the previous one, was used to seal a papyrus document in contrast to the two presented fiscal bullae (nos. 97a-b), which served as receipts. The inscription is divided between two registers by a double lines and is surrounded by a single circular border line.

The Hebrew inscription reads:

בשלשת / למכס

bšlšt / lmks

"In the third (year), for the custom/tribute"

Line 1.

bšlšt — "In the third year", of the king whose name is not mentioned.

Line 2.

lmks — "For the custom/tribute". The prefix *lamed* stands for the word: "For", similar to the formula found on the Samaria ostraca (Rainey 1967). The term *mks*, in Akkadian *miksu*, is a fixed contribution or offering which is collected for the treasury of God and the priests. The "tribute" is well attested in the Bible: *wyhy hmks lhʾ mn hṣʾn ... wytn mšh ʾt mks trwmt hʾ lʾlʿzr hkhn* "And the Lord's tribute of sheep was ... And Moses gave the tribute, which was the Lord's gift, to ʾElʿazar the priest" (Num. 31:37–41). Another lit. meaning of the word *mks* is "Custom-officer", an interpretation which is less probable in this case.

100. In the 10th (Year, from the City of) ʾArubboth, [Ish]maʿʾel ...

A fragmentary bulla made of black clay, measuring 15.0x9.3 mm. On the back of the bulla the imprint of the texture of the papyrus to which the bulla was affixed is visible, along with grooves where the cord which tied the papyrus ran. This bulla, like the previous two, was used to seal a papyrus document in contrast with the two presented fiscal bullae (nos. 97a-b), which served as receipts. The field is divided into four registers by a single and two double lines and surrounded by a double framing line. The right side of the third register and the lower forth register are missing.

The Hebrew inscription reads:

+ בעשרת / הׄארבת / [יש]מׄעאל / (למלך)

+ bʿśrt / h̊ʾrbt / [yš]m̊ʿʾl / (lmlk)

"In the tenth (year, from) the city of ʾArubboth, [Ysh]maʿʾel (to the King)"

Line 1.
\+ *bʿśrt* — "In the tenth (regnal year)", of the king whose name is omitted.

Line 2.
hʾrbt — "The (city of) ʾArubboth", literally meaning "windows". The reading of the first letter *he*, the definite article, is based on the preserved and visible upper horizontal bar of the letter. This is the name of a city mentioned only once in the Bible as the seat of Ben Hesed, governor of Solomon's third district (I Kgs. 4:10). According to the location of the 3rd district, ʾArubboth is to be identified with Khirbet el-Ḥamam found within the boundaries of Manasseh in the hill country (Zertal 1992:466). This is probably the city of Rabbah mentioned in Sheshonk's list (biblical Shishak), 11th in the list before Ta'anach, Shunem and Beth-Shean. According to Alt (1953:76–89), the district of ʾArubboth is in fact the district of Narbata of the Hellenistic period.

Line 3.
(yš)mʿʾl — "Yishmaʿʾel" is the only possible reconstruction of a theophoric personal name. It means "The God (Yahweh) will listen", similar to names such as "ʾElishamaʿ and Yishmaʿ. Six persons in the Bible bear this name (Gen. 16:15; I Chr. 8:38; II Chr. 19:11; II Kgs. 25:25, etc.). This is also a common name in the Hebrew epigraphic material and was recorded twenty times by Davies (1991:380) and once on an ostracon from Judah (Deutsch and Heltzer 1995, 77:2). The name occurs on two additional bullae in this group, nos. 56 and 82 above.

The forth register is missing but it probably contained the term *lmlk*, comparable to the previous three bullae.

Two bullae belonging to our group, published by Avigad[26]

101.

ב 26 / שנה / אלתלד / למלך

b 26 / šnh / ʾltld / lmlk

"In the 26th year (from the city of) Eltolad, to the king"

102.

לֹאחֹאב / אֹבֹסי

l̇ʾḥʾb / *ʾḃsẏ*

"Belonging to ʾAḥʾab (son of) *ʾbsy*" (sic.)

26. Avigad 1990:262–266; WSS 421, 424.

Summary and conclusions to Chapter Three

One hundred and nine hitherto unpublished Hebrew bullae were presented in the third chapter. Fourteen bullae are of high officials, including six different titles: "King of Judah" (no. 1), "Daughter of the King" (no. 14), "Servant of Hezekiah" (nos. 2–4), "Servant of the King" (nos. 7–10), "Who is over the house" (nos. 5–6), and "Governor of the city" (nos. 11–13). Four other bullae bear the term "For the King" (nos. 97a-b, 98, 101). All the titles are known from the Bible. Bullae bearing titles are 13% of the whole group. Seven bullae are sealed with seals which belonged to a king, four high officials and two individuals known from the Bible:

No. 1. "ʾAḥaz son of Yehotam, King of Judah" (II Kgs. 15:38).

Nos. 2–4. Three anonymous servants of "King Hezekiah" (II Kgs. 16:20).

No. 9. "Natanmelek servant of the King" (The eunuch in II Kgs. 23:11).

No. 25. "ʾAḥiqam son Shapan" (II Kgs. 22:12).

No. 30. "ʾElyaqim (son of) Ḥilqiyahu" (Who is over the House, II Kgs. 11:18).

Five bullae (two identical), bear the names of four cities: Lachish (no. 97a-b), "Naṣib" (no. 98), "Arubboth" (no.100), and "Eltolad" (101). Six bullae are dated (nos. 97a–100).

The group contains, for the first time, bullae which belonged to women (five items, nos. 14–17). This constitute only 4.35 % of the whole group.

The onomasticon includes 115 different names. In 51 names appear the theophoric element *yhw* which are 45% of the whole group. In five names appears the shortened theophoric element *yh* which are 4.35% of the whole group. Six names includes the shortened theophoric suffix *y* which are 5.2% of the whole group. Consequently, the majority of 54.55% of the names bear the Judean Yahwistic theophoric element *yhw* or its shortened forms *yh* or *y*. Twelve names include the theophoric element *ʾl* and five names have the suffix ʾ. Especially noteworthy is the fact that the North-Israeli Yahwistic theophoric element *yw* is not found among the names on the Hebrew bullae, in our group or in the previously published ones.

Four new, previously unpublished personal names were also presented: *ʾyʿm* (no. 55), *mqmyhw* (no. 64), *mnḥmw* (no. 71) and *ʾlykn* (no. 89).

Iconography on Hebrew bullae is rare and only sixteen examples in our group are iconic (13.9%). These include two or four-winged cobra snakes, *uraei* (nos. 35, 48, 86), a bird (no. 28), a sphinx (nos. 46a-b), a fish (no. 65), quadrupeds (nos. 32, 37, 41?, 51), a winged solar-disk (no. 67), pomegranates (66a-b), and four-winged beetles (nos. 70, 91). The floral and geometrical decoration motifs which served as field dividers are more common (See plates IX–XIII).

This is a group of bullae belonging to the same archive. The earliest bulla in the group is that of "Ahaz son of Yehotam, King of Judah" dating to around 732/1–716/5 B.C.E. The bullae belonging to the "servants of Hezekiah" (nos. 2–4), are to be dated to around 716/5–687/6 B.C.E. The two bullae belonging to "ʾAḥiqam son Shapan" and "ʾElyaqim (son of) Ḥilqiyahu" (nos. 25, 30) are also contemporary with king Hezekiah. The latest datable bulla is that of "Natanmelek the servant of the King" (the eunuch), the servant of king Josiah, ca. 640–609 B.C.E. This is probably also the king to which the dating on the fiscal bullae are referring (nos. 97–101).

The number of the previously published bullae was 376. To this are to be added 109 bullae from the Moussaieff collection presented here, another bulla mentioned above (note no. 6), the recently published bulla of King Hezekiah (Cross 1999), twenty bullae from the Hecht Museum collection (chapter two, 18), two bullae from the Borowsky private collection (chapter two, 17) and a bulla from the Bible Lands Museum collection (chapter two, 15, no. 1). The entire corpus list 510 examples in total, omitting damaged or worn bullae on which the inscriptions are missing.

The List of Bullae in Chapter Three

לאחז (בן) יהותם, מלך יה(ו)דה	1.	*lʾḥz (bn) yhwtm, mlk yhdh*
ליהוזרח בן חלקיהו עבד חזקיהו	2.	*lyhwzrḥ bn ḥlqyhw ʿbd ḥzqyhw*
לעזריהו בן יהואח עבד חזקיהו	3.	*lʿzryhw bn yhwʾḥ ʿbd ḥzqyhw*
.... עבד חזקיהו	4.	*.... ʿbd ḥzqyhw*
לאדניהו אשר על הבית	5.	*lʾdnyhw ʾšr ʿl hbyt*
[ל]מבט[חיהו] אשר ע[ל הבית]	6.	*[l]mbṭ[ḥyhw] ʾšr ʿ[l hbyt]*
לאביהו עבד המלך	7.	*lʾbyhw ʿbd hmlk*
לגדליהו עבד המלך	8.	*lgdlyhw ʿbd hmlk*
לנתנמלך עבד המלך	9.	*lntnmlk ʿbd hmlk*
לעזריהו עבד המלך	10.	*lʿzryhw ʿbd hmlk*
לטבשלם שר הער	11.	*lṭbšlm śr hʿr*
לפקדיהו שר הער	12.	*lpqdyhw śr hʿr*
שר הער	13.	*śr hʿr*
לנויה בת המלך	14.	*lnwyh bt hmlk*
לאחמיה בת מתן	15a.	*lʾhmyh bt mtn*
לאחמיה בת מתן	15b.	*lʾhmyh bt mtn*
לשלמה בת שבניהו	16.	*lšlmh bt šbnyhw*
... בת פקח	17.	*... bt pqḥ*
לאחאב בן אחמלך	18a.	*lʾḥʾb bn ʾḥmlk*
לאחאב בן אחמלך	18b.	*lʾḥʾb bn ʾḥmlk*
לאחאב (בן) ...	19.	*lʾḥʾb (bn) ...*
אחיא בן מתניהו	20.	*ʾḥyʾ bn mtnyhw*
לאחיא בן מאמן	21.	*lʾḥyʾ bt mʾmn*
אחיאם בן שלם	22.	*ʾḥyʾm bn šlm*
לאחיעזר (בן) אריהו	23.	*lʾḥyʿzr (bn) ʾryhw*
לאחיקם בן [א]חי[הו]	24.	*lʾḥyqm bn [ʾ]ḥy[hw]*
לאחיקם בן שפן	25.	*lʾḥyqm bn špn*
לאחמלך (בן) מקניהו	26.	*lʾḥmlk (bn) mqnyhw*
לאליה (בת/בן) אליאב	27.	*lʾlyh (bt/bn) ʾlyʾb*
לאליהו	28.	*lʾlyhw*
לאליהו (בן) אדניהו	29.	*lʾlyhw (bn) ʾdnyhw*
לאליקם (בן) חלקיהו	30.	*lʾlyqm (bn) ḥlqyhw*
לאלסמך (בן) אבא	31.	*lʾlsmk (bn) ʾbʾ*
לאלרם נ.., בן ירמיהו	32.	*lʾlrm n... bn yrmyhw*
לאלשמע בן מלכיהו	33.	*lʾlšmʿ bn mlkyhw*
לאלשמע בן שעל	34.	*lʾlšmʿ bn šʿl*
לאמריהו בן אסף	35.	*lʾmryhw bn ʾsp*
לאפרח (בן) נחמיהו	36.	*lʾprḥ (bn) nḥmyhw*
לאריהו (בן) עזר	37.	*lʾryhw (bn) ʿzr*
לאשיהו (בן) שעל	38.	*ʾšyhw (bn) šʿl*
לבניהו בן נריהו בן פקח	39.	*lbnyhw bn nryhw bn pqḥ*
לבקש בן בניהו	40.	*lbqš bn bnyhw*
להושעיהו (בן) ראיהו	41.	*lhwšʿyhw (bn) rʾyhw*

להושעיהו בן שמעיהו	42.	*lhwšʿyhw bn šmʿyhw*
להצל בן שחר	43.	*lhṣl bn šḥr*
לזכר בן טביהו	44.	*lzkr bn ṭbyhw*
לחגב בן אמריהו	45.	*lḥgb bn ʾmryhw*
לטביהו (בן) חני	46a.	*lṭbyhw (bn) ḥny*
לטביהו (בן) חני	46b.	*lṭbyhw (bn) ḥny*
ליאזניהו	47.	*lyʾznyhw*
ידעיהו	48.	*ydʿyhw*
ליהואב בן שפט	49.	*lyhwʾb bn špṭ*
ליהועז בן אלעשה	50a.	*lyhwʿz bn ʾlʿśa*
ליהועז בן אלעשה	50b.	*lyhwʿz bn ʾlʿśa* (not identical)
ליהוקם (בן) חגי	51.	*lyhwqm (bn) ḥgy*
ליועליהו בן שבנא	52.	*lywʿlyhw bn šbnʾ*
ליקמיהו בן אסף	53.	*lyqmyhw bn ʾsp*
ירם (בן) נריהו	54.	*yrm (bn) nryhw*
לירמיהו בן איעם	55.	*lyrmyhw bn ʾyʿm*
לישמעאל בן שפן	56.	*lyšmʿʾl bn špn*
למיאמן (בן) משלם	57.	*lmyʾmn (bn) mšlm*
למליהו (בן) נחמיהו	58.	*lmlyhw (bn) nḥmyhw*
למלכיהו בן יועליהו	59.	*lmlkyhw bn ywʿlyhw*
למעשיהו בן חצפ..	60.	*lmʿśyhw bn ḥṣp..*
למצרי (בן) שבניהו	61a.	*lmṣry (bn) šbnyhw*
למצרי (בן) [שבניהו]	61b.	*lmṣry (bn) [šbnyhw]*
למתניהו (בן) אמריהו	62.	*lmtnyhw (bn) ʾmryhw*
למתניהו בן אריהו	63.	*lmtnyhw bn ʾryhw*
לנחם בן מקמיהו	64.	*lnḥm bn mqmyhw*
לנחמיהו (בן) יהואב	65.	*lnḥmyhw (bn) yhwʾb*
לנרא (בן) מלכיהו	66a.	*lnrʾ (bn) mlkyhw*
לנרא (בן) מלכיהו	66b.	*lnrʾ (bn) mlkyhw*
לנרא בן משלם	67.	*lnrʾ bn mšlm*
לסמך (בן) רפא	68.	*lsmk (bn) rpʾ*
לסמך בן שפטיהו	69.	*lsmk bn špṭyhw*
לסעדיהו (בן) ...	70.	*lsʿdyhw (bn) ...*
עבדיה (בן) מנחמו	71.	*ʿbdyh (bn) mnḥmw*
לעבדיהו בן אחאב	72.	*ʿbdyhw (bn) ʾḥʾb*
לעזר (בן) אחא	73.	*lʿzr (bn) ʾḥʾ*
לעזריהו בן ...עז	74.	*lʿzryhw bn ...ʿz*
לעזריקם בן מכי	75.	*lʿzryqm bn mky*
לעכבר בן פלטי	76a.	*lʿkbr bn plṭy*
לעכבר בן פלטי	76b.	*lʿkbr bn plṭy*
לעכבר בן פלטי	76c.	*lʿkbr bn plṭy*
לעליהו בן הצליהו	77.	*lʿlyhw bn hṣlyhw*
לעשיהו (בן) שבנא	78.	*lʿśyhw (bn) šbnʾ*
לפלטיהו (בן) שכניהו	79.	*lplṭyhw (bn) šknyhw*
לפלטיהו ...ל.יהו	80.	*lplṭyhw ...l.yhw*
לפלטיהו (בן) ...	81.	*lplṭyhw (bn) ...*
לפשחר בן ישמעאל	82.	*lpšḥr bn yšmʿʾl*
לצפן בן עזריקם	83.	*lṣpn bn ʿzryqm*
לצפניה (בן) מיאמן	84.	*lṣpnyh (bn) myʾmn*
לשבניהו (בן) מחסיהו	85.	*lšbnyhw (bn) mhsyhw*
לשכניהו (בן) אלעשה	86.	*lšknyhw (bn) ʾlʿśa*

לשלם בן אליקם	87.	*lšlm bn ʾlyqm*
לשלמה (בן/בת) ישעיהו	88.	*lšlmh (bn/bt) yšʿyhw*
לשלמיהו בן אליכן	89.	*lšlmyhw bn ʾlykn*
לשמעיהו (בן) צפניהו	90.	*lšmʿyhw (bn) ṣpnyhw*
לשפט בן ידעיהו	91.	*lšpṭ bn ydʿyhw*
לשפן בן חגב	92.	*lšpn bn ḥgb*
לשפן בן עזרקם	93.	*lšpn bn ʿzrqm*
לשפן (בן) רפאיהו	94.	*lšpn (bn) rpʾyhw*
... בן בעדיהו	95.	*... bn bʿdyhw*
..א.. (בן) סמכי	96.	*..ʾ.. (bn) smky*
ב 14 שנה, ראשנה, לכש, למלך	97a.	*b 14 šnh, rʾšnh, lkš, lmlk*
ב 14 שנה, ראשנה, לכש, למלך	97b.	*b 14 šnh, rʾšnh, lkš, lmlk*
ב 20 שנה, נצב, למלך	98.	*b 20 šnh, nṣb, lmlk*
בשלשת, למכס	99.	*bšlšt, lmks*
בעשרת, הארבת, [יש]מעאל, (למלך)	100.	*bʿśrt, hʾrbt, [yš]mʿʾl, (lmlk)*

Bullae belonging to our group, published by Avigad (1990:262–266)

ב 26 שנה, אלתלד, למלך	101.	*b 26 šnh, ʾltld, lmlk*
לתחת בן בסי (sic.) **(אחאב אבסי)**	102.	*ltḥt bn bsy (sic.) (ʾḥʾb ʾbsy)*

Indexes for Chapter Three

Personal Names

אבא	*ʾbʾ* — 31
אביהו	*ʾbyhw* — 7
אדניהו	ʾdnyhw — 5, 29
אחא	*ʾḥʾ* — 73
אחאב	*ʾḥʾb* — 18a-b, 19, 72
אחז	*ʾḥz* — 1
אחיא	*ʾḥyʾ* — 20, 21
אחיאם	*ʾḥyʾm* — 22
אחיהו	*ʾḥyhw* — 24
אחיעזר	*ʾḥyʿzr* — 23
אחיקם	*ʾḥyqm* — 24, 25
אחמיה	*ʾḥmyh* — 15a-b
אחמלך	*ʾḥmlk* — 18a-b, 26
איעם	*ʾyʿm* — 55
אליאב	*ʾlyʾb* — 27
אליה	*ʾlyh* — 27
אליהו	*ʾlyhw* — 28, 29
אליכן	*ʾlykn* — 89
אליעז	*ʾlyʿz* — 74?
אליקם	*ʾlyqm* — 30, 87
אלסמך	*ʾlsmk* — 31
אלעז	*ʾlʿz* — 74?
אלעשה	*ʾlʿśh* — 50a-b, 86
אלרם	*ʾlrm* — 32
אלשמע	*ʾlšmʿ* — 33, 34
אמריהו	*ʾmryhw* — 35, 46, 62
אסף	*ʾsp* — 35, 53
אפרח	*ʾprḥ* — 36
אריהו	*ʾryhw* — 23, 37, 63
אשיהו	*ʾšyhw* — 38
בניהו	*bnyhw* — 39, 40
בסי (אבסי)	*bsy [ʾbsy (sic.)]* — 102
בעדיהו	*bʿdyhw* — 95
בקש	*bqš* — 40
גדליהו	*gdlyhw* — 8
הושע	*hwšʿ* — 41?
הושעיהו	*hwšʿyhw* — 41?, 42
הצל	*hṣl* — 43
הצליהו	*hṣlyhw* — 77
זכר	*zkr* — 44
חגב	*ḥgb* — 45, 92
חגי	*ḥgy* — 51
חזקיהו	*ḥzqyhw* — 2, 3, 4
חלקיהו	*ḥlqyhw* — 2, 30
חני	*ḥny* — 46a-b
חצפ...	*ḥṣp..* — 60
טביהו	*ṭbyhw* — 44, 46a-b
טבשלם	*ṭbšlm* — 11
יאזניהו	*yʾznyhw* — 47
ידעיהו	*ydʿyhw* — 48, 91
יהואב	*yhwʾb* — 49, 65
יהואח	*yhwʾḥ* — 3
יהוזרח	*yhwzrḥ* — 2
יהועז	*yhwʿz* — 50a-b, 74?
יהוקם	*yhwqm* — 51
יהותם	*yhwtm* — 1
יועליהו	*ywʿlyhw* — 52, 59
יקמיהו	*yqmyhw* — 53
ירם	*yrm* — 54
ירמיהו	*yrmyhw* — 32, 55
ישמעאל	*yšmʿʾl* — 56, 82, 100
ישעיהו	*yšʿyhw* — 88
מאמן	*mʾmn* — 21
מבטחיהו	*mbṭḥyhw* — 6
מחסיהו	*mḥsyhw* — 85
מיאמן	*myʾmn* — 57, 84
מכי	*mky* — 75
מליהו	*mlyhw* — 58
מלכיהו	*mlkyhw* — 33, 59, 66a-b
מנחמו	*mnḥmw* — 71
מעשיהו	*mʿśyhw* — 60
מצרי	*mṣry* — 61a-b
מקמיהו	*mqmyhw* — 64
מקניהו	*mqnyhw* — 26
משלם	*mšlm* — 57, 67
מתן	*mtn* — 15a-b
מתניהו	*mtnyhw* — 20, 62, 63
נויה	*nwyh* — 14
נחם	*nḥm* — 64
נחמיהו	*nḥmyhw* — 36, 58, 65
נרא	*nrʾ* — 66a-b, 67
נריהו	*nryhw* — 39, 54

נתנמלך *ntnmlk* — 9
סמך *smk* — 68, 69
סמכי *smky* — 96
סעדיהו *sʿdyhw* — 70
עבדיהו *ʿbdyhw* — 71
עזר *ʿzr* — 37, 73
עזריהו *ʿzryhw* — 3, 10, 74
עזריקם *ʿzryqm* — 75, 83
עזרקם *ʿzrqm* — 93
עכבר *ʿkbr* — 76a-c
עליהו *ʿlyhw* — 77
עשיהו *ʿśyhw* — 78
פלטי *plṭy* — 76a-c
פלטיהו *plṭyhw* — 79, 80, 81
פקדיהו *pqdyhw* — 12
פקח *pqḥ* — 17, 39
פשחר *pšḥr* — 82
צפן *ṣpn* — 83
צפניה *ṣpnyh* — 84
צפניהו *ṣpnyhw* — 90
ראיהו? *rʾyhw?* — 41
רפא *rpʾ* — 68
רפאיהו *rpʾyhw* — 94
שבנא *šbnʾ* — 52, 78
שבניהו *šbnyhw* — 16, 61a, (61b), 85
שחר *šḥr* — 43
שכניהו *šknyhw* — 79, 86
שלם *šlm* — 22, 78
שלמה *šlmh* — 16, 88
שלמיהו *šlmyhw* — 89
שמעיהו *šmʿyhw* — 42, 90
שעל *šʿl* — 34, 38
שפט *špṭ* — 49, 91
שפטיהו *špṭyhw* — 69
שפן *špn* — 25, 56, 92, 93, 94
תחת (אחאב) *tḥt [ʾḥʾb (sic.)]* — 102
..א.. *..ʾ..* — 96
..יהו *..yhw* — 80
..עז *..ʿz* — 74

Royal names

אחז *ʾḥz* — 1
חזקיהו *ḥzqyhw* — 2, 3, 4
יהותם *yhwtm* — 1

Toponyms

יהדה *yhdh* — 1
לכש *lkš* — 97a-b
נצב *nṣb* — 98
ארבת *ʾrbt* — 100
אלתלד *ʾltld* — 101

Titles

אשר על הבית *ʾšr ʿl hbyt* — "Who is over the house" — 5, 6
בת המלך *bt hmlk* — "Daughter of the king" — 14
למלך *lmlk* — "For the king" — 97a-b, 98, 101
מלך יהדה *mlk yhdh* — "King of Judah" — 1
עבד המלך *ʿbd hmlk* — "Servant of the king" — 7, 8, 9, 10
עבד חזקיהו *ʿbd ḥzkyhw* — "Servant of Hezekiah" — 2, 3, 4
שר הער *śr hʿr* — "Governor of the city" — 11, 12, 13

Words

בן *bn* — "Son" — 2, 3, 18a-b, 20, 21, 22, 24, 25, 33, 34, 35, 39, 40, 42, 43, 44, 45, 49, 50a-b, 52, 53, 55, 56, 59, 60, 63, 64, 67, 69, 72, 74, 75, 76a-c, 77, 82, 83, 87, 88?, 89, 91, 92, 93, 95, 102

בת *bt* — "Daughter" — 14, 15a-b, 16, 17, 27?, 88?

מכס *mks* — "Customs" — 99

עשרת *ʿśrt* — "Tenth" — 100

ראשנה *rʾšnh* — "First" — 97a-b

שלשת *šlšt* — "Three (masc.)" — 99

שנה *šnh* — "Year" — 97a-b, 98, 101

Numerals

14 — 97a-b

20 — 98

26 — 101

BIBLIOGRAPHY

Aharoni, Y. 1966. The Use of Hieratic Numerals in Hebrew Ostraca and the Shekel Weight. *BASOR* 184:13–19.

Aharoni, Y. 1975. *Investigations at Lachish: The Sanctuary and the Residency. (Lachish V).* Tel Aviv.

Aharoni, Y. 1981. *Arad Inscriptions.* Jerusalem.

AHL — Avigad, N., Heltzer, M. and Lemaire, A. in press: *Catalogue of the West Semitic Seals in the Hecht Museum.* Haifa.

Ahlström, G.W. 1993. The Seal of Shema^{c}. *Scandinavian Journal of the Old Testament* 7:208–215.

Albright, W.F. 1943. *The Excavation of Tell Beit Mirsim.* Vol. 3: *The Iron Age. AASOR* 21–22:73.

Alt, A. 1953. *Kleine Schriften* 2.

ANET — Pritchard, J.B. ed., 1969. *Ancient Near Eastern Texts Relating to the Old Testament.* Third Edition with Supplement. Princeton.

Avi-Yonah, M. and Stern, E. (eds.) 1978. *Encyclopedia of Archaeological Excavations in the Holy Land.* Vol. 4. London. p. 1062.

Avigad, N. 1950. Epigraphical Gleanings from Gezer. *PEQ* 82:43–46.

Avigad, N. 1953. The Epitaph of a Royal Steward from Siloam Village. *IEJ* 3:137–152.

Avigad, N. 1958. An Early Aramaic Seal. *IEJ* 8:228–230.

Avigad, N. 1963. Two Newly Found Hebrew Seals. *IEJ* 13:322–324.

Avigad, N. 1964. Seals and Sealings. *IEJ* 14:190–194.

Avigad, N. 1972. Two Hebrew Inscriptions on Wine-Jars. *IEJ* 22:1–9.

Avigad, N. 1975. New Names on Hebrew Seals. *EI* 12:66–71 (Hebrew).

Avigad, N. 1976. New Light on *na^{c}ar* Seals. *Magnalia Dei.* The Mighty Acts of God. (eds. F.M. Cross et al.) Studies Presented to J. Bright. Garden City: 294–300.

Avigad, N. 1978. The King's Daughter and the Lyre. *IEJ* 28:146, Pl. 26:C.

Avigad, N. 1978a. Baruch the Scribe and Yerahme'el the King's Son. *IEJ* 28:52–56.

Avigad, N. 1979. A Group of Hebrew Seals from the Hecht Collection, in: *Festschrift Rëuben R. Hecht.* Jerusalem:119–126.

Avigad, N. 1986. *Hebrew Bullae from the Time of Jeremiah.* Jerusalem.

Avigad, N. 1987. The Contribution of Hebrew Seals to an Understanding of Israelite Religion and Society; in Miller, P.D., Hanson, P.D. and McBride, D.S. (eds.), *Ancient Israelite Religions: Essays in Honor of F.M. Cross.* Philadelphia:195–208.

Avigad, N. 1989. Another Group of West-Semitic Seals from the Hecht Collection. *Michmanim* 4:7–21.
Avigad, N. 1989a. Two Seals of Woman and Other Hebrew Seals. *EI* 20:90–96 (Hebrew).
Avigad, N. 1990. Two Hebrew "Fiscal" Bullae. *IEJ* 40:262–266.
Avigad, N. 1992. A New Bulla of a Moabite Scribe. *EI* 23:92–93 (Hebrew).
Avigad, N. 1994. The "Governor of the City" Bulla, in: Geva, H. ed., *Ancient Jerusalem Revealed*. Jerusalem:138–140.
Avigad, N. 1997. *Corpus of West Semitic Stamp Seals*. (Revised and completed by B. Sass). Jerusalem.
Avigad, N., Heltzer, M. and Lemaire, A. *Catalogue of the West Semitic Seals in the Hecht Museum*. Haifa. (in press)
Avishur, Y. and Heltzer, M. 1996. *Studies on the Royal Administration, in Israel in the Light of Epigraphic sources*. Jerusalem (Hebrew).
Barkay, G. 1993. A Bulla of Ishmael, the King's Son. *BASOR* 290–291:109–114.
Barkay, G. 1994. A Second "Governor of the City" Bulla, in: Geva, H. ed., *Ancient Jerusalem Revealed*. Jerusalem:141–144.
Barnett, R.D. 1967. Layard's Nimrud Bronzes and their Inscriptions. *Eretz-Israel* 8:6*.
Beer-Sheba I — Aharoni, Y. 1973. ed., *Beer-Sheba I: Excavations at Tel Beer-Sheba, 1969–1971 Seasons*. Tel Aviv.
Beit-Arieh, I. 1986–7. The Ostracon of Aḥiqam from Ḥorvat ʿUza. *Tel Aviv* 13–14:32–38.
Beit-Arieh, I. 1988–9. Ḥorvat ʿUza — 1988, *ESI* 7–8:181.
Beit-Arieh, I. and Cresson, B. 1985. An Edomite Ostracon From Ḥorvat ʿUza. *Tel Aviv* 12:96–101.
Bennett, C.M. 1966. Fouilles d'Umm el-Biyara. Rapport préliminaire. *RB* 73:372–403.
Bennett, C.M. 1974. Excavations at Buseirah, Southern Jordan. *Levant* 6:1–24.
Bliss, F.J. 1900. Second Report on the Excavations at Tell ej-Judeideh. *PEFQS* 32:199–222.
Bordreuil, P. 1986. *Catalogue des sceaux ouest-sémitiques inscrits*. Paris.
Bordreuil, P. 1992. Sceaux inscrits des pays du Levant, *Supplément au dictionnaire de la Bible*. fasc. 66, cols. 86–212, Paris.
Bordreuil, P. and Lemaire, A. 1976. Nouveaux sceaux hébreux, araméens et ammonites. *Semitica* 26:45–63.
Bordreuil, P. and Lemaire, A. 1982. Nouveaux sceaux hébreux, araméens. *Semitica* 32:21–34.
Bordreuil, P. and Pardee, D. 1988. Le papyrus du marzeaḥ. *Semitica* 38:49–68.
Bracke, J.M. 1992. Pashhur, in: *The Anchor Bible Dictionary*. Vol. 5:171–172.
Clermont-Ganneau, C. 1883. Sceaux et cachets israélites, phéniciens et syriens. *JA* 1:123–159.
Clermont-Ganneau, C. 1902. Archaeological and Epigraphic Notes on Palestine. *PEFQS* 34:260–282.
Collon, D. 1990. *Near Eastern Seals*. London.
Cowley, A. 1923. *Aramaic Papyri of the Fifth Century B.C.E.* Oxford.
Cross, F.M. 1996. A Papyrus Recording a Divine Legal Decision and the Root *rḥq* in Biblical

and Near Eastern Legal Usage; in: Fox, M.V. et al., *Texts, Temples, and Traditions, A Tribute to Menahem Haran*. Winona Lake:311–320.

Cross, F.M. 1999. King Hezekiah's Seal Bears Phoenician Imagery, *Biblical Archaeology Review*. Vol. 25, no. 2:42–45, 60.

Davies, G.I. 1991. *Ancient Hebrew Inscriptions, Corpus and Concordance*. Cambridge.

Deutsch, R. 1998. First Impression; What We Learn from Ahaz's Seal. *BAR* 24, no. 3:54–56, 62.

Deutsch, R. 1999. A Royal Ammonite Seal Impression. in: Avishur, Y. and Deutsch, R. (eds.): *Michael; Historical, Epigraphical and Biblical Studies in Honor of Prof. Michael Heltzer*. Tel Aviv–Jaffa:121–125.

Deutsch, R. and Heltzer, M. 1994. *Forty New Ancient West Semitic Inscriptions*. Tel Aviv–Jaffa.

Deutsch, R. and Heltzer, M, 1995. *New Epigraphic Evidence from the Biblical Period*. Tel Aviv-Jaffa.

Deutsch, R. and Heltzer, M. 1997. *Windows to the Past*. Tel Aviv–Jaffa.

DHL — Overbeck, B. and Meshorer, Y., 1993. *Das Heilige Land*. München.

Diringer, D. 1934. *Le Iscrizioni Antico-Ebraiche Palestinesi*. Firenze.

Driver, G.R. 1945. A New Israelite Seal. *PEQ* 77:5.

Even-Shoshan, A. 1990. *A New Concordance of the Bible*. Jerusalem (Hebrew).

Fulco, W.J. 1979. A Seal from Umm el-Qanafid, Jordan: *gʾlyhw ʿbd hmlk*. *Orientalia* 48:107–108.

Fuller, R. 1992. Shecaniah, in: *The Anchor Bible Dictionary*. Vol. 5:1173–1174.

Galil, G. 1996. *The Chronology of the Kings of Israel and Judah*. Leiden.

Galling, K. 1941. Beschriftete Bildsiegel des ersten Jahrtausends v. Chr. vornehmlich aus Syrien und Palästina. *ZDPV* 64:121–202.

Geraty, L.T. 1985. The Andrews University Madaba Plains Project: A Preliminary Report on the First Season at Tell el-ʿUmeiri. *Andrews University Seminary Studies*. 23:85–110.

Gitin, S., Dothan, T. and Naveh, J. 1997. A Royal Dedicatory Inscription from Ekron. *IEJ* 47:1–16.

Giveon, R. 1961. Two New Hebrew Seals and their Iconographic Background. *PEQ* 93:38–43.

Giveon, R. 1988. *Scarabs from Recent Excavations in Israel*. Göttingen.

Glueck, N. 1940. The Third Season of Excavations at Tell el-Kheleifeh. *BASOR* 79:2–18.

Gophna, R. and Porat, Y. 1972. The Land of Ephraim and Manasseh. In: Kochavi, M., ed.: *Judaea Samaria and the Golan*. Jerusalem:196–213 (Hebrew).

Guthe, H., Erman, A. and Kautzsch, E. 1906. Ein Siegelstein mit hebräischer Unterschrift vom Tell el-Mutesellim. *MNDPV* 5:33–35.

Hazor II — Yadin, Y, et al., 1959. *Hazor II: An Account of the Second Season of Excavations in 1956*. Jerusalem (Hebrew).

Heltzer, M. and Ohana, M. 1978. *The Extra-Biblical Tradition of Hebrew Personal Names*. Haifa.

Herodotus — The *History*, Translated by David Grene, 1988, University of Chicago. Chicago — London.

Herr, L. 1978. *The Scripts of Ancient Northwest Semitic Seals.* Missoula.

Hestrin, R. and Dayagi-Mendels, M. 1974. A Seal Impression of a Servant of King Hezekiah. *IEJ* 24:27–29.

Hestrin, R. and Dayagi-Mendels, M. 1979. *Inscribed Seals.* Jerusalem.

Kalai, Z. 1968. Naṣib, in: *Encyclopaedia Biblica.* Vol. 5:913–914 (Hebrew).

Kennedy, J.M. 1992. "Obadiah", in: *The Anchor Bible Dictionary.* Vol. 5:1–2. New-York.

Kimchi, D. 1991. *Encyclopedia of Men and Women in the Bible.* Tel-Aviv.

Kornfeld, W. 1978. *Onomastica Aramaica aus Ägypten.* Vienna.

Lachish I — Torczyner, H. et al., 1938. *Lachish I: The Lachish Letters.* London.

Lachish III — Tufnell, O. et al., 1953. *Lachish III: The Iron Age.* London.

Lachish V — Aharoni, Y. 1975. *Investigations at Lachish: The Sanctuary and the Residency.* Tel Aviv.

Layard, A.H. 1853. *Discoveries in the Ruins of Nineveh and Babylon.* London.

Lemaire, A. 1980. Notes d'épigraphie nord-ouest sémitiques. *Semitica* 30:19, Pl. I:b.

Lemaire, A. 1983. Nouveaux sceaux nord-ouest sémitiques. *Semitica* 33:27–30, Pls. I–III.

Lemaire, A. 1985. Sept sceaux nord-ouest sémitiques inscrits. *EI* 18:29*–32*.

Lemaire, A. 1991. Notes d'épigraphie nord-ouest sémitique. *Semitica* XL:39–54.

Lemaire, A. 1995. Name of Israel's Last King Surfaces in a Private Collection. *BAR* 21:48–52, no. 6.

Lemaire, A. 1999. (Book review: Deutsch, Robert. 1997. *Messages From the Past*). *Bibliotheca Orientalis* LVI No. 1/2:174–176.

Levy, M.A. 1869, *Siegel und Gemmen mit aramäischen, phönizischen, althebräischen, himjarischen, nabathäischen und altsyrischen Inschriften.* Breslau.

Maisler (Mazar), B. 1951. The Excavations at Tell Qasile: Preliminary Report III. *IEJ* 1:194–218.

Martin, M.F. 1964. Six Palestinian Seals. *RSO* 39:203–210.

Meshel, Z. 1978. *Kuntillet ʿAjrud, a Religious Center from the Time of the Judaean Monarchy on the Border of Sinai.* Jerusalem (Israel Museum Cat. no. 175).

Meshorer, Y. 1982. *Ancient Jewish Coinage.* New York. Vol. I:115–117, Pls.1–3.

Milik, J.T. 1959. Notes d'épigraphie et de topographie palestiniennes. I: l'ostracon de l'ophel et la topographie de Jérusalem. *RB* 66:550–53.

Millard, A.R. 1988, in: Buchanan, B. and Moorey, P.R.S. *Catalogue of Near Eastern Seals in the Ashmolean Museum III: The Iron Age Stamp Seals (c. 1200–350 BC).* Oxford.

Moscati, S. 1951. *L'Epigrafia ebraica antica.* Rome.

MPY — Mommsen, H., Perlman, I. and Yellin, J. 1984. The Provenience of the *lmlk* Jars. *IEJ* 34:89–113.

Naṣbeh I — McCown, C.C. 1974. *Tell en-Naṣbeh* I: *Archaeological and Historical Results.* Berkeley & New Haven.

Naveh, J. 1970. The Scripts in Palestine and Transjordan in the Iron Age, *Near Eastern Archaeology in the Twentieth Century*, Essays in Honor of Nelson Glueck, ed. J.A. Sanders. Garden City:277–283.

Naveh, J. 1994. *Origins of the Alphabets; Introduction to Archaeology*. Jerusalem.

Naveh, J. 1996. Gleanings of Some Pottery Inscriptions. *IEJ* 46:44–51.

Noth, M. 1927. Das Krongut der israelitischen Könige und seine Verwaltung, *ZDPV* 50:240–244.

O'Connell, K.G. 1977. An Israelite Bulla from Tell el-Ḥesi. *IEJ* 27:197–199.

On. — Klosterman, E. 1966. *Eusebius, Das Onomastikon der Biblischen Ortsnamen*. Hildesheim.

Overbeck, B. and Meshorer, Y. 1993. *Das Heilige Land*. München.

Prignaud, J. 1978. Scribes et Graveurs à Jérusalem vers 700 av. J. C., in: Moorey, R. and Parr, P. (eds.), *Archaeology in the Levant: Essays for Kathleen Kenyon*. Warminster:136.

Pritchard, J.B. 1959. *Hebrew Inscriptions and Stamps from Gibeon*. Philadelphia.

Rainey, A.F. 1967. The Samaria Ostraca in the Light of Fresh Evidence. *PEQ* 99:32–41.

Rainey, A.F. 1981. Three Additional Texts, in: Aharoni, Y. *Arad Inscriptions*. Jerusalem:122–125.

Ramat Raḥel — Aharoni, Y. 1962. *Excavations at Ramat Raḥel, Seasons 1959–60*. Roma.

Reade, J.E. 1995. Cubic bronze weight, in: Curtis, J.E. and Reade, J.E. eds. *Art and Empire; Treasures from the British Museum*. London:195.

Reifenberg, A.1938. Some Ancient Hebrew Seals. *PEQ* 70:113–116.

Reifenberg, A. 1942. Ancient Hebrew Seals III. *PEQ* 74:109–112.

Robinson, E. 1841. *Biblical Researches in Palestina, Mount Sinai and Arabia Petraea*. Vol. II and III. London.

Rosenbaum, J. and Seger, J.D. 1986. Three Unpublished Ostraca from Gezer. *BASOR* 264:51–60.

Rowe. A. 1936. *A Catalogue of Egyptian Scarabs, Scaraboids, Seals and Amulets in the Palestine Archaeological Museum*. Le Caire.

Saarisalo, A. 1931. Topographical Researches in the Shephelah. *JPOS* 11:98–104.

Sass, B. 1993. The Pre-Exilic Hebrew Seals: Iconism vs. Aniconism, in: Sass, B. and Uehlinger, C. eds. *Studies in the Iconography of Northwest Semitic Inscribed Seals*. Fribourg:194–256.

Samaria I — Reisner, G.A., Fisher, C.S. and Lyon, D.G., 1924. *Harvard Excavation at Samaria*, Vol. I. Harvard.

Schröder, P. 1880. Drei Siegelsteine mit phoenizischen Aufschriften. *ZDMG* 34:681–684.

Schumacher, G. and Steuernagel, C. 1908. *Tell el Mutesellim*. Leipzig.

Schneider, T. 1994. A Biblical Name on a City of David Bulla: Azariah son of Hilkiah (High Priest?), in: Geva, H. ed., *Ancient Jerusalem Revealed*. Jerusalem:62–63.

Segal, J.B. 1957. An Aramaic Ostracon from Nimrud. *Iraq* 19:139–45.

Sellers, O.R. and Albright, W.F. 1931. The First Campaign of Excavations at Beth-Zur. *BASOR* 43:2–13.

Sendschirli V — Von Luschan, F. and Andrae, W. 1943. *Ausgrabungen in Sendschirli V: Die Kleinfunde von Sendschirli*. Berlin.

Shiloh, Y. 1981. The City of David Archaeological Project: The Third Season. *BA* 44:161–170.

Shiloh, Y. 1986. A Group of Hebrew Bullae from the City of David. *IEJ* 36:16–28.

Shoham Y. 1994. A Group of Hebrew Bullae from Yigal Shiloh's Excavation in the City of David, in: Geva, H. ed.: *Ancient Jerusalem Revealed*. Jerusalem:55–61.
Syon, D. 1992-3. The coins from Gamla — Interim Report. *INJ* 12:34–55.
Thiele, E.R. 1983. *The Mysterious Numbers of the Hebrew Kings*. Chicago (Third revised edition).
Torrey, C.C. 1923. A Few Ancient Seals. *AASOR* 2–3:103–108.
Torrey, C.C. 1940. A Hebrew Seal from the Reign of Ahaz. *BASOR* 79:27–28.
Tufnell, O. et al., 1953. *Lachish III: The Iron Age*. London.
Ussishkin, D. 1992. Lachish, in: *The Anchor Bible Dictionary*. Vol. 5:114–126.
Ussishkin, D. 1994. Gate 1567 at Megiddo and the Seal of Shemaᶜ, Servant of Jeroboam; in Coogan M.D., Exum, J.C. and Stager, L.E. eds.: *Scripture and Other Artifacts*. Louisville.
Vattioni, F. 1969. I Sigilli ebraici. *Biblica* 50:357–388.
Vattioni, F. 1971. I Sigilli, le monete e gli avori aramaici. *Augustinianum* 11:47–69.
Vaughn, A.G. 1996. *The Chronicler's Account of Hezekiah: The Relationship of Historical Data to a Theological Interpretation of 2 Chronicles 29–32*. (Unpublished Ph.D. dissertation, Princeton Theological Seminary).
Vincent, L.H. 1903. Notes d'épigraphie palestinienne. *RB* 12:604–612.
Willett, T.W. 1992. Haggiah, in: *The Anchor Bible Dictionary*. Vol. III:23.
Wright, W. 1882. On Three Gems Bearing Phoenician Inscriptions. *PSBA* 4:54.
Yadin, Y. 1967. A Note on the Nimrud Bronze Bowls. *Eretz-Israel* 8:6*.
Zadok, R. 1988. *The Pre-hellenistic-Israelite Antroponomy and Prosopography*. Leuven.
Zertal, A. 1992. Arubboth, in: *The Anchor Bible Dictionary*. Vol. 1:465–467.

ABBREVIATIONS

A — Avigad, N. 1986. *Hebrew Bullae from the Time of Jeremiah*. Jerusalem.
AASOR — *Annual of the American Schools of Oriental Research*
AHL — Avigad, N., Heltzer, M. and Lemaire, A. *Catalogue of the West Semitic Seals in the Hecht Museum*. Haifa. (in press)
ANET — *Ancient Near Eastern Texts Relating to the Old Testament*
BA — *Biblical Archaeologist*
BAR — *Biblical Archaeology Review*
BASOR — *Bulletin of the American Schools of Oriental Research*
EI — *Eretz Israel*
ESI — *Excavations and Surveys in Israel*
IAA — *Israel Antiquities Authority*
IEJ — *Israel Exploration Journal*
INJ — *Israel Numismatic Journal*
JA — *Journal Asiatique*
JPOS — *Journal of the Palestine Oriental Society*
MNDPV — *Mitteilungen und Nachrichten des Deutschen Palästina-Vereins*
PEFQS — *Palestine Exploration Fund, Quarterly Statement*
PEQ — *Palestine Exploration Quarterly*
PSBA — *Proceedings of the Society of Biblical Archaeology*
RB — *Revue Biblique*
RSO — *Rivista degli Studi Orientali*
S — *Shoham, Y. 1994.*
WSS — *West Semitic Seals* — Avigad, N. 1997. *Corpus of West Semitic Stamp Seals*. (Revised and completed by B. Sass). Jerusalem.
ZDMG — *Zeitschrift den Deutschen Morgenländischen Gesellschaft*
ZDPV — *Zeitschrift den Deutschen Palästina-Vereins*

	1	2	3	4	5	6	7	8	9	10	11	12	13
ʾ													
b													
g													
d													
h													
w													
z													
ḥ													
ṭ													
y													
k													
l													
m													
n													
s													
ʿ													
p													
ṣ													
q													
r													
š													
t													

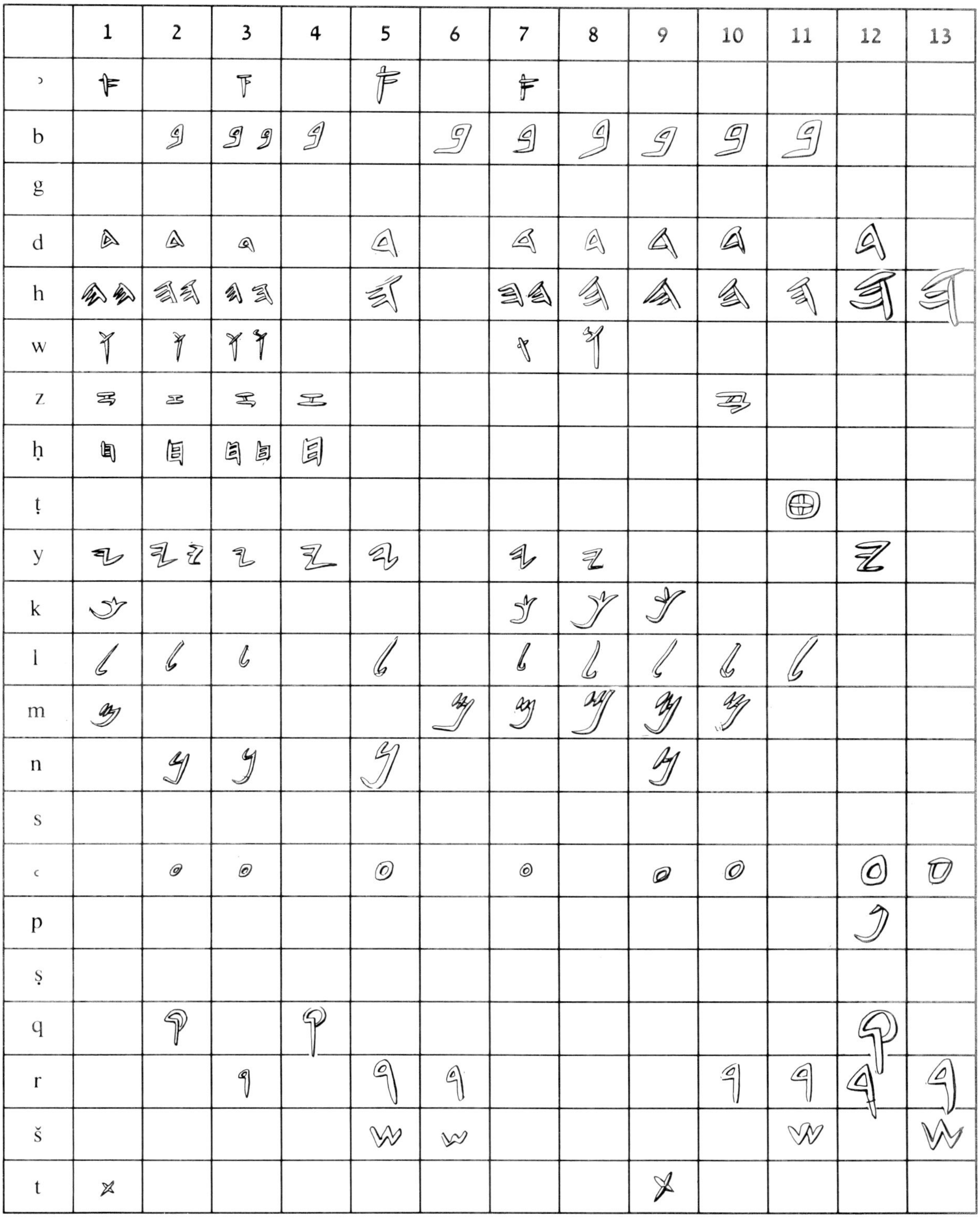

	14	15	16	17	18	19	20	21	22	23	24	25	26
ʾ													
b													
g													
d													
h													
w													
z													
ḥ													
ṭ													
y													
k													
l													
m													
n													
s													
ʿ													
p													
ṣ													
q													
r													
š													
t													

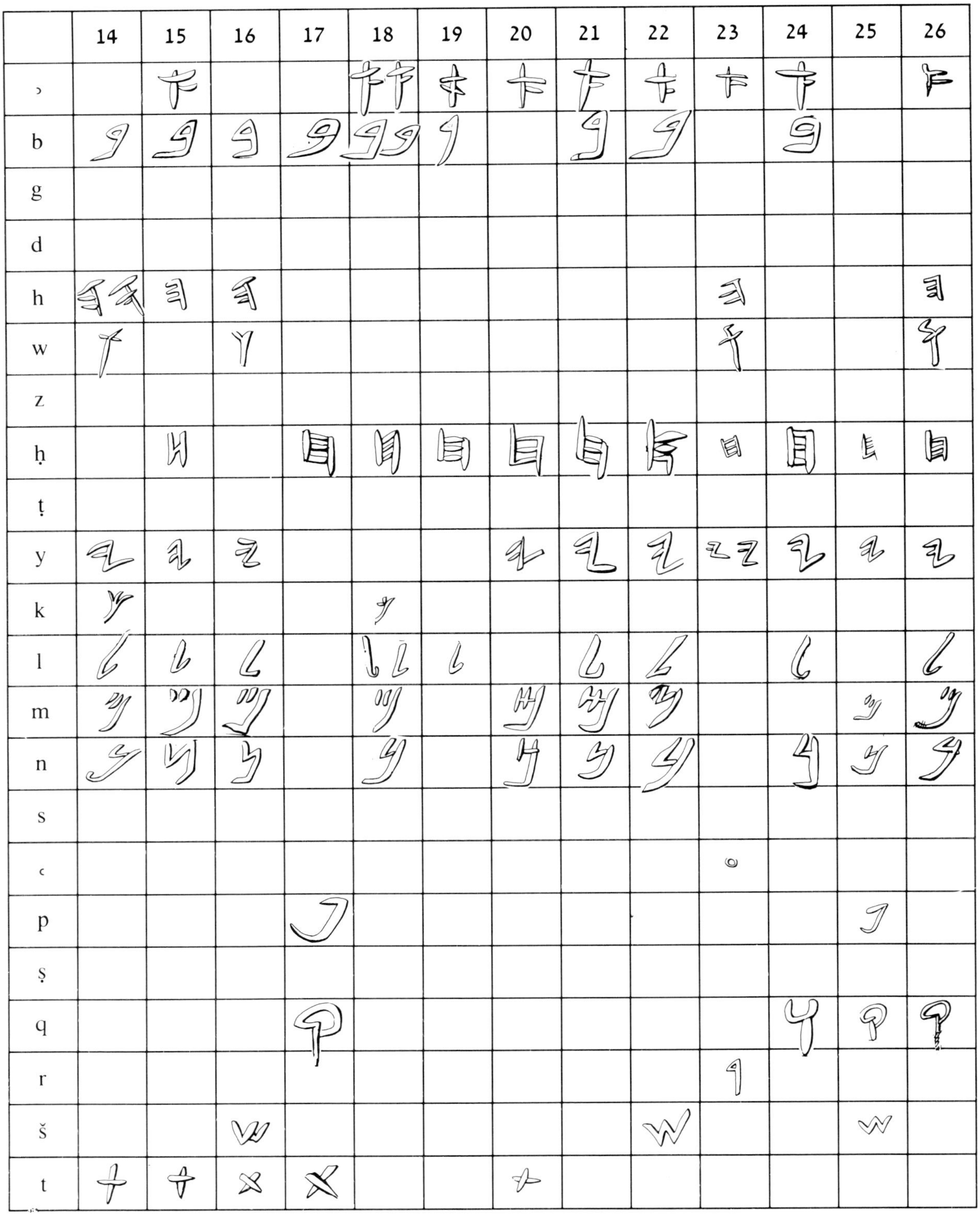

	27	28	29	30	31	32	33	34	35	36	37	38	39
ʾ													
b													
g													
d													
h													
w													
z													
ḥ													
ṭ													
y													
k													
l													
m													
n													
s													
ʿ													
p													
ṣ													
q													
r													
š													
t													

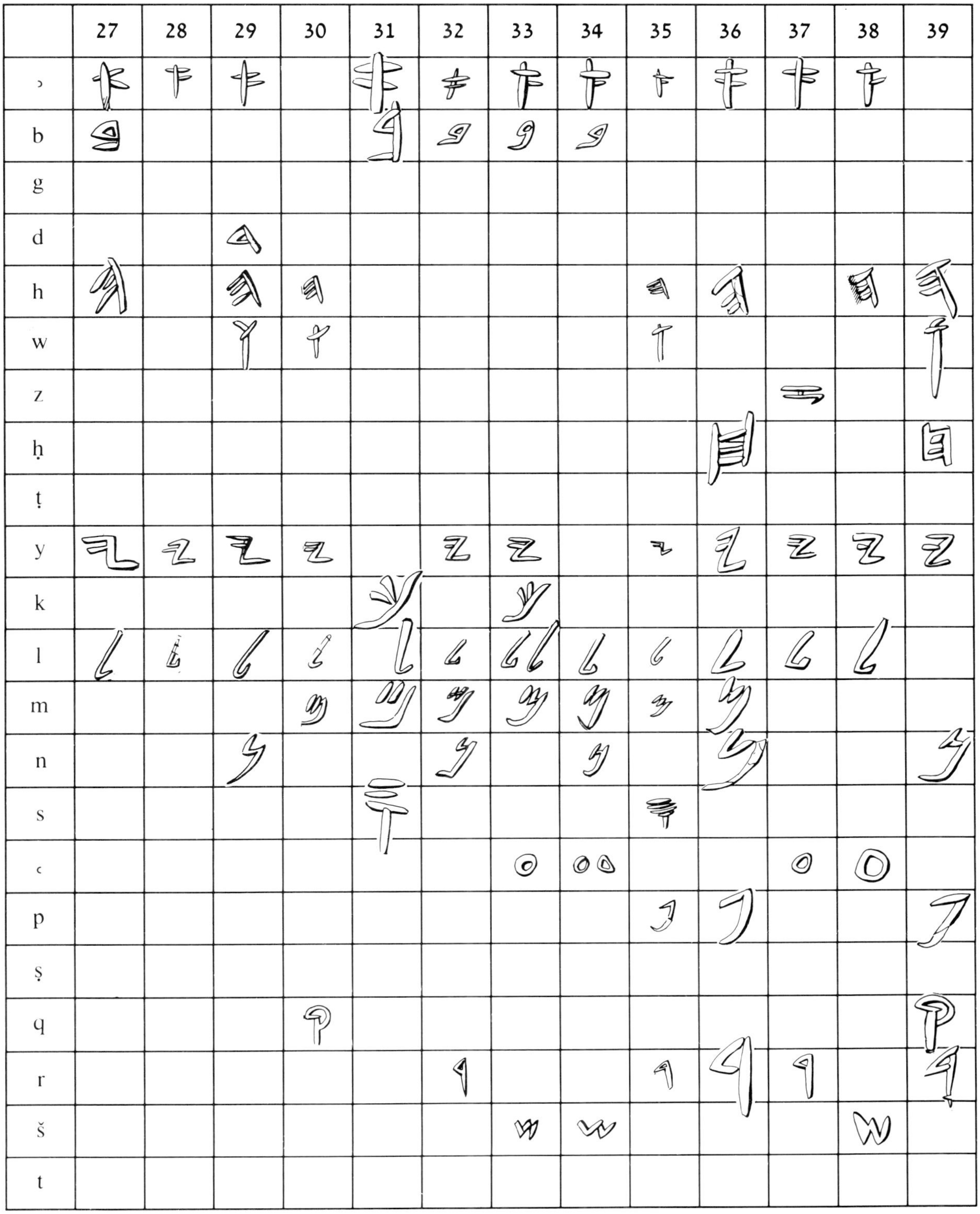

	40	41	42	43	44	45	46	47	48	49	50	51	52
ʾ													
b													
g													
d													
h													
w													
z													
ḥ													
ṭ													
y													
k													
l													
m													
n													
s													
ʿ													
p													
ṣ													
q													
r													
š													
t													

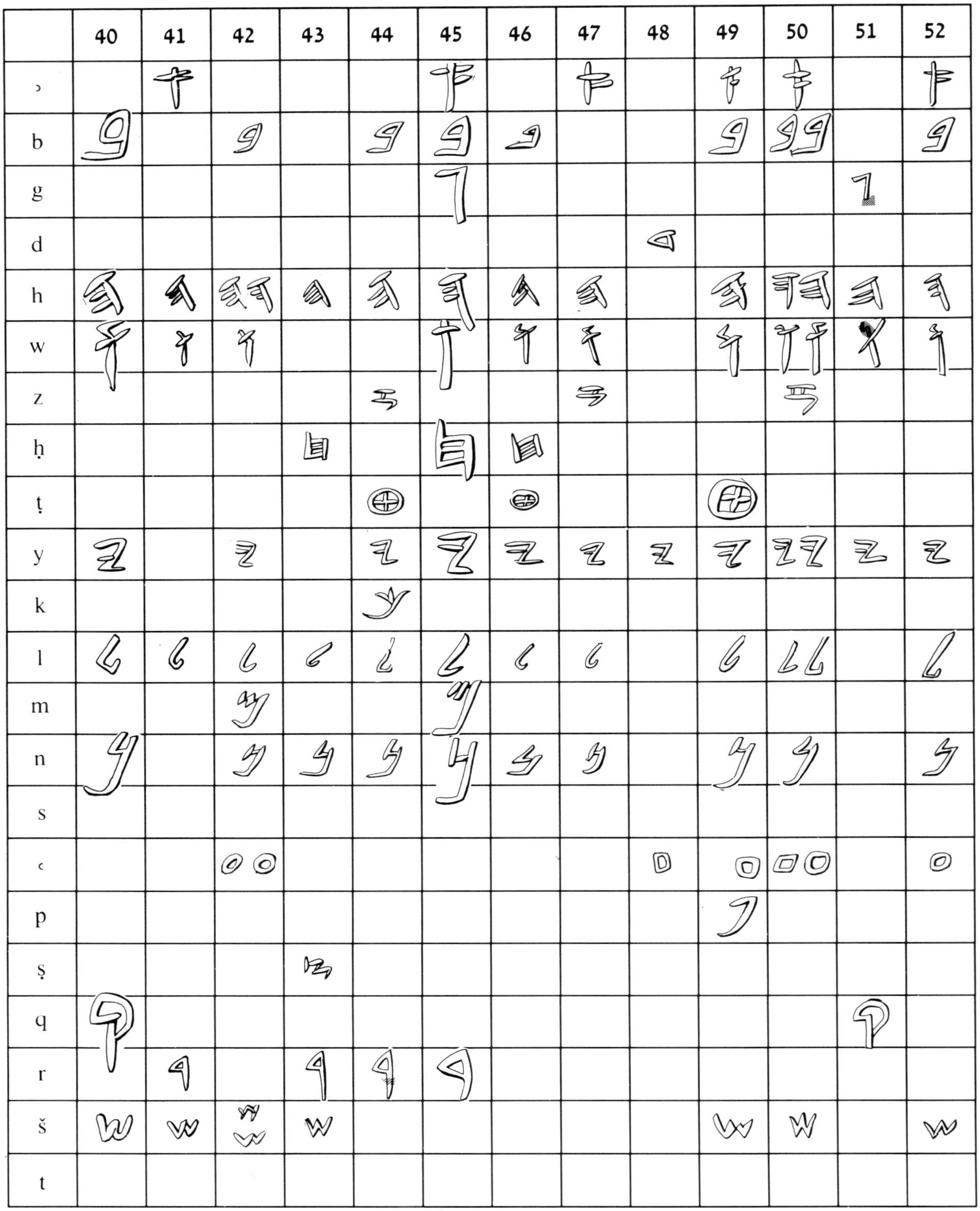

	53	54	55	56	57	58	59	60	61	62	63	64	65
ʾ													
b													
g													
d													
h													
w													
z													
ḥ													
ṭ													
y													
k													
l													
m													
n													
s													
ʿ													
p													
ṣ													
q													
r													
š													
t													

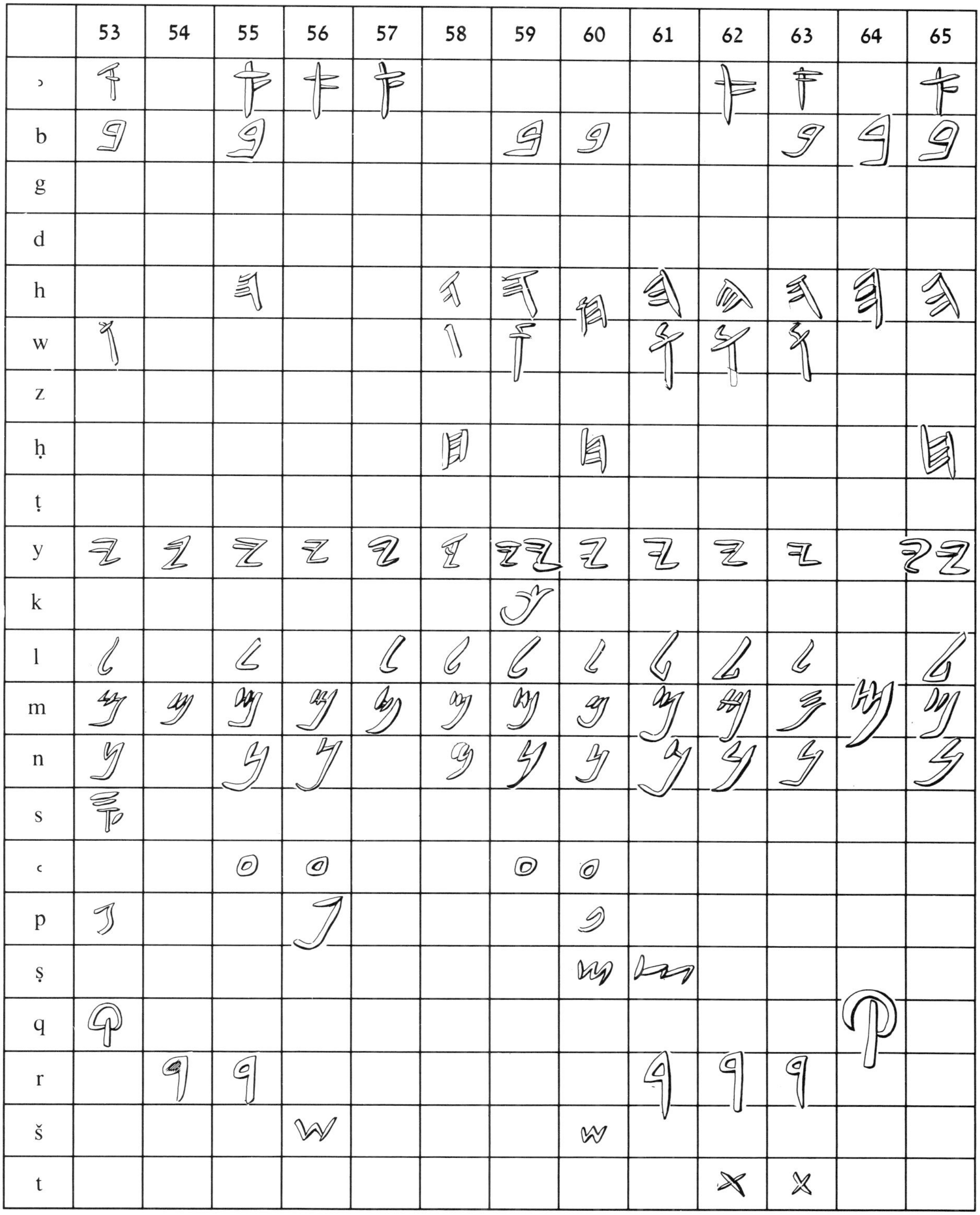

	66	67	68	69	70	71	72	73	74	75	76	77	78
ʾ													
b													
g													
d													
h													
w													
z													
ḥ													
ṭ													
y													
k													
l													
m													
n													
s													
ʿ													
p													
ṣ													
q													
r													
š													
t													

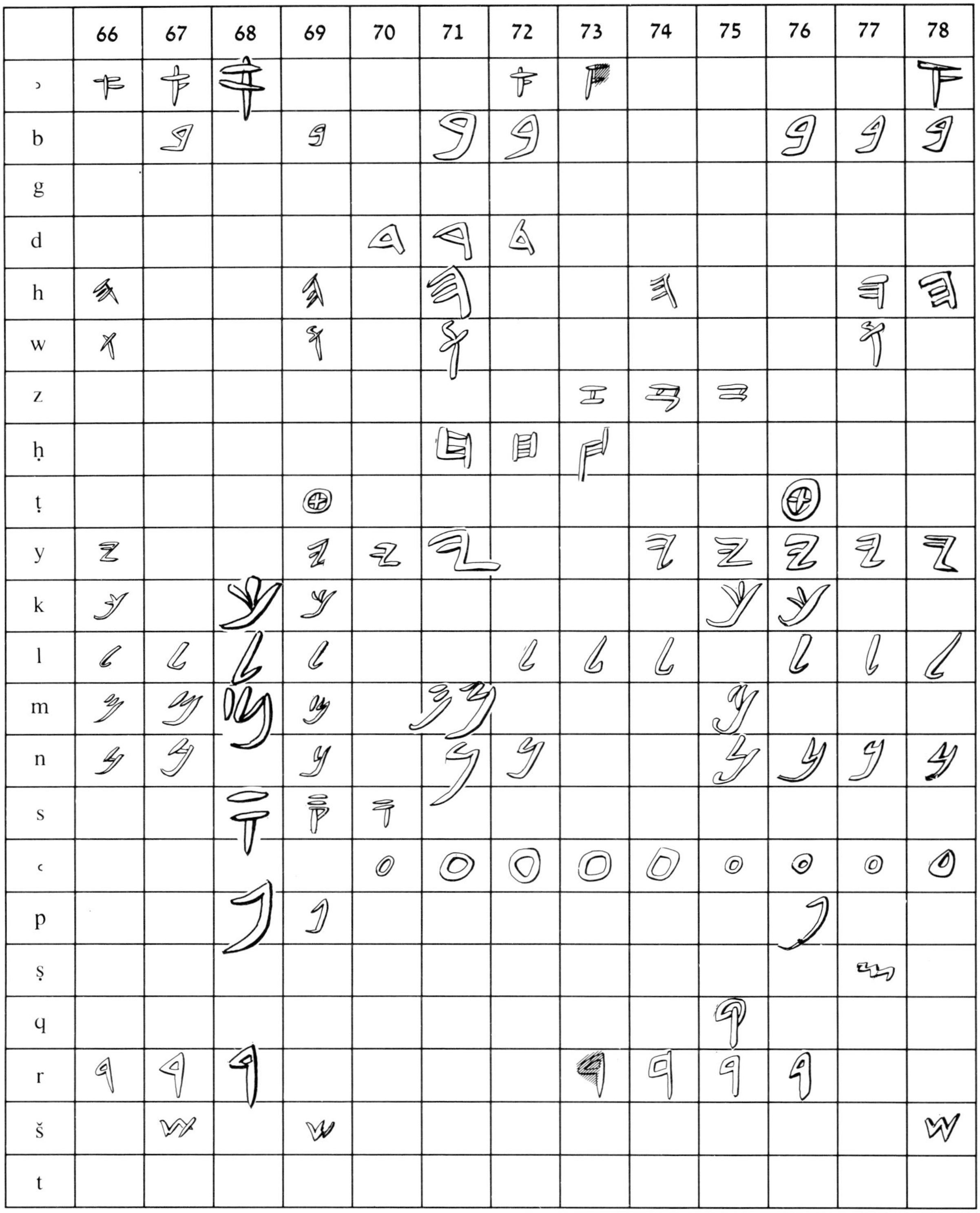

VII

	79	80	81	82	83	84	85	86	87	88	89	90	91
ʾ													
b													
g													
d													
h													
w													
z													
ḥ													
ṭ													
y													
k													
l													
m													
n													
s													
ʿ													
p													
ṣ													
q													
r													
š													
t													

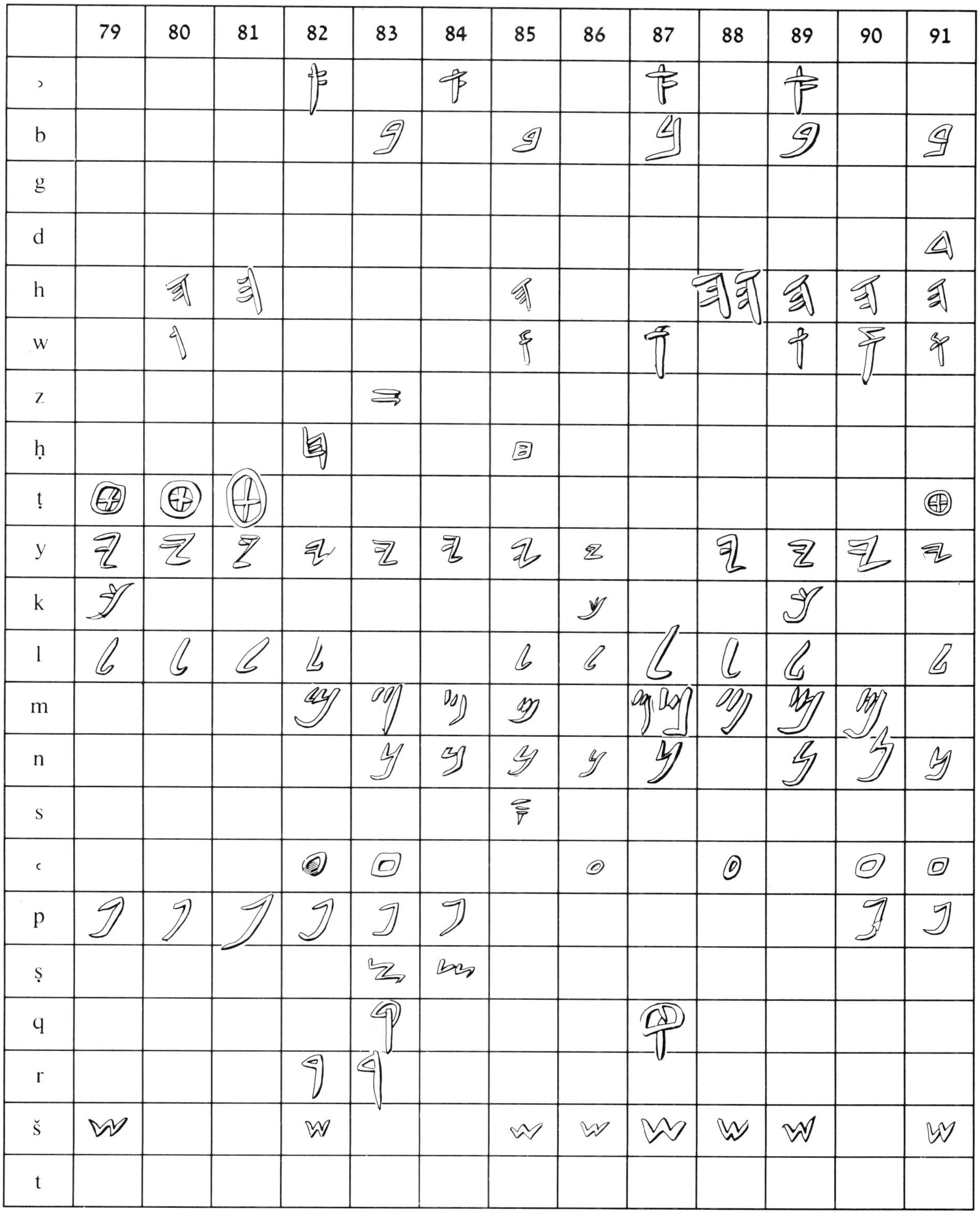

VIII

	92	93	94	95	96	97	98	99	100	101	102
ʾ											
b											
g											
d											
h											
w											
z											
ḥ											
ṭ											
y											
k											
l											
m											
n											
s											
ʿ											
p											
ṣ											
q											
r											
š											
t											

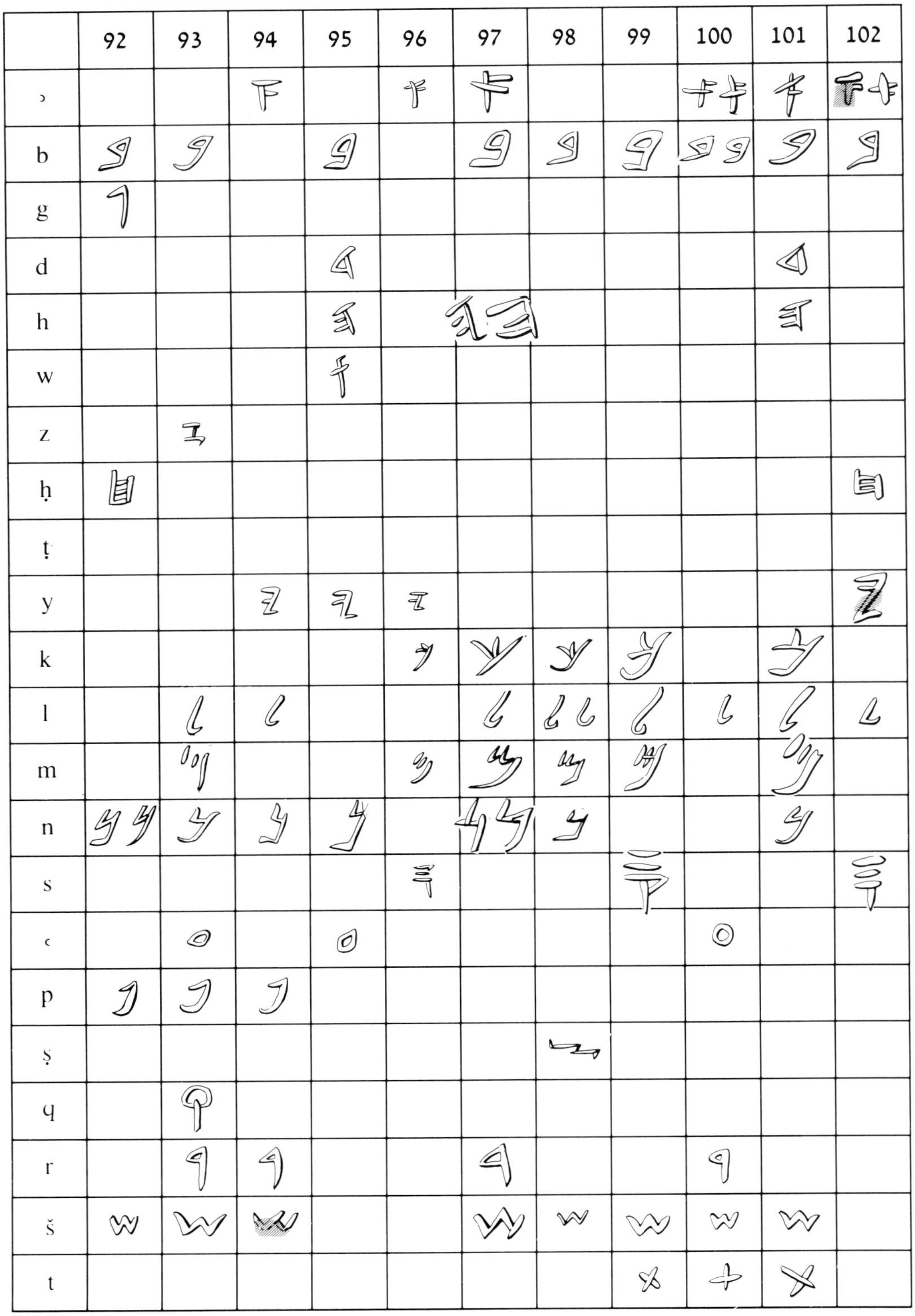

IX

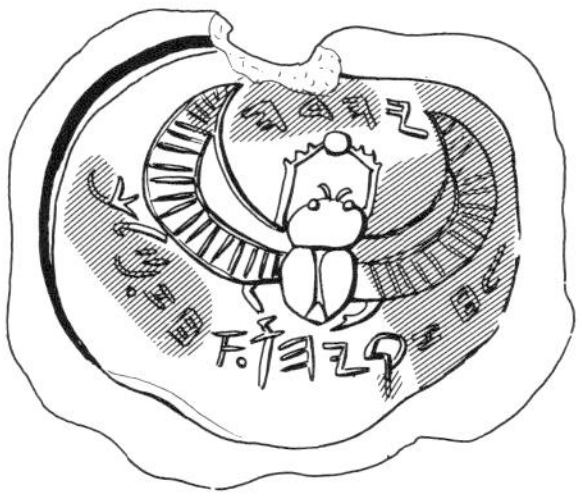

Avigad 1986, 199.

no. 70

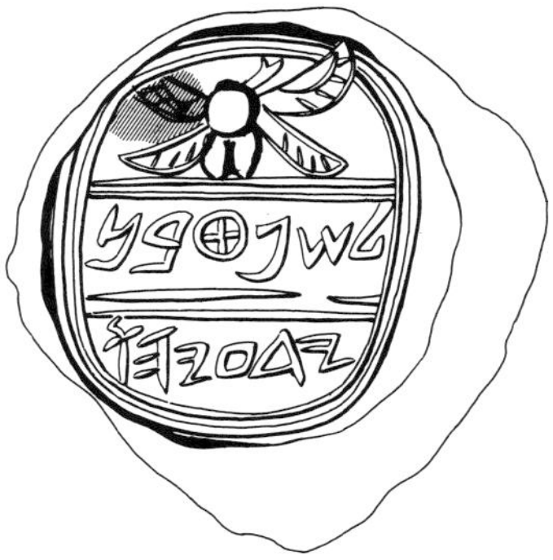

no. 91

no. 35

no. 86

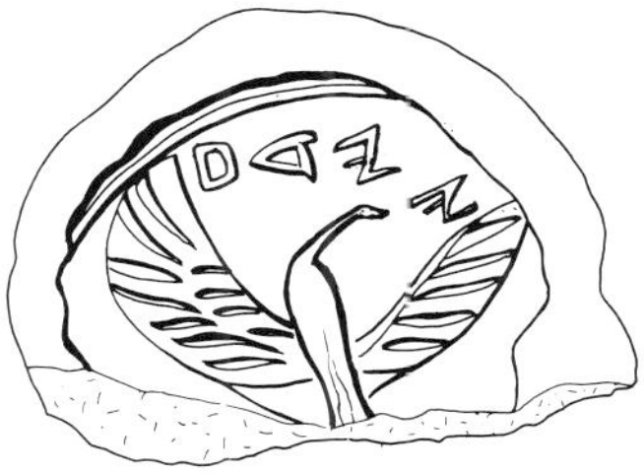

no. 48

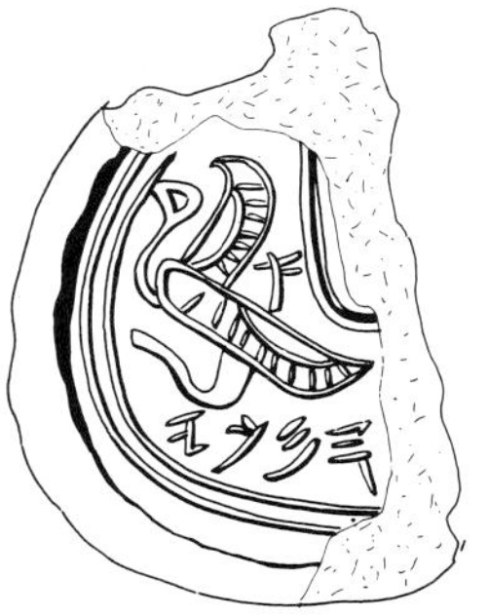

no. 96

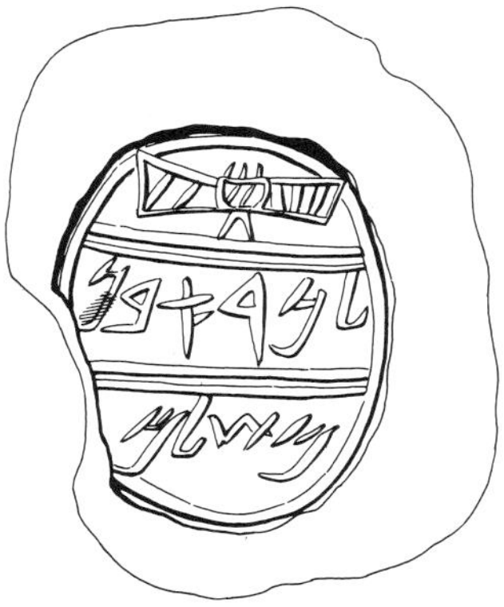

no. 67

no. 46

no. 28

The iconography: Two-winged beetle: A199; Four-winged beetle: 70, 91; Two-winged *uraeus*: 48, 96; Four-winged *uraeus*: 35, 86; Winged solar disc: 67; Sphinx: 46; Bird (with human face?): 28.

X

no. 32

no. 37

no. 51

no. 65

no. 38

no. 92

no. 102

The iconography: Does: 32, 37, 51; Fish: 65; Palm branch: 38, 92, 102.

XI

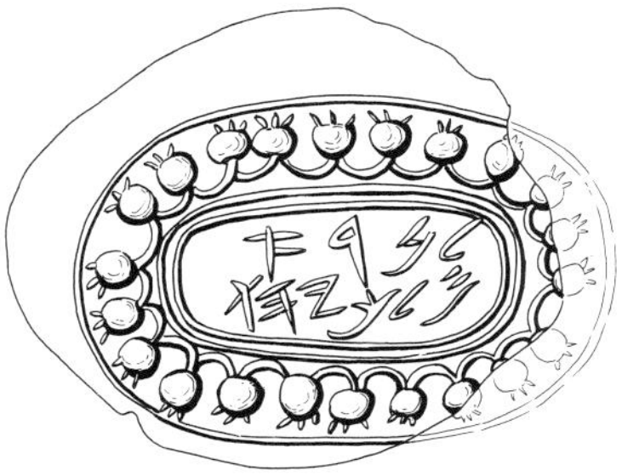

no. 66

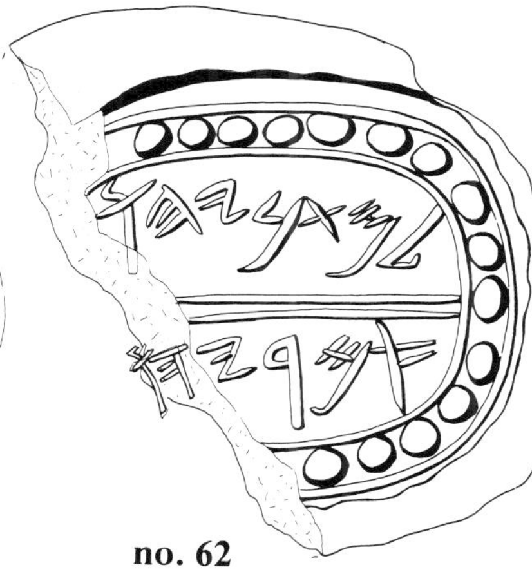

no. 62

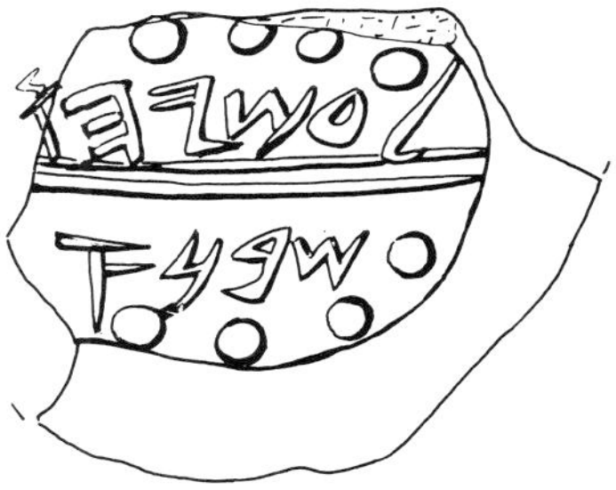

no. 78

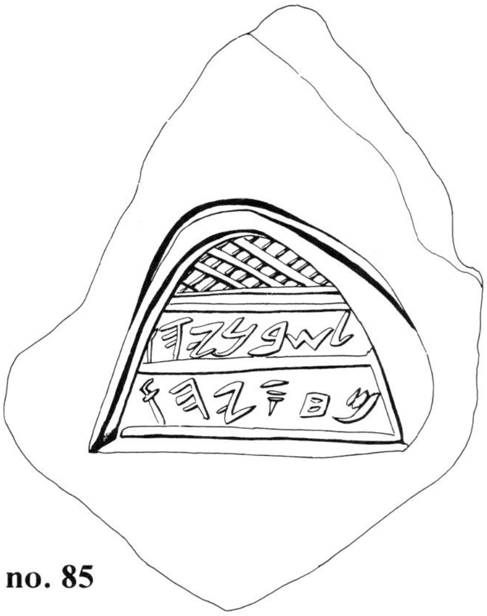

no. 85

no. 24

no. 82

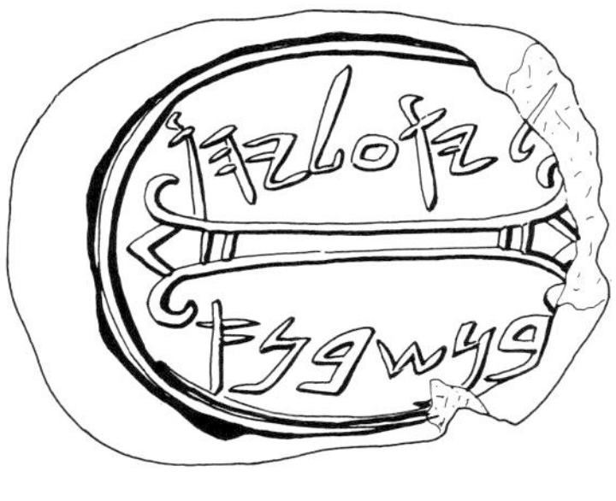

no. 52

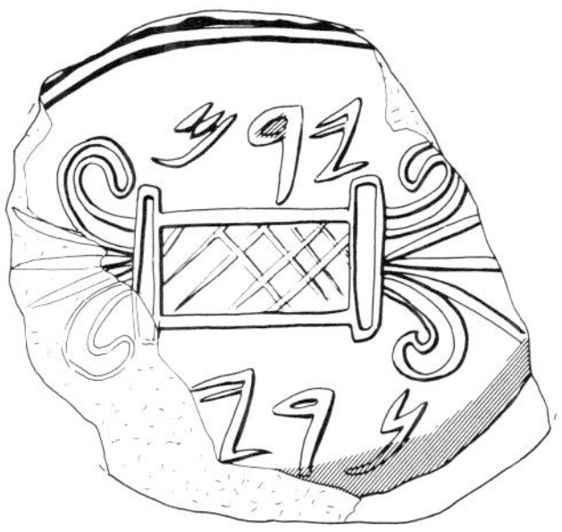

no. 54

The iconography: Pomegranates: 66; Dots: 62, 78; Net: 85; Dentate pattern: 24; Rectangular framed zigzag pattern: 82; Palmette 52, 54.

XII

no. 47

no. 7

no. 21

no. 49

no. 93

no. 8

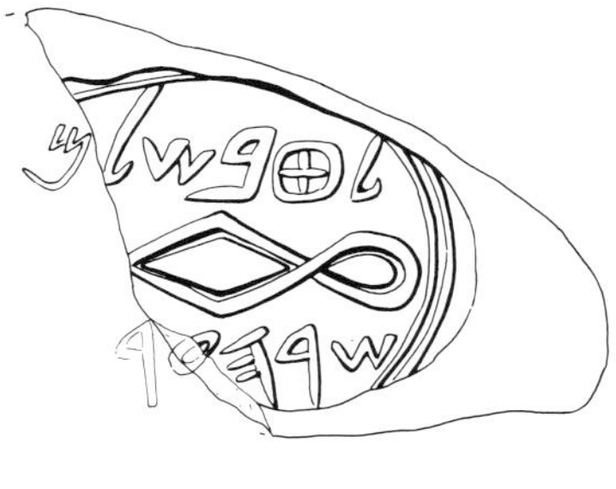

no. 11

no. 59

The iconography: Lotus-bud field divider with four petals: 47; Lotus-bud with two petals 7, 21, 49, 93; Double lotus-bud: 59; Schematic lotus-bud: 8, 11.

XIII

no. 61

no. 15

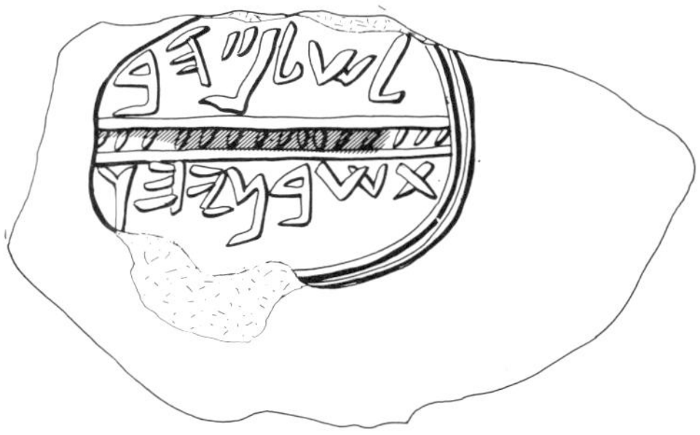

no. 16

no. 36

no. 55

no. 64

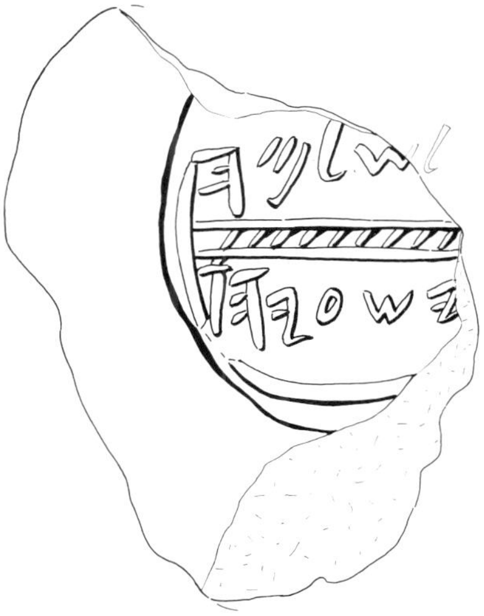

no. 88

The iconography: Double line with dotted ends: 61; Ladder-pattern: 16, 36, 55, 64, 88.

XIV

Thermoluminescence analysis report for bulla no. 76c

Ralf Kotalla "Laboratory"
Authentication ceramic art objects by thermoluminescence

Kätzling 2
D-72401 Haigerloch Germany
Tel. -49-7474 -9536-0
Fax -49-7474-9536-10
Car -49-171-622 8521

E-mail: kotalla@gbc.de(internet)
http://www.gbc.de/kotalla
Eurofilestransfer 49-7474-953616

Thermoluminescence - Report

No.: 961263

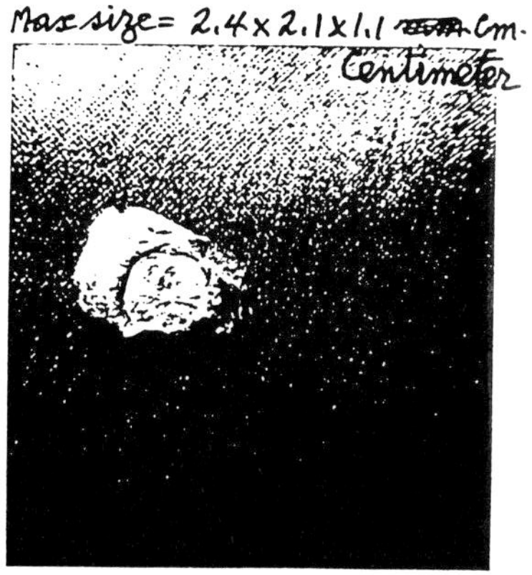

Haigerloch, 31. Dezember 1996

Report on Thermoluminescence Authenticity Tests

The analysis carried out on the samples from the object depicted on page 1 with the Tl no.961263 were executed using the thermoluminescenc method, and produced the following results:

1. Analysis Result:

a: ---------------fired in antiquity---------------------

On the basis of standard methods and techniques used in the thermoluminescence process, I calculate the last time of firing of the object samples to be:

b: . 2700 Years old (+/- 20% of the overall age)

2. Object: Seal of terracotta

H.= 2,4 cm

3. Origin: Orient

Assumed age on the basis of stylistic characteristics appr. 2700 years. The photograph of the object enclosed on page 1 was taken by myself.

4. Sampling:

1.-Sample: innerside fragment 2.-Sample: innerside fragment

5. Comments:

The samples were taken from a place which, in my experience, permits a reliable statement to be made of the overall object. The enclosed graphs form a constituent part of the expertise and reflect only excerpts from the complete catalogue of measurements.

Ralf Kotalla

The expertise is only valid if accompanied by the stamp of the laboratory and the signature of Mr. Ralf Kotalla.

XV

Thermoluminescence analysis report for bulla no. 85

RESEARCH LABORATORY FOR ARCHAEOLOGY
AND THE HISTORY OF ART
6 KEBLE ROAD, OXFORD OX1 3QJ
TEL: (01865) 515211
FAX: (01865) 273932

REPORT ON THERMOLUMINESCENCE ANALYSIS

made on sample .581y39......

ORIGIN OF SAMPLE

The sample was obtained in ...powder............... form, on ..8. January. 1997.......

by ...Doreen Stoneham of the Laboratory, Oxford...............................

The object from which the sample was taken was presumed to be:

a small fragment of terracotta (date unknown)...............................

It was reported to me that the position of sampling was:

on curved face...

The following samples have also been obtained from this object:

none...

A photograph was available at the time of sampling and this was annotated with the sample number and signed.

RESULT

Using standard methods and techniques it is estimated that the material of the sample was last fired:

between 1100 and 1800 years ago..

This result is considered **consistent** with the suggested period of manufacture of the object concerned. The result is given in good faith; however the Laboratory takes no responsibility for financial loss incurred through an erroneous report being given.

Research Laboratory for Archaeology
and the History of Art
Oxford University

SPECIAL COMMENT

More precise dating is not possible due to lack of environmental information.

Date ....10 February 1997...... *Signed* ...D. Stoneham

This report should carry the laboratory stamp and be signed by M. Tite or D. Stoneham.

AC

NOTES

(i) If the object has suffered restoration it should be borne in mind that the component parts may be of differing antiquity. This report refers only to the part from which the sample was obtained.

(ii) The analysis refers to the date of last firing. This may be different from the date of manufacture if the object has been refired. In some cases it is possible to determine whether or not this has been the case, and where this is so the result is stated under 'Special Comment'.

(iii) In making this report it is assumed that the sample has not been exposed to irradiation with X-rays, γ-rays or neutrons.

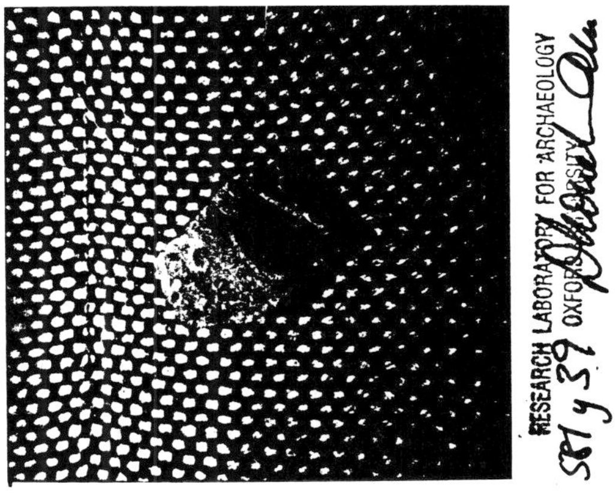

XVI

The Royal Bullae

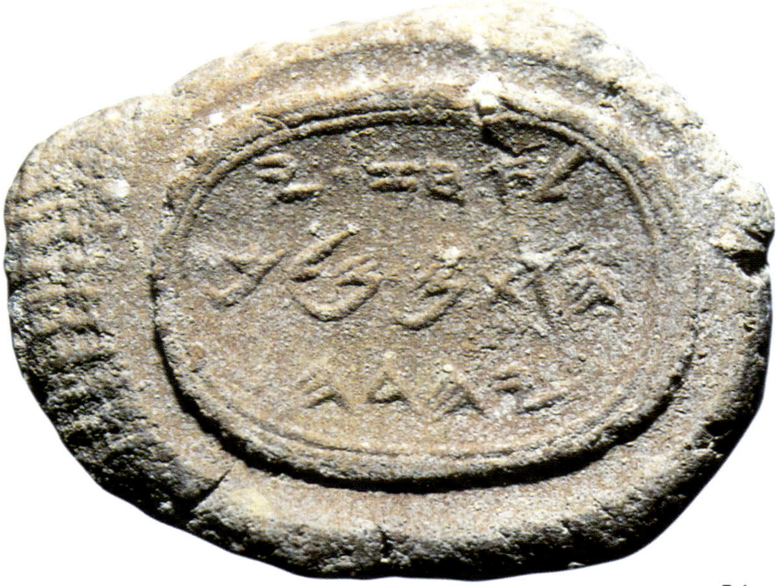

7:1

Shlomo Moussaieff collection

Belonging to Aḥaz (son of) Yehotam, King of Judah

7:1

Yoav Sasson collection

[Belonging to Ḥeze]kiah (son of) A[ḥaz K]ing of J[udah]

XVII

The Royal Bullae

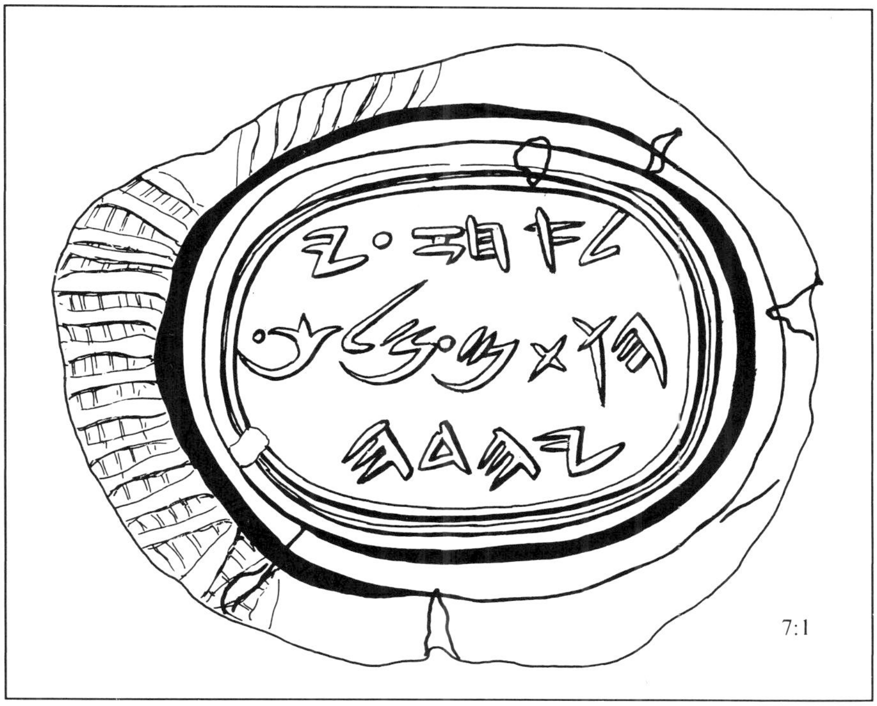

Belonging to Aḥaz (son of) Yehotam, King of Judah

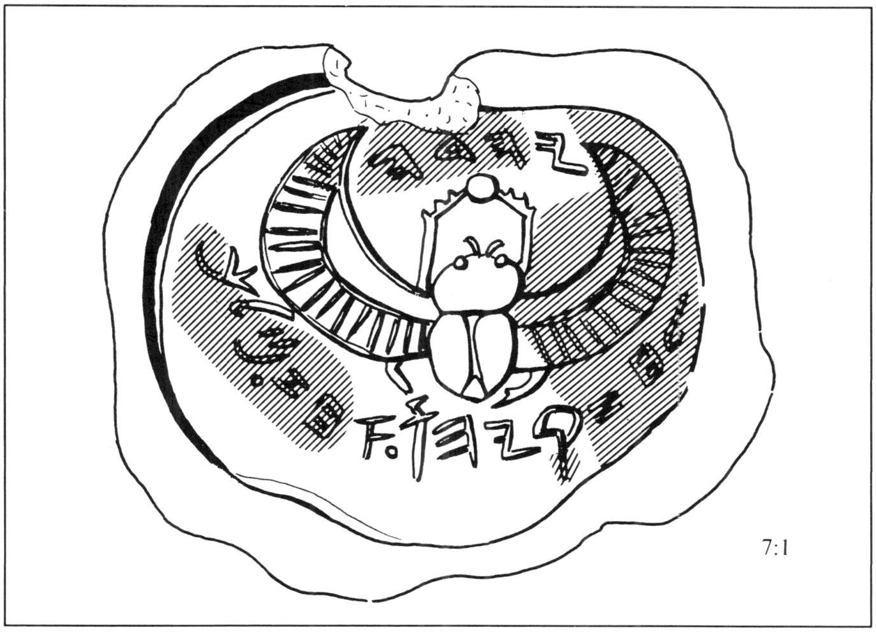

[Belonging to Ḥeze]kiah (son of) A[ḥaz K]ing of J[udah]